Wildlife of Lake Washington

Photography and Narrative by
Aaron Baggenstos

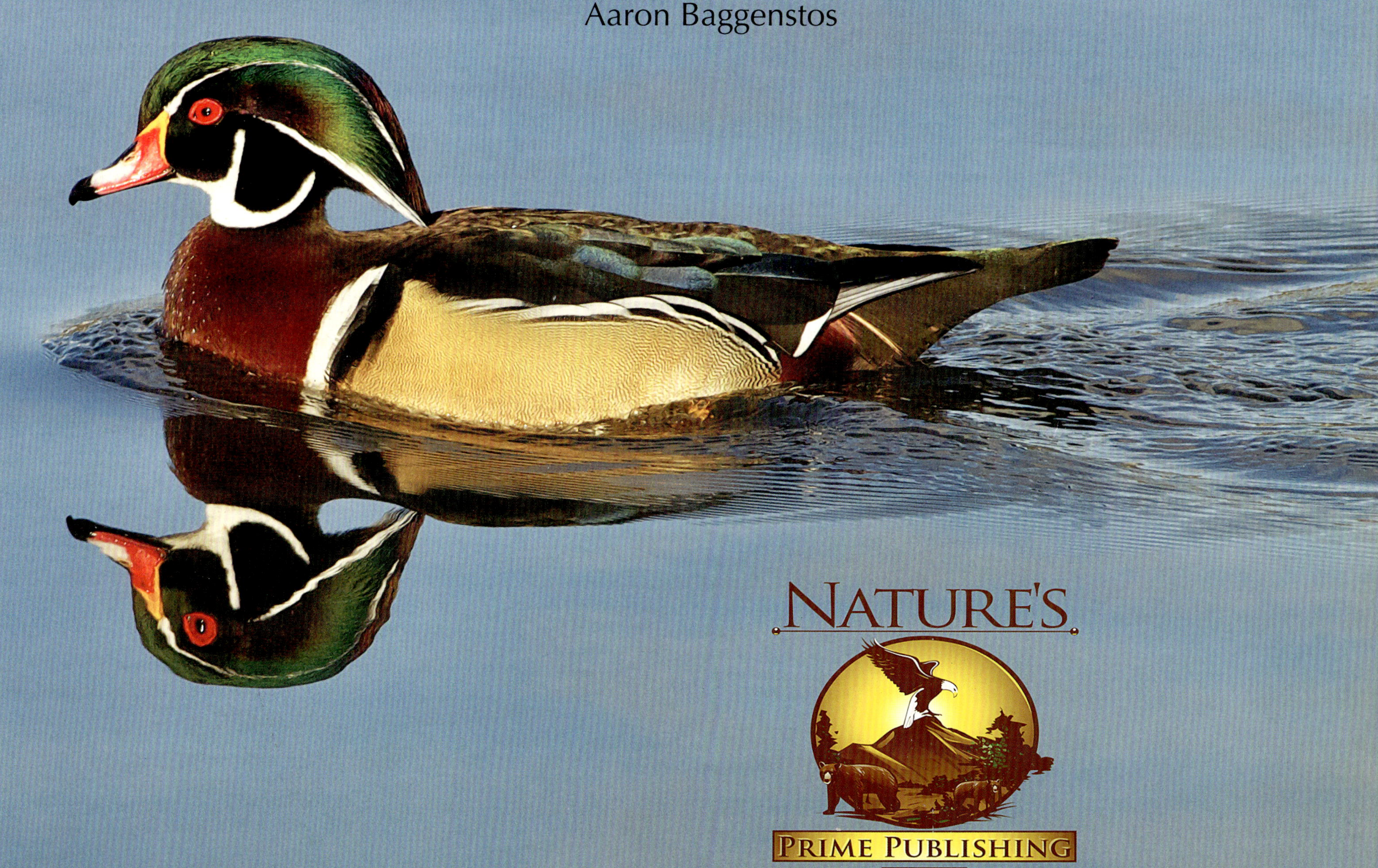

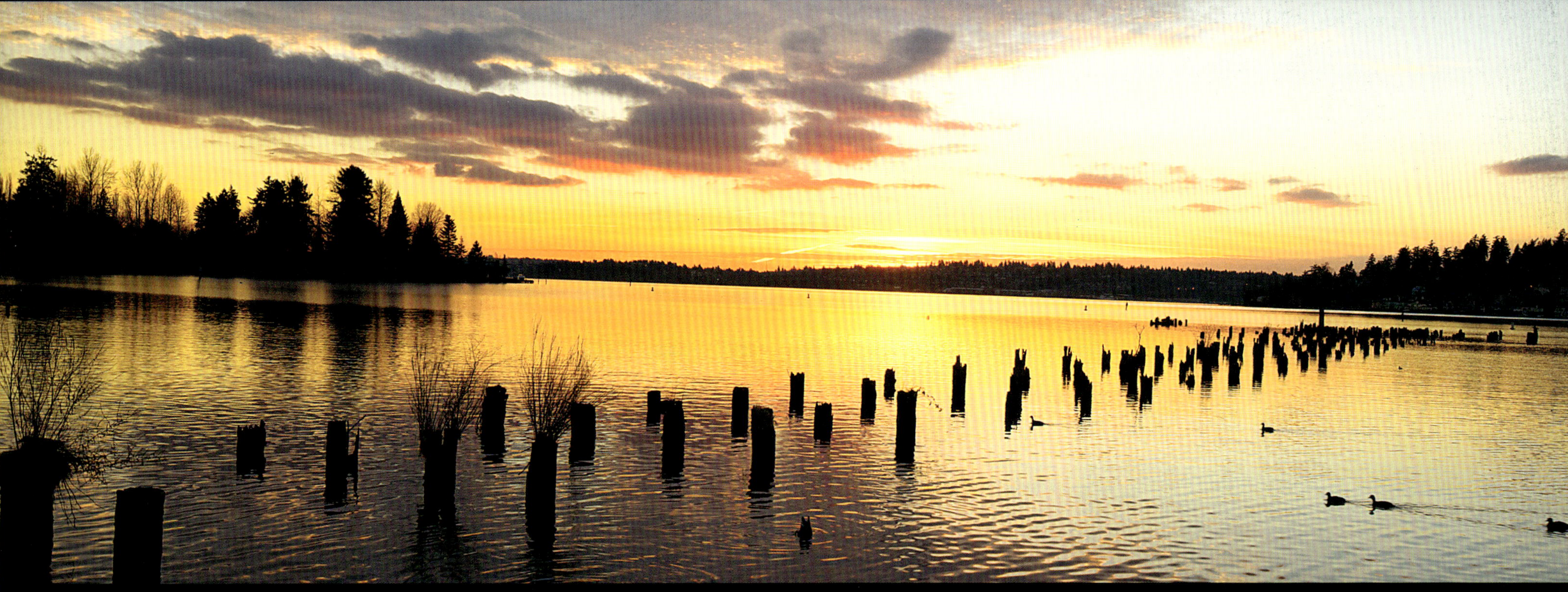

Above: Ducks swim through a stunning January sunset on Lake Washington's Juanita Bay.

Photography and Narrative by Aaron Baggenstos

ISBN # 978-0-9838856-0-3

Created, produced, and designed in the United States.

Printed in China through Palace Press International.

Nature's Prime Publishing
Kirkland, Washington
www.aaronbaggenstos.com

To my mother and father for inspiring infinite possibility.

Forward

Washington State is a unique and extraordinary place to observe and learn about wildlife. Its varied landscape and weather, proximity to the Pacific Ocean, and location on the migratory route of many wildlife species produce an incredible biological diversity few states can match. In a relatively small area, Washington contains most of the ecosystems found in the Western United States and some, for example the Olympic Rainforest, that are found nowhere else in the United States. Each of these unique ecosystems is home to a different mix of spectacular creatures and create a broad range of wildlife experiences.

Biodiversity is fragile. If we destroy the places where wild creatures live we will destroy the creatures themselves. Roughly 90 percent of Washington's old growth trees have been logged leaving a mere 10 percent. Currently, Washington is home to around 30 species of endangered wildlife, meaning they are seriously threatened with extinction throughout all or a significant portion of their range within the state. Thankfully, through the work of a small number of dedicated individuals and organizations over the state's history, a series of over 120 state parks and over 30 wildlife refuges have been established to support our hundreds of species of wildlife. Although protected, these areas are still at risk and susceptible to human impact and poaching. Most of our state's undeveloped land is unprotected. A greater effort needs to be made to protect these lands and if I have my way the number of wildlife refuges will double in the next 10 years.

This book intends to give you a better appreciation for the Lake Washington region, this wonderful state, and the amazing animals that inhabit it. You will have a greater understanding of the incredible biodiversity that exists just outside our homes in an urban area where over a million people live and work. My guess is that you will find animals in this book you were not aware inhabited the Lake Washington region. My hope is it will inspire you to get outside to search for and enjoy these magnificent animals who are your neighbors.

Enjoy,

Aaron Baggenstos

Lake Washington

Lake Washington is one of Washington State's largest natural lakes. At 22 miles long with a maximum depth of 214 feet, it provides precious habitat for some of Washington's most fascinating wildlife. The lake and its dozens of parks support over 200 species of birds as well as numerous species of mammals, reptiles, amphibians, insects, and fish. Some of these animals call the lake and its surrounding areas home, while others temporarily visit during migration.

You will notice that I take a lot of my photographs at Juanita Bay Park because it is close to my home, but any park in the region is a great place to look for the birds and animals in this book. I have placed trees marking my favorite parks on the map to the right and I have noted specific locations throughout the book where you are more likely to see certain species. However, it is important to know that birds and animals sometimes travel great distances for food, shelter, and migration and cannot always be found in the same places. The best way to find what you are looking for is through research, time, and even a little bit of luck.

I always pay special attention not to disturb the wildlife I photograph. My long telephoto lens enables me to intimately capture my subjects from a safe distance, and a good pair of binoculars can do the same thing for you at an affordable price.

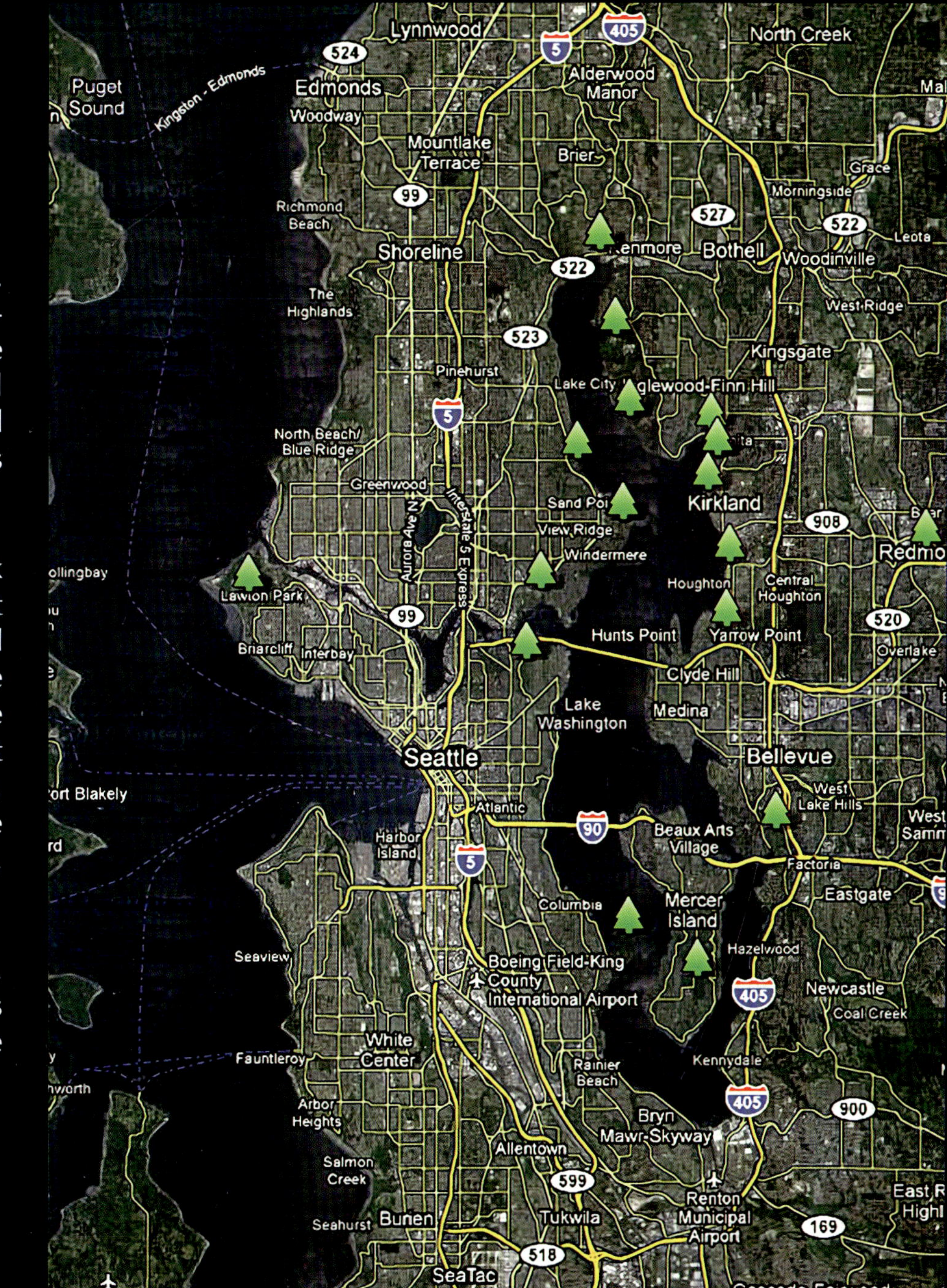

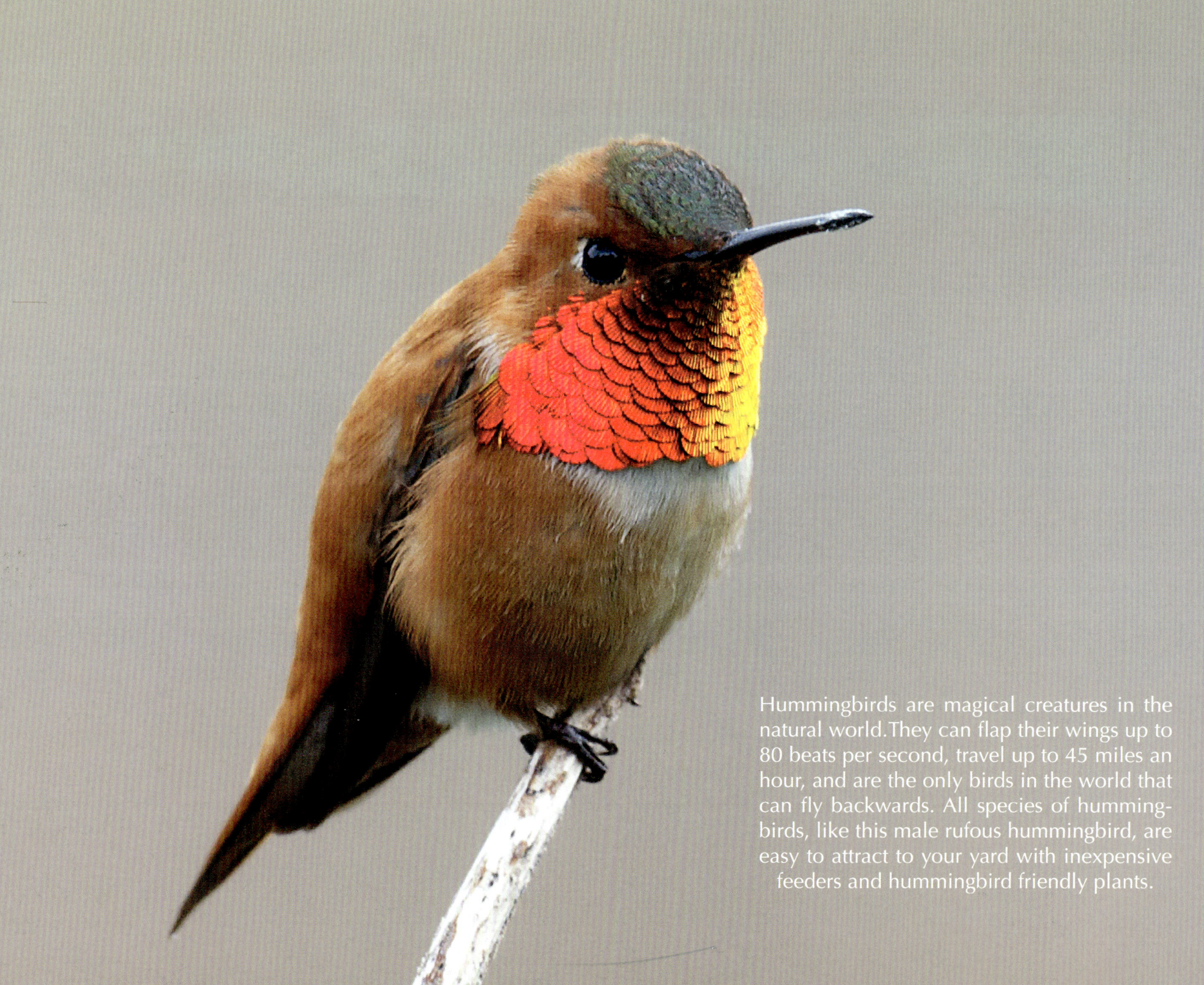

Hummingbirds are magical creatures in the natural world. They can flap their wings up to 80 beats per second, travel up to 45 miles an hour, and are the only birds in the world that can fly backwards. All species of hummingbirds, like this male rufous hummingbird, are easy to attract to your yard with inexpensive feeders and hummingbird friendly plants.

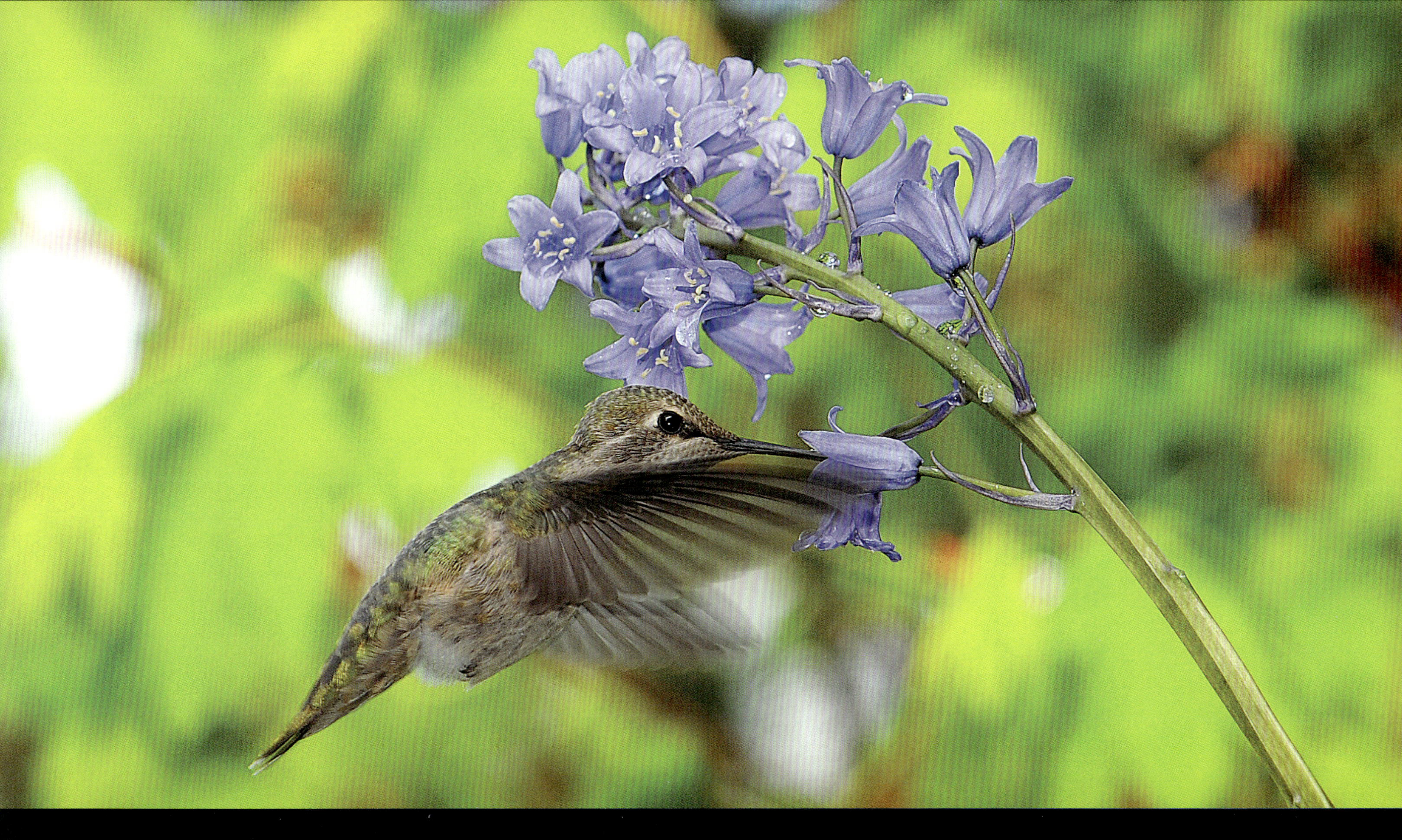

Above: In Kirkland, a female Anna's Hummingbird hovers in place while it collects nectar for energy.

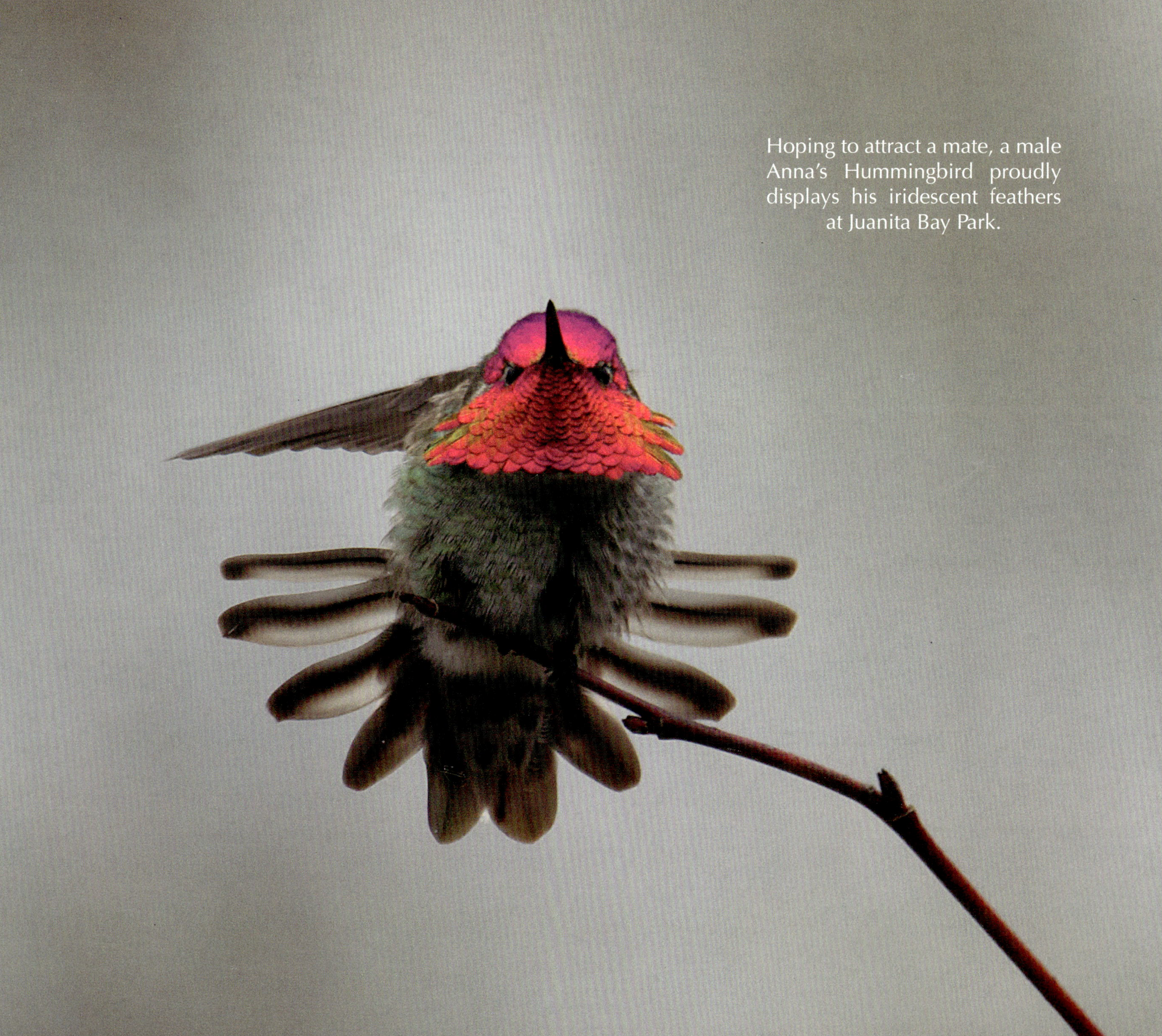

Hoping to attract a mate, a male Anna's Hummingbird proudly displays his iridescent feathers at Juanita Bay Park.

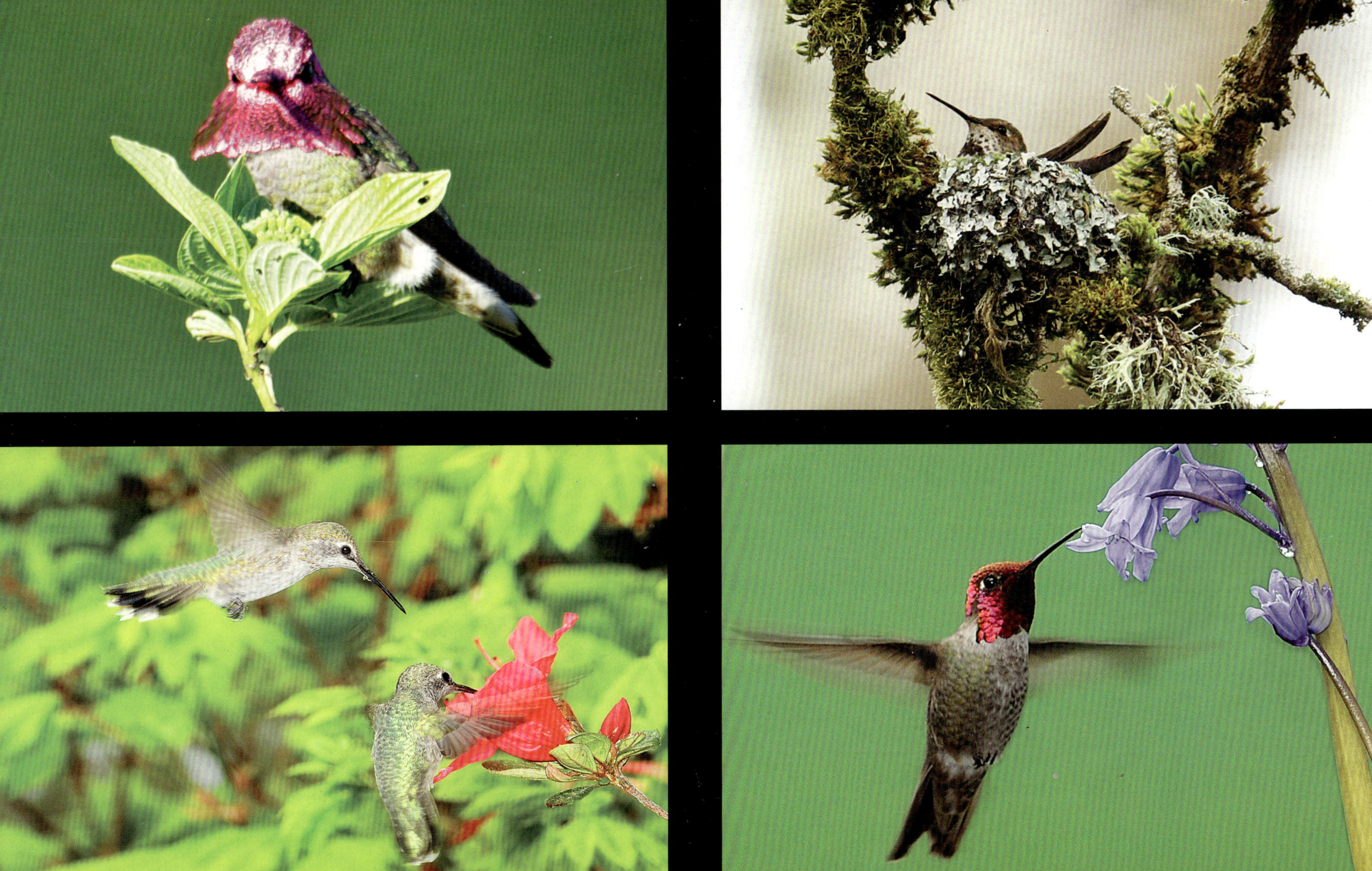

Top Left: On display, this male Anna's Hummingbird glimmers in the sunlight. *Top Right*: A female rufous hummingbird incubates her eggs which are about the size of Tic-Tacs. *Bottom Left*: Two female Anna's Hummingbirds share a flower for nectar. *Bottom Right*: A male Anna's Hummingbird collects nectar.

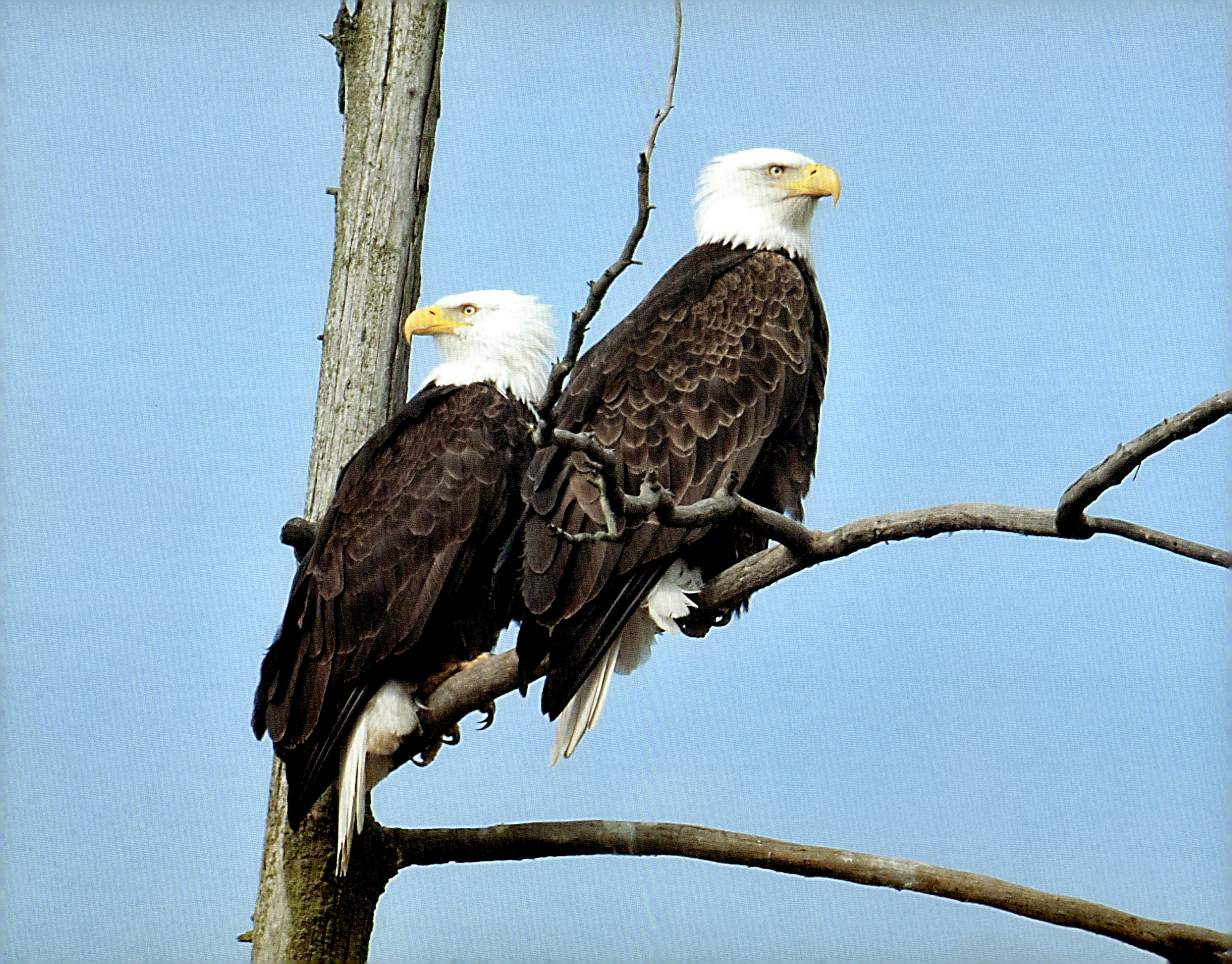

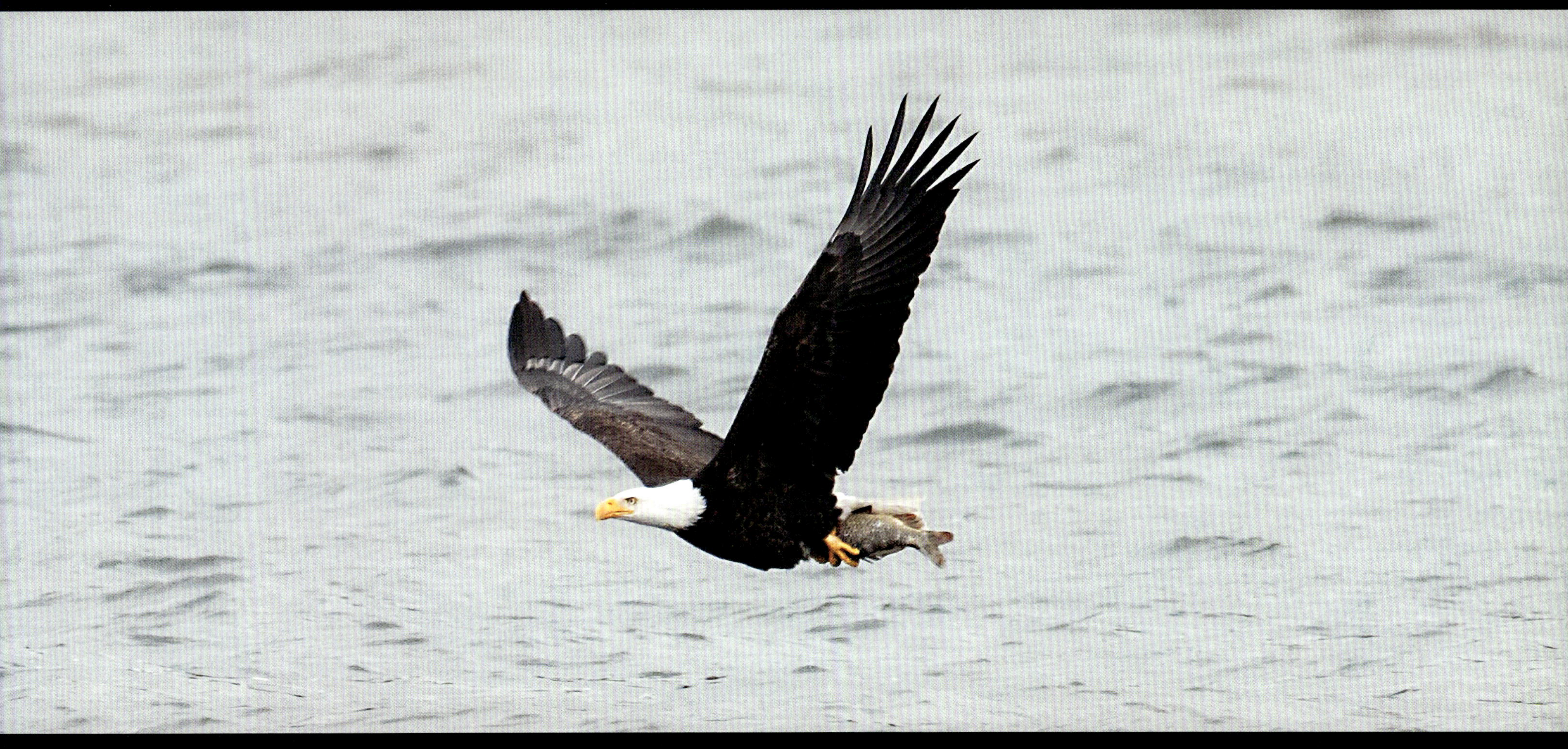

Facing Page: In 1967, with the dramatic decline in its population, the bald eagle was declared an endangered species. Habitat destruction, illegal poaching, and contamination of its food source by the pesticide DDT threatened its very existence. Thankfully, we as a nation stood up to protect this majestic icon. In 2007, After 40 years of federal protection, it was removed from the endangered species list after an astonishing recovery. It is now not only a symbol of America, but of our dedication to preserve the natural world and the creatures that inhabit it.

Above: A bald eagle gains elevation above a gloomy Lake Washington after a successful fishing trip.

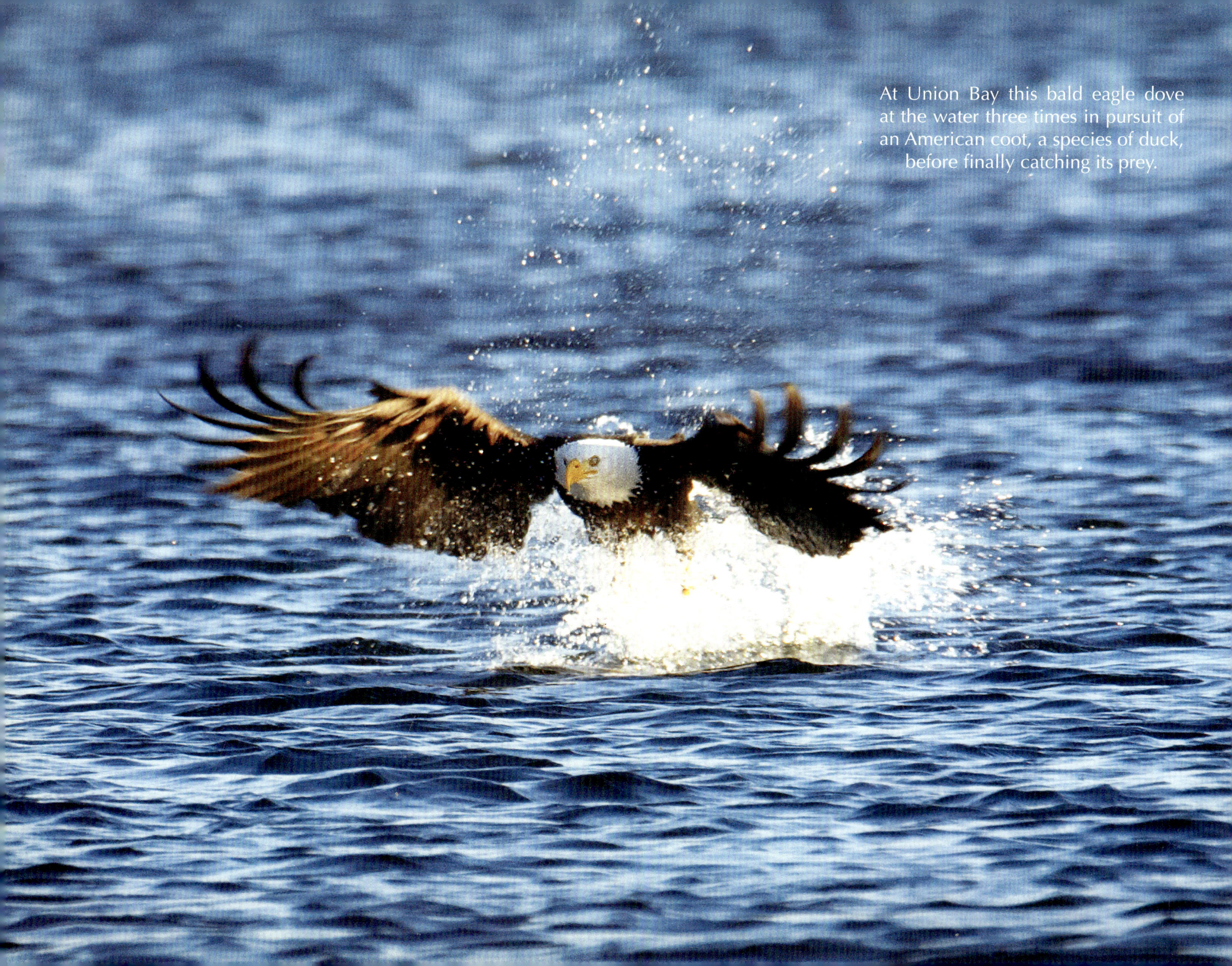

At Union Bay this bald eagle dove at the water three times in pursuit of an American coot, a species of duck, before finally catching its prey.

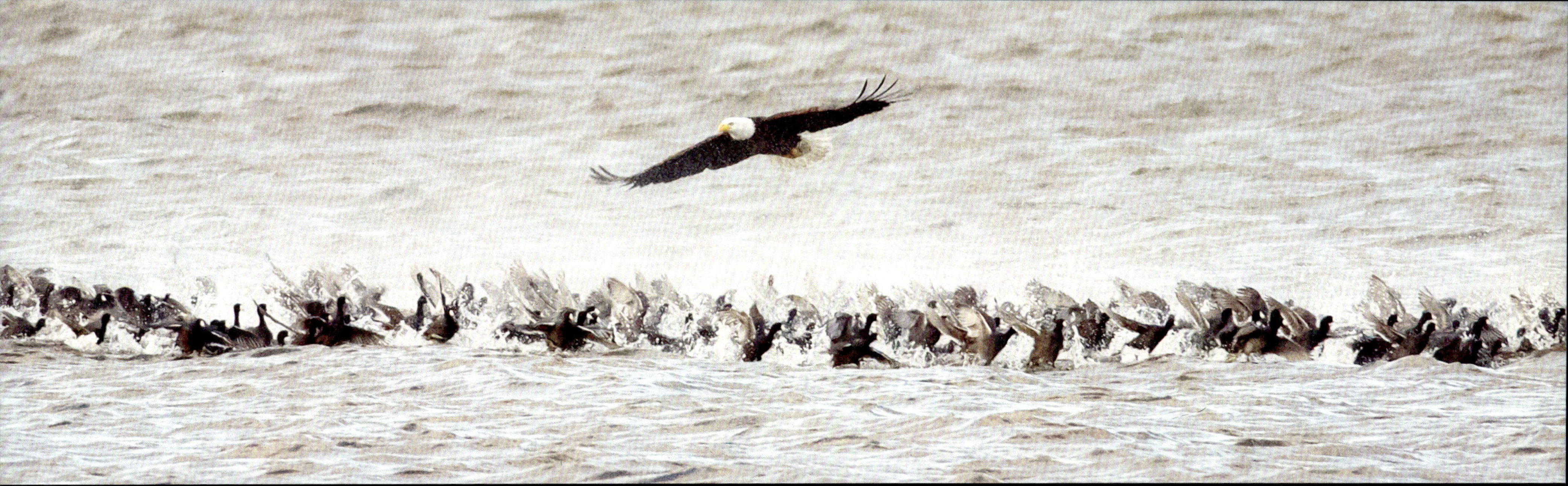

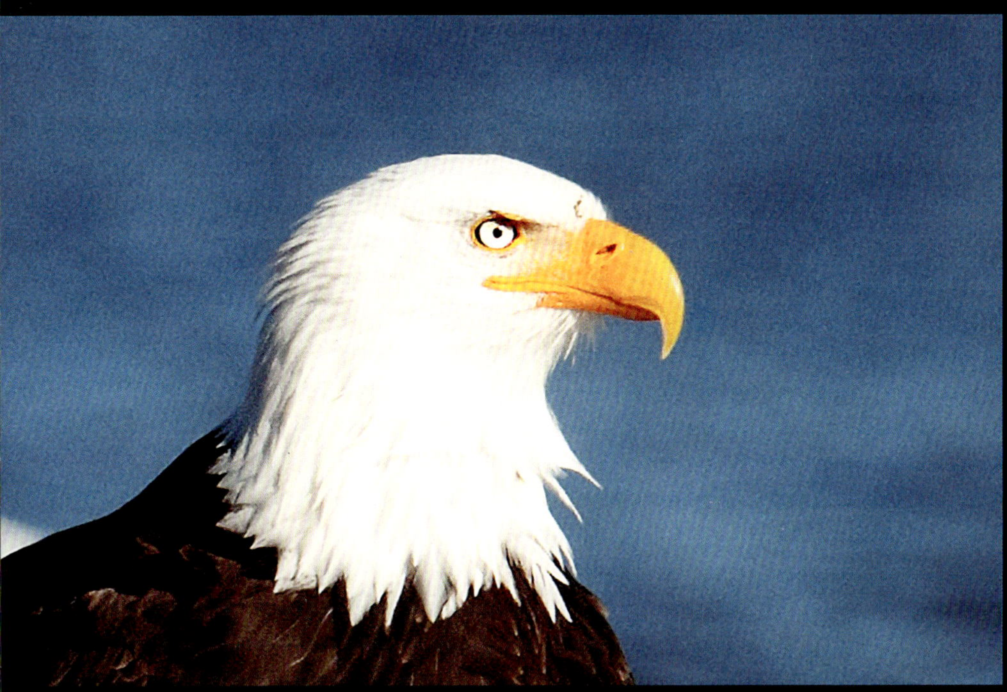

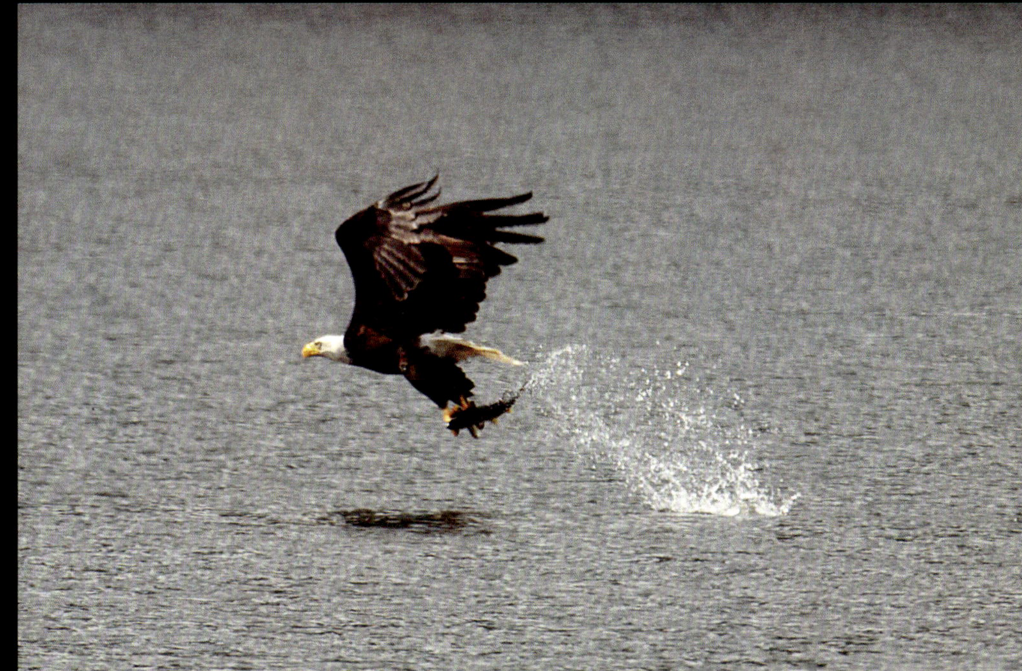

Top: A bald eagle stalks a "raft" of American coots, one of its favorite meals. *Bottom Left*: Eagles are renowned for their excellent eyesight. They can see fish in the water from several hundred feet in the air. *Bottom Right*: In the last three years, with hundreds of hours in the field, I have only captured a handful of photographs of a bald eagle catching a fish at this close range.

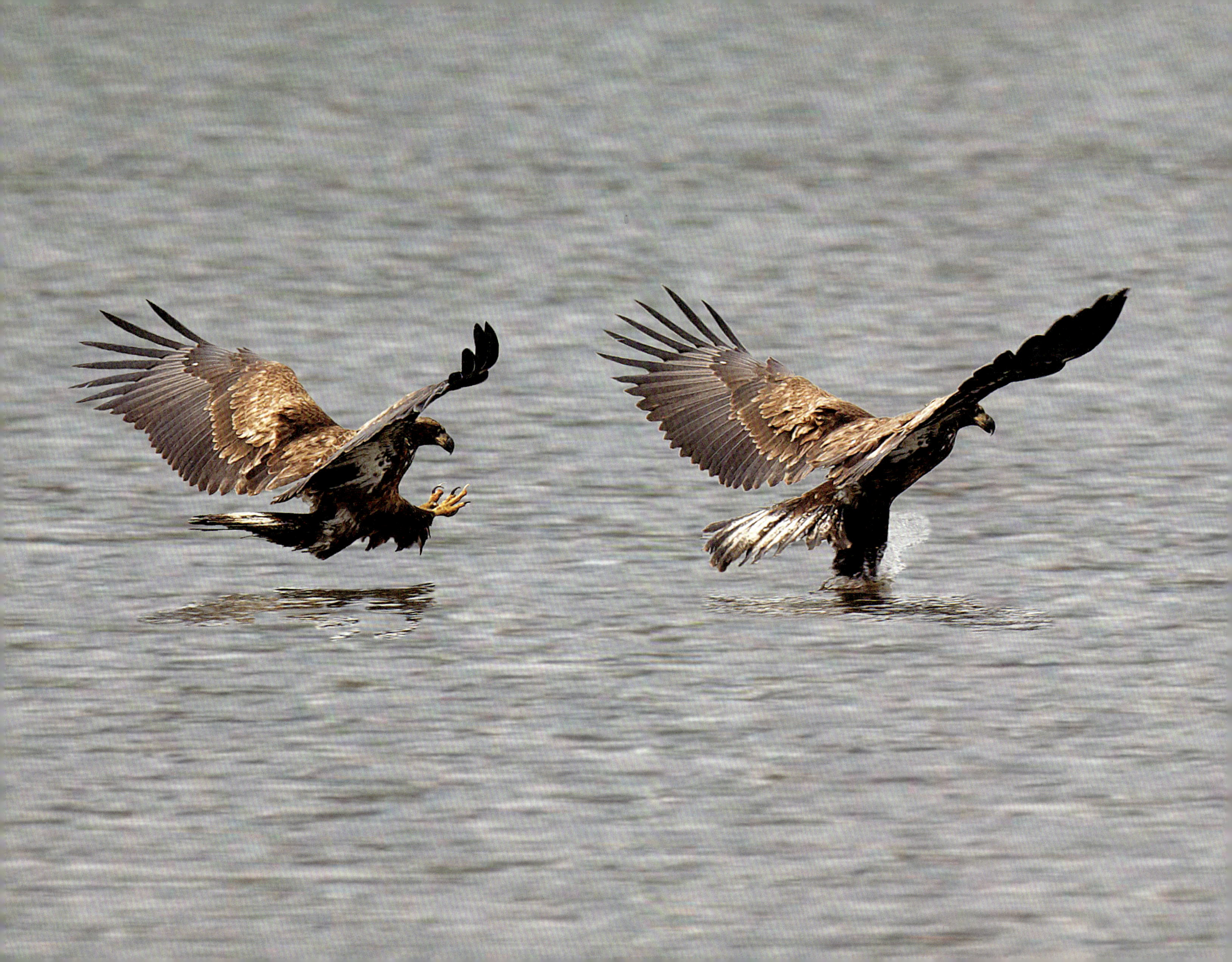

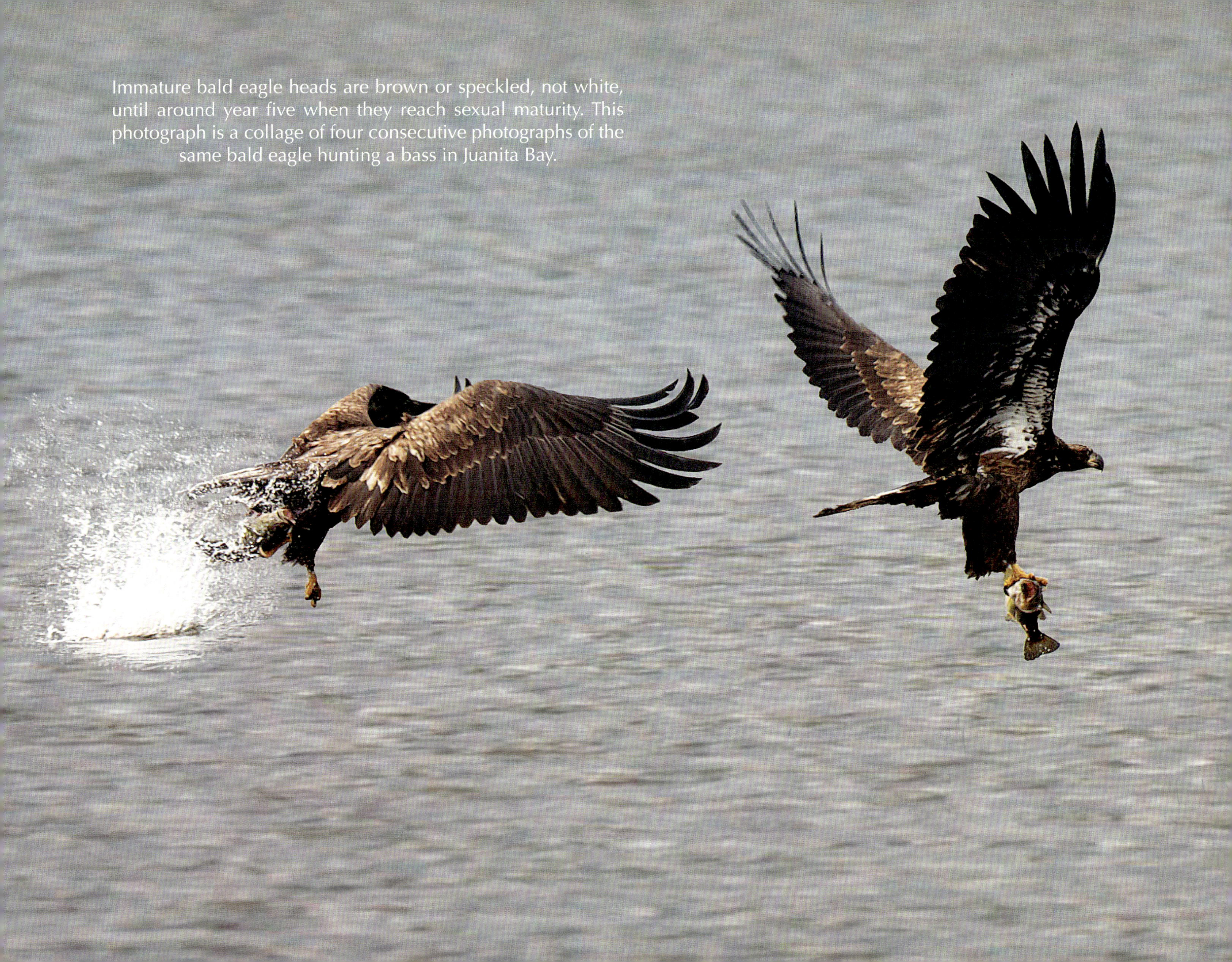

Immature bald eagle heads are brown or speckled, not white, until around year five when they reach sexual maturity. This photograph is a collage of four consecutive photographs of the same bald eagle hunting a bass in Juanita Bay.

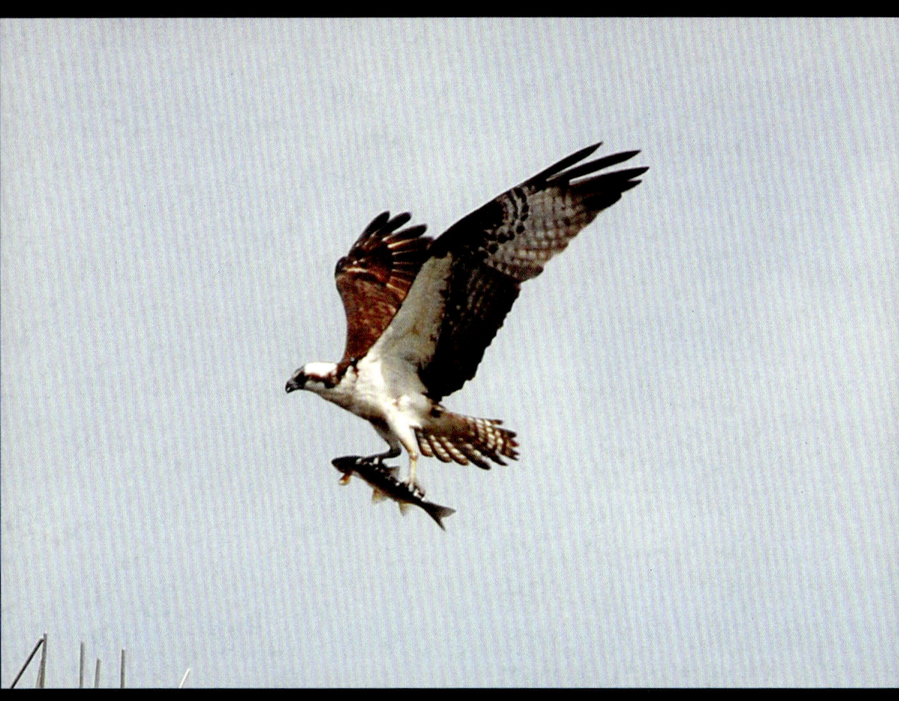

Above: Ospreys make around 99 percent of their diet from fish. They hunt by diving into the water from 30 to 100 feet up creating a spectacular show of splashing water that is very exciting to observe. Ospreys are migratory birds that nest in North America and travel hundreds of miles south during the winter. Ospreys build large stick nests close to water on telephone poles and a variety of artificial platforms. In May of 2011 a pair even chose to build a nest on top of a large NOAA ship's mast that was docked on the lake.

Facing Page: An osprey emerges from the lake after a disappointing unsuccessful hunt.

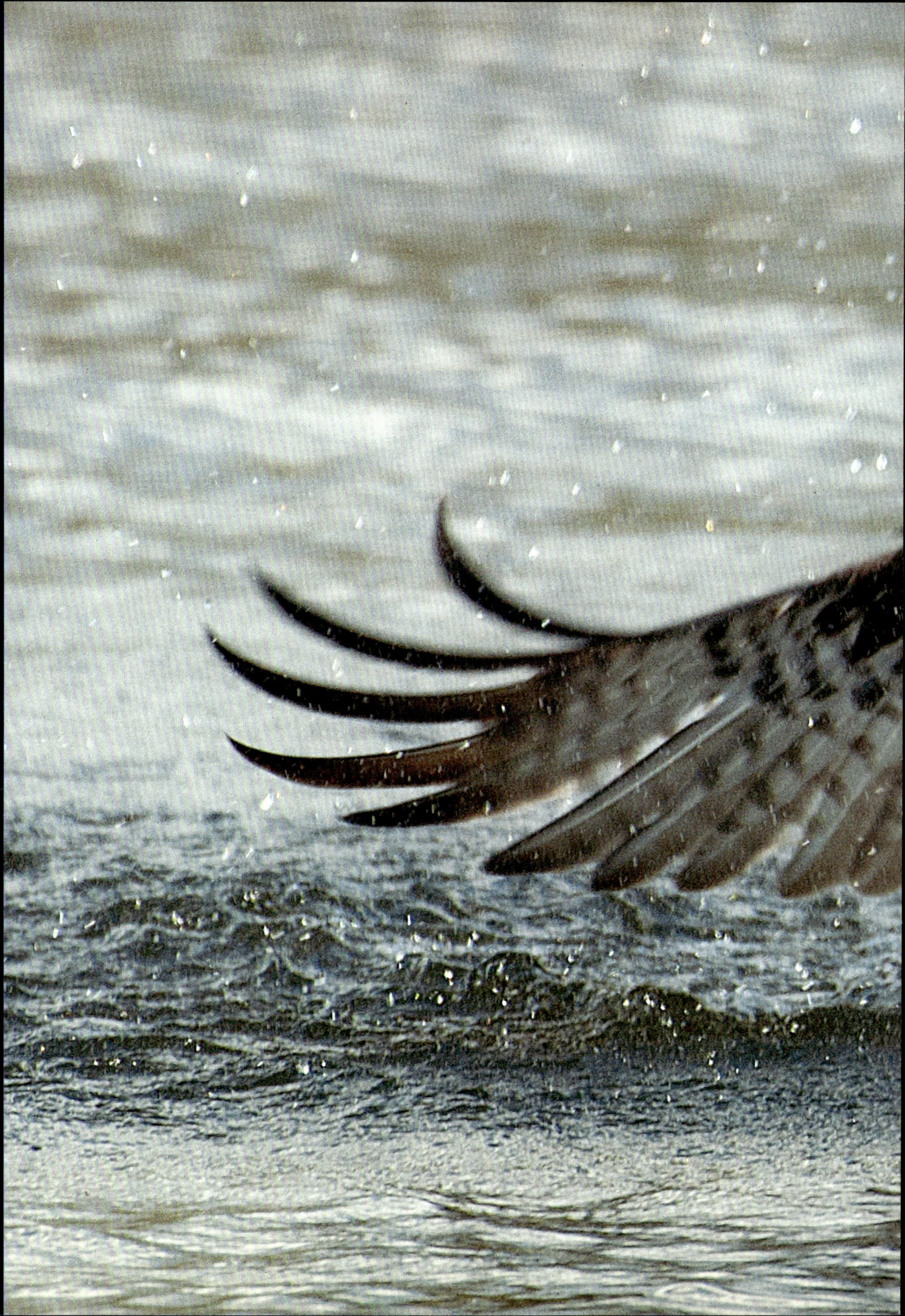

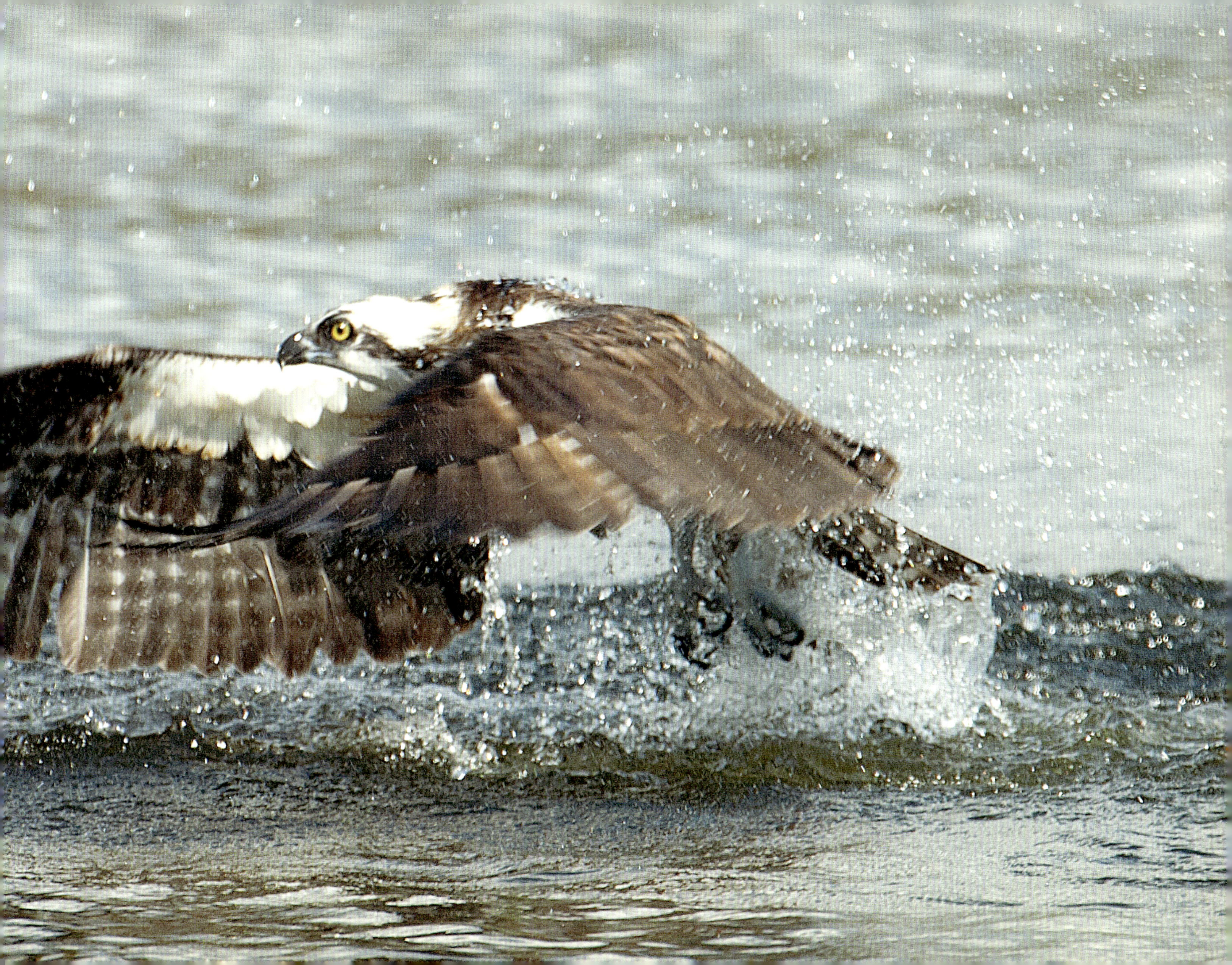

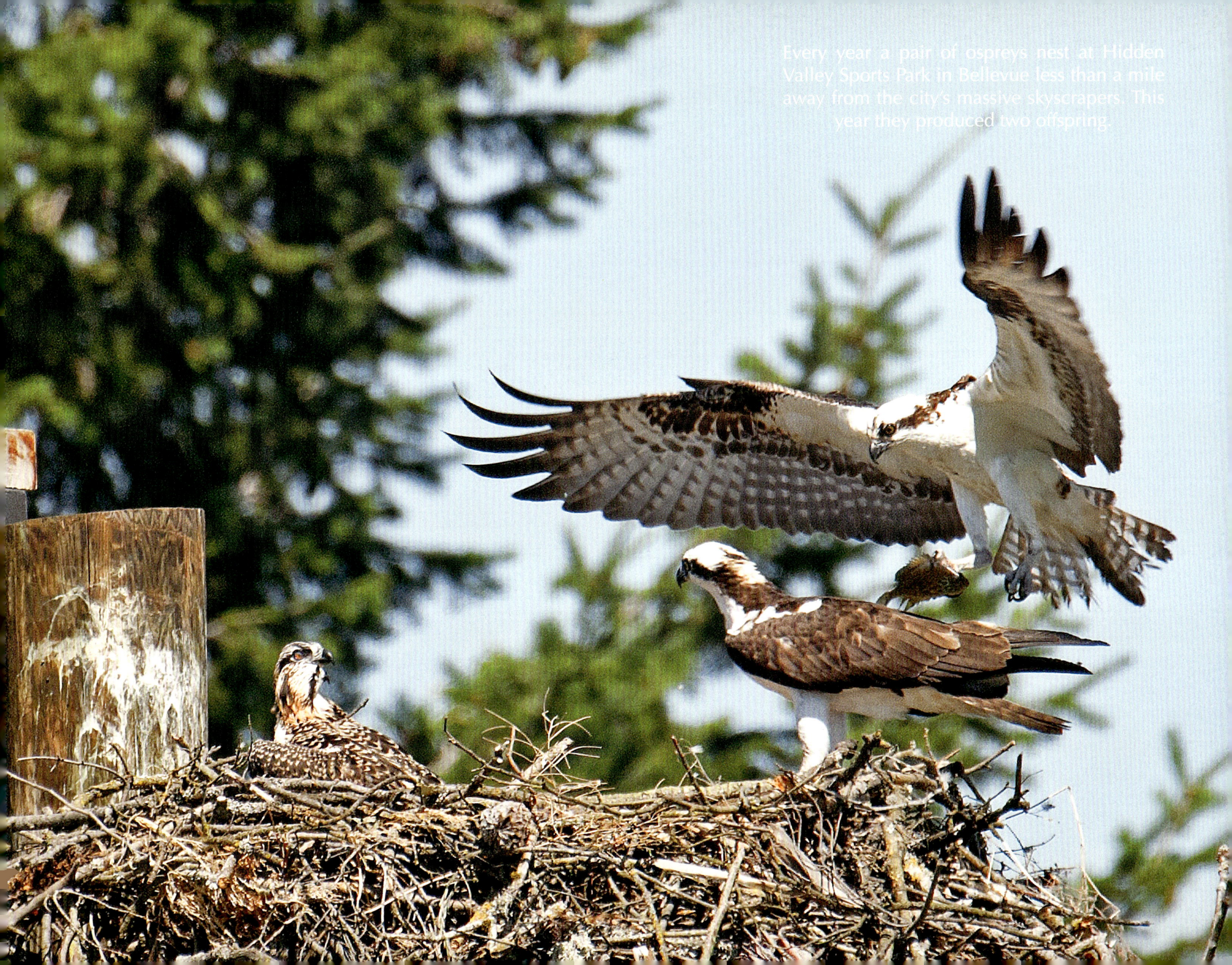

Every year a pair of ospreys nest at Hidden Valley Sports Park in Bellevue less than a mile away from the city's massive skyscrapers. This year they produced two offspring.

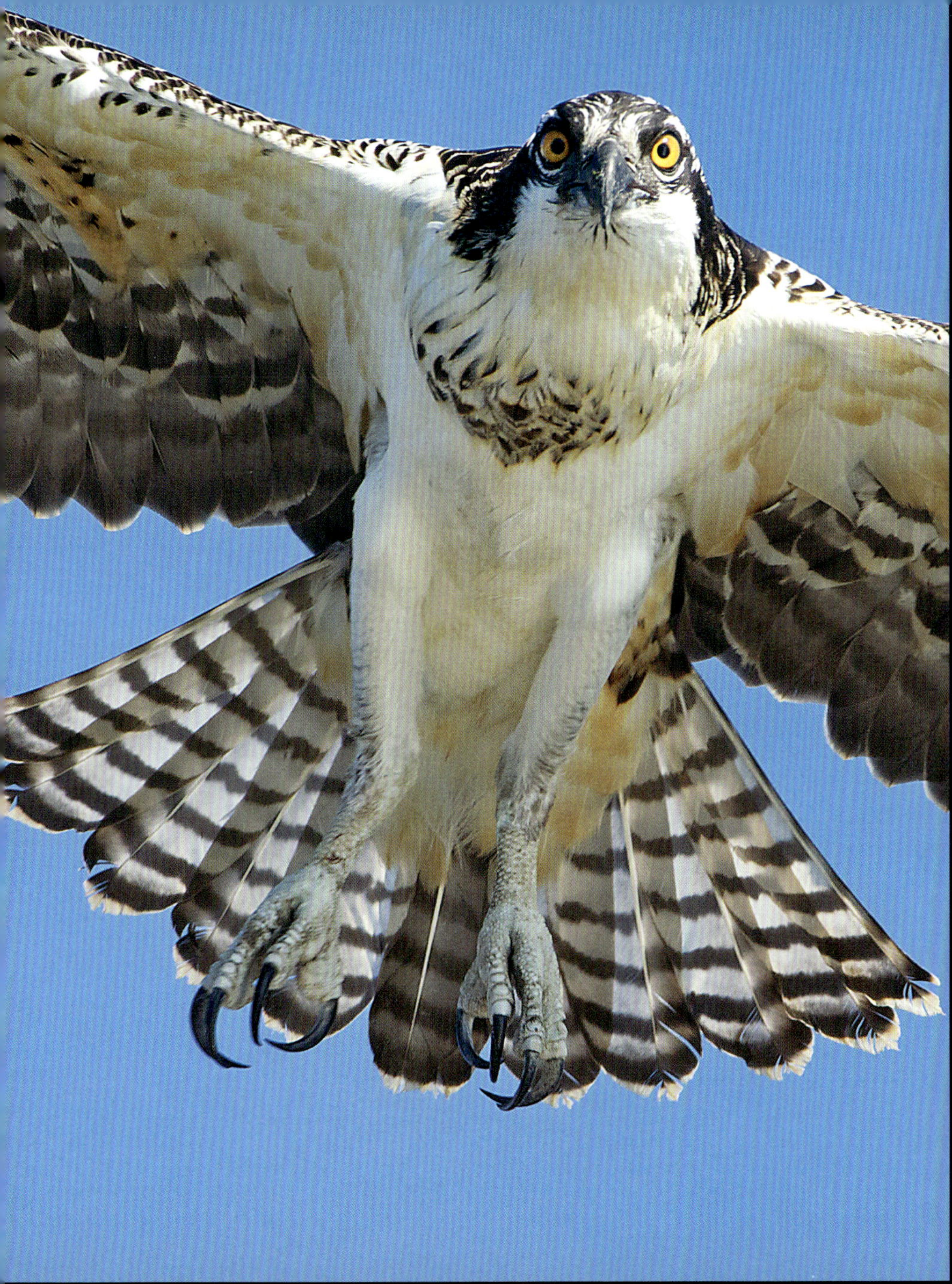

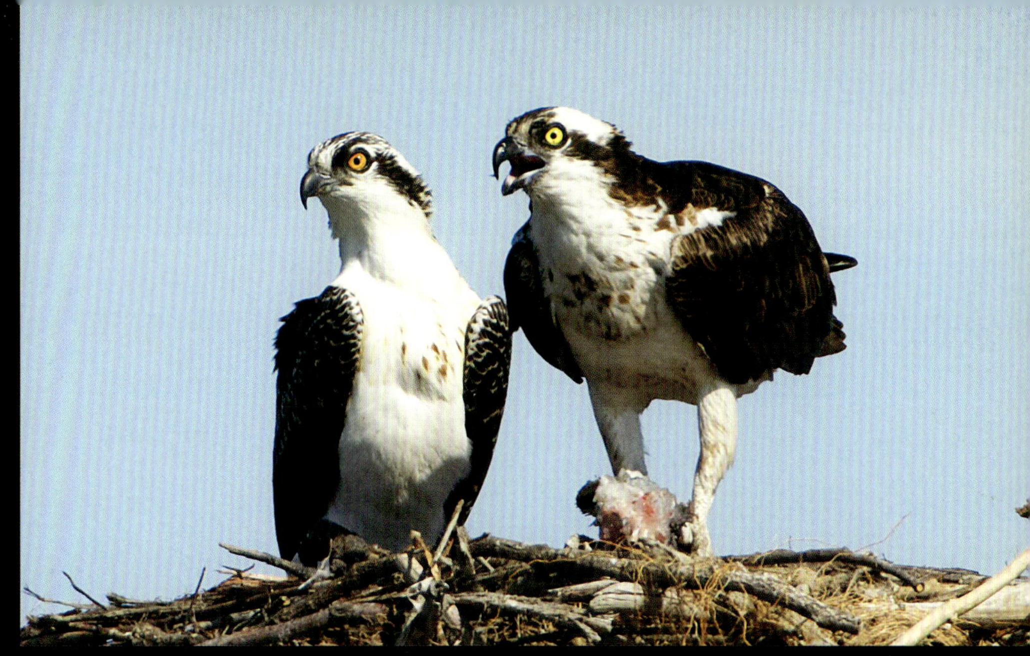

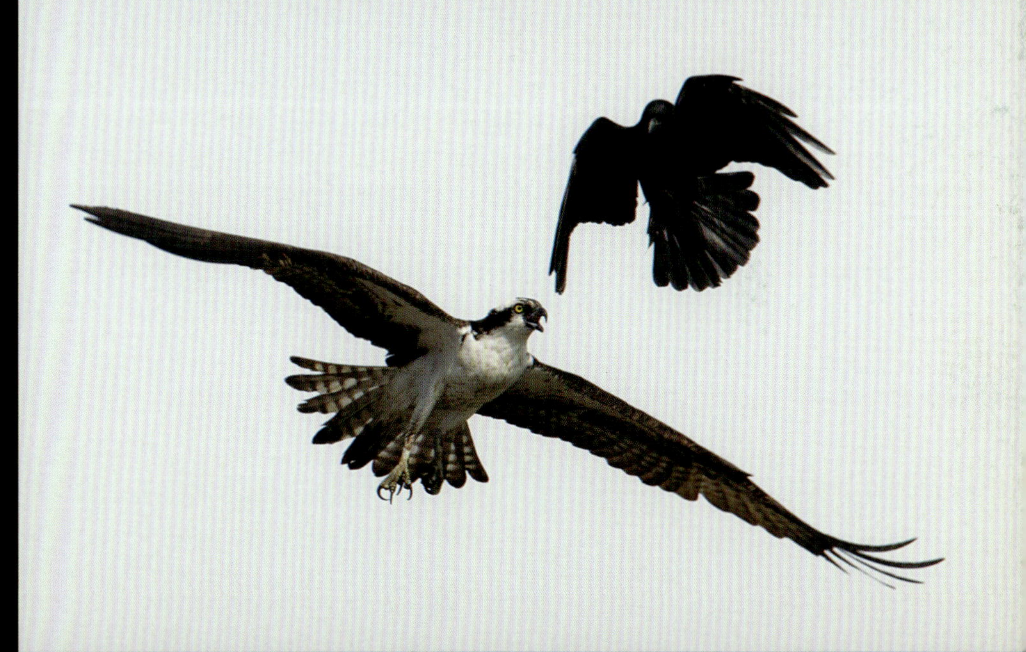

Above Left: Ospreys have massive talons designed perfectly for catching fish. *Top Right*: Juvenile and parent share their nest with a half eaten fish. *Bottom Right*: A crow and osprey engage in a territorial aerial battle.

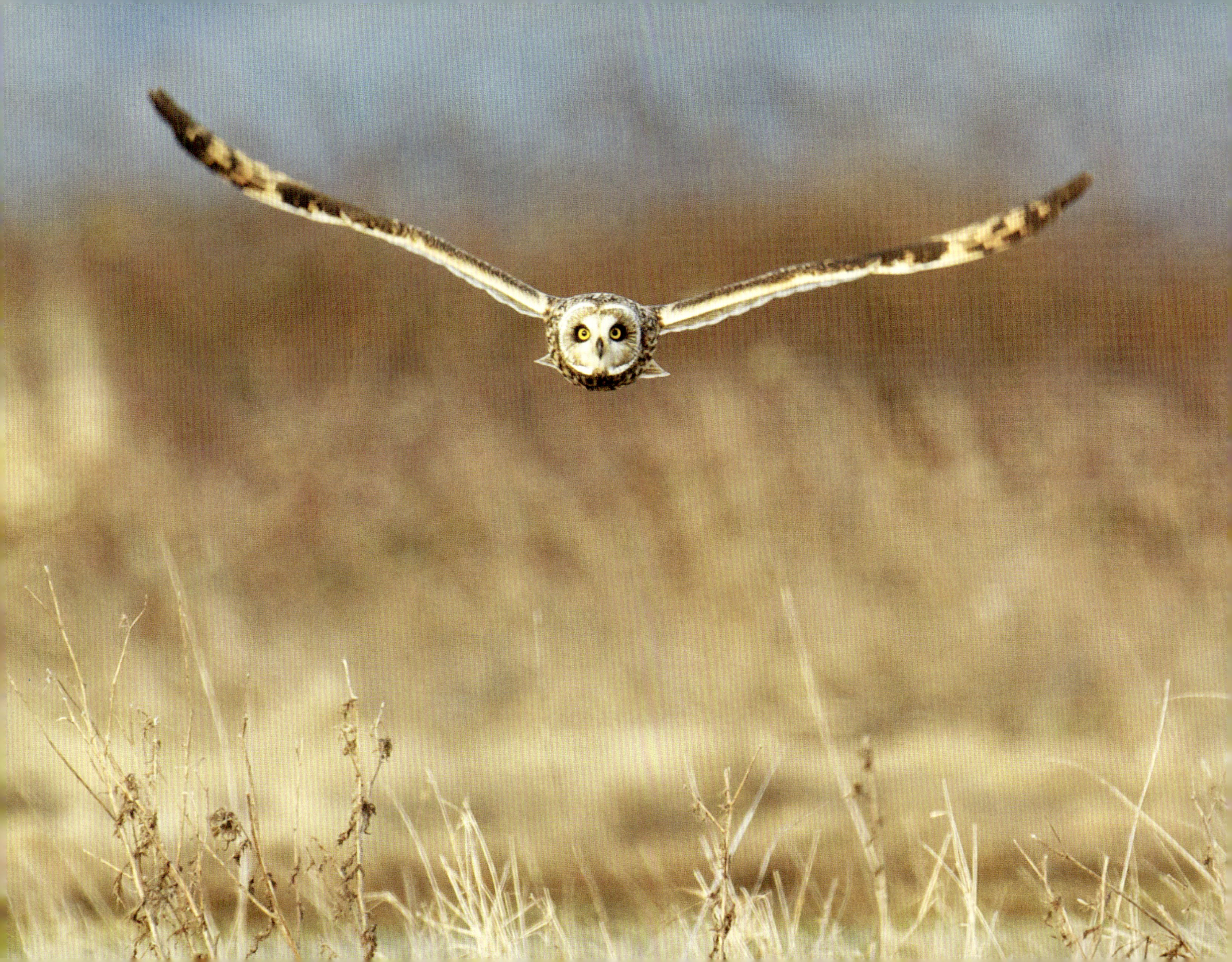

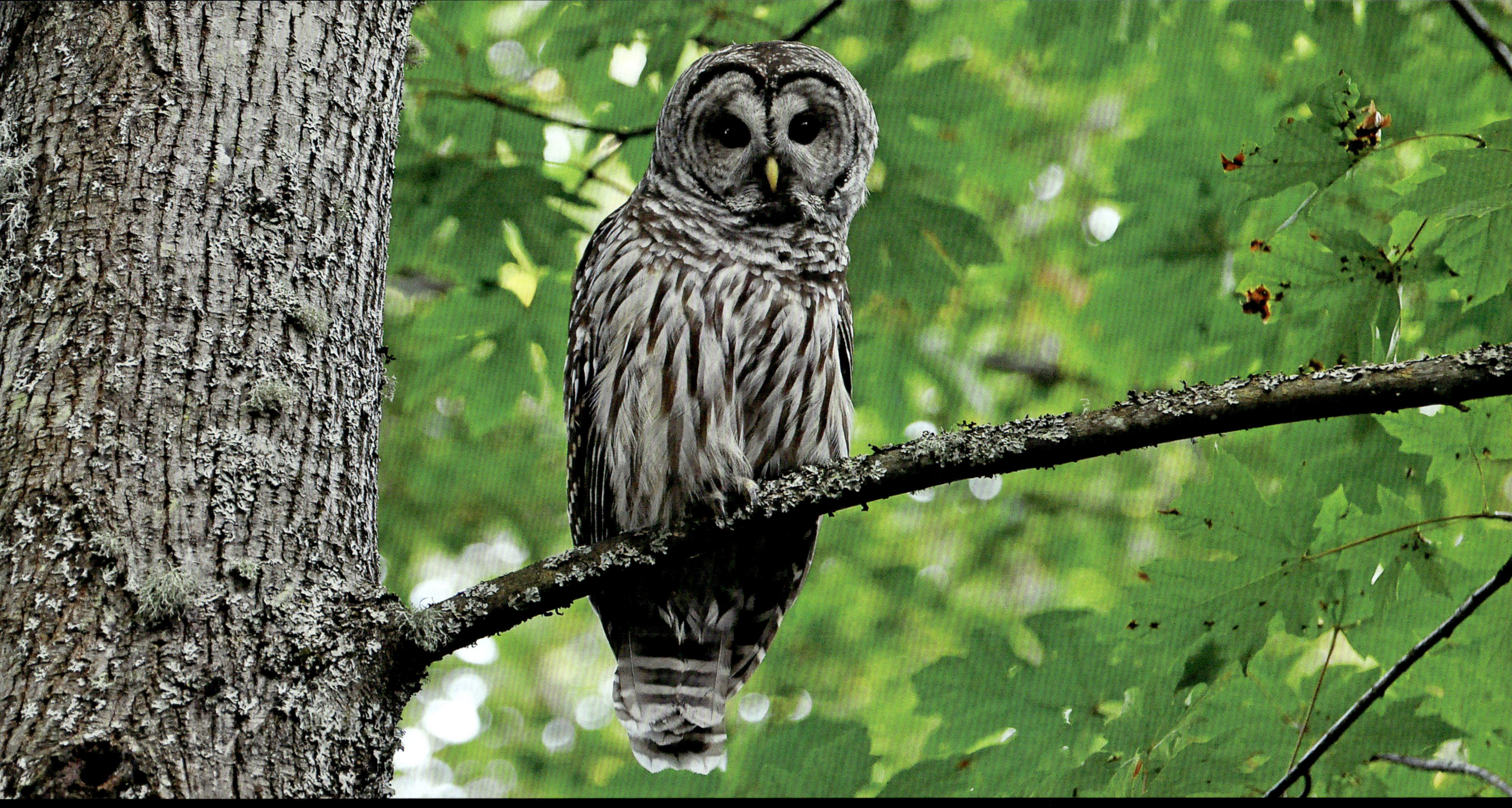

Facing Page: Owls have captivated our imaginations for centuries. They are symbols of wisdom, mystery, and mysticism. Some Native American tribes honored them as the keepers of spirits. Since most species are almost entirely active at night they are incredibly difficult to find and more so to photograph. My encounters with them have been sheer chance, or because I've waited motionless in a camouflaged blind for hours at a time for them to show themselves. Every encounter leaves me with a powerful reverence that renews my sense of wonder about these incredible birds. A short-eared owl blessed me with its presence to get this shot as it hunted a grassy field for rodents. Marymoor Park in Redmond at dusk and dawn is a great place to look for these owls.

Above: Owls have a humanlike presence. It was an exhilarating experience to photograph this barred owl in Discovery Park as it prepared for its nightly hunt.

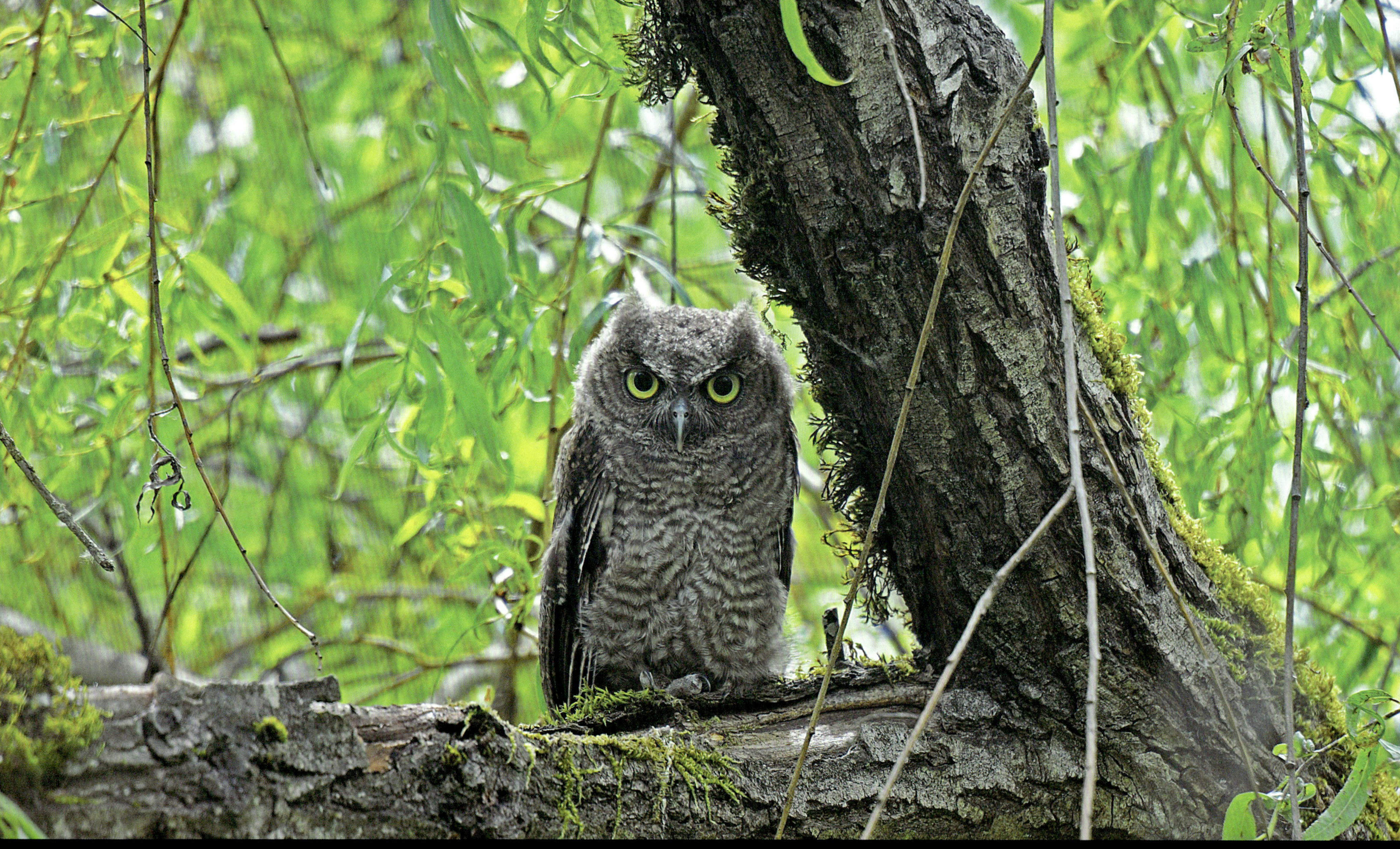

Above: One morning in August this elusive western screech owl provided me a rare and intimate look. I always thank mother nature when I have an uncommon wildlife encounter such as this.

Facing Page: I visited this barn 15 to 20 times and spent dozens of hours without success before I was able to photograph this barn owl. I sat motionless for four hours in the pitch black one night before it finally showed its face. The scream of a barn owl at night when you are alone is horrifying.

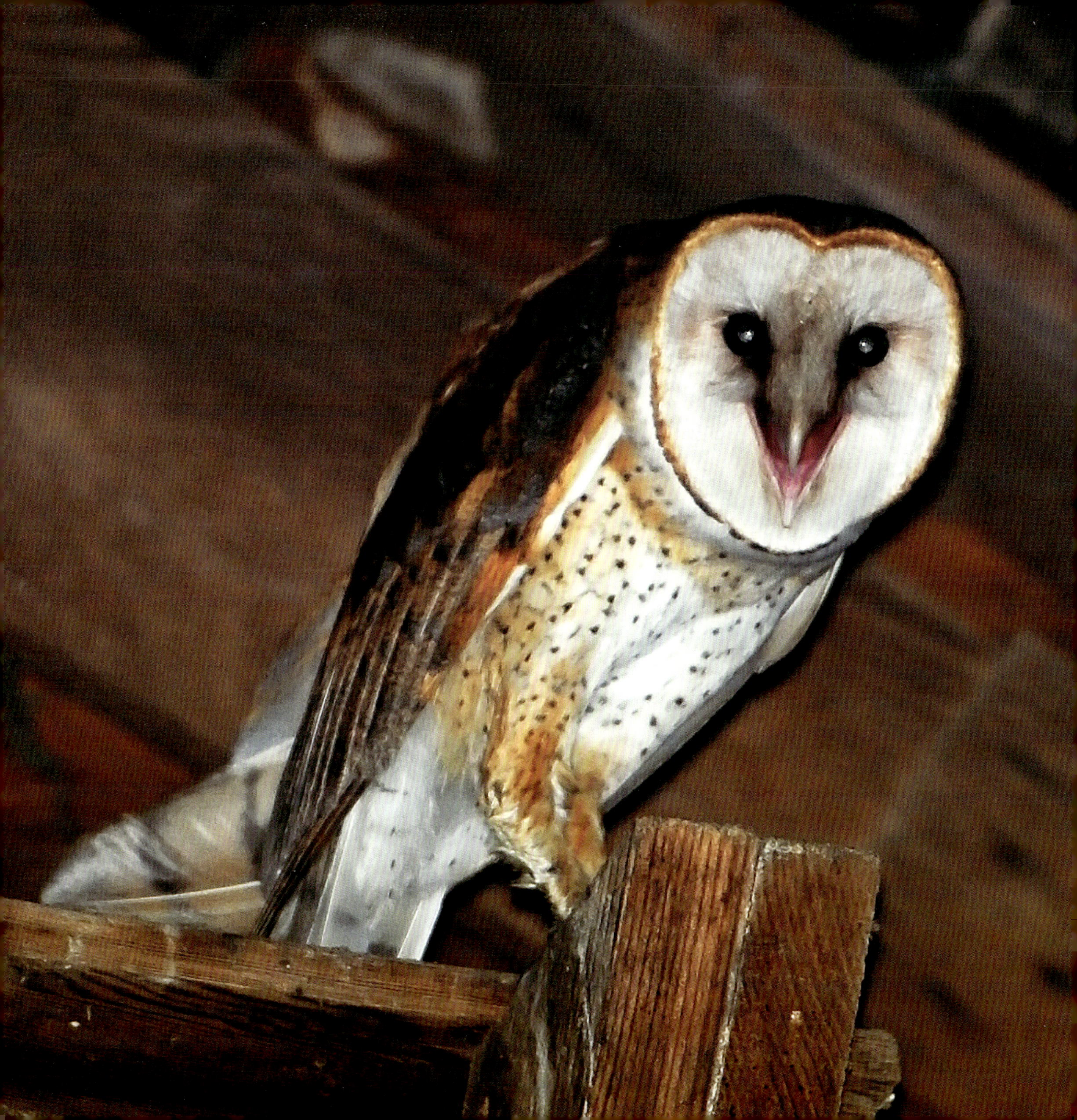

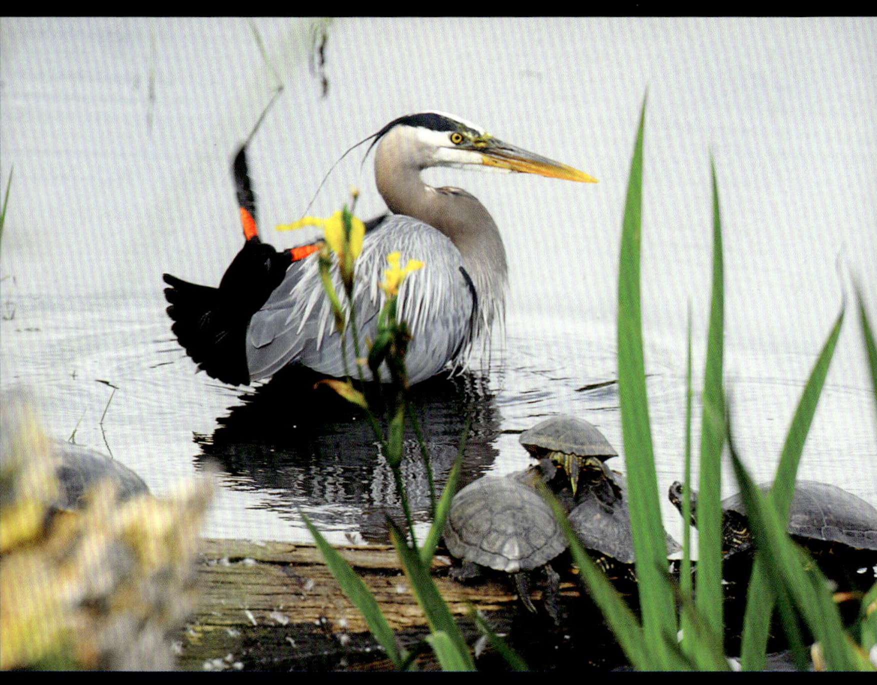

Above: A red-winged blackbird flies into a beautiful composition of great blue heron and turtles, making this photo truly unique.

Right: It is always suspenseful to watch great blue herons hunt and they are common throughout the Lake Washington region. They wait motionless along the water's edge ready to dive head-first into the water to catch a meal. This was an unusually large catch.

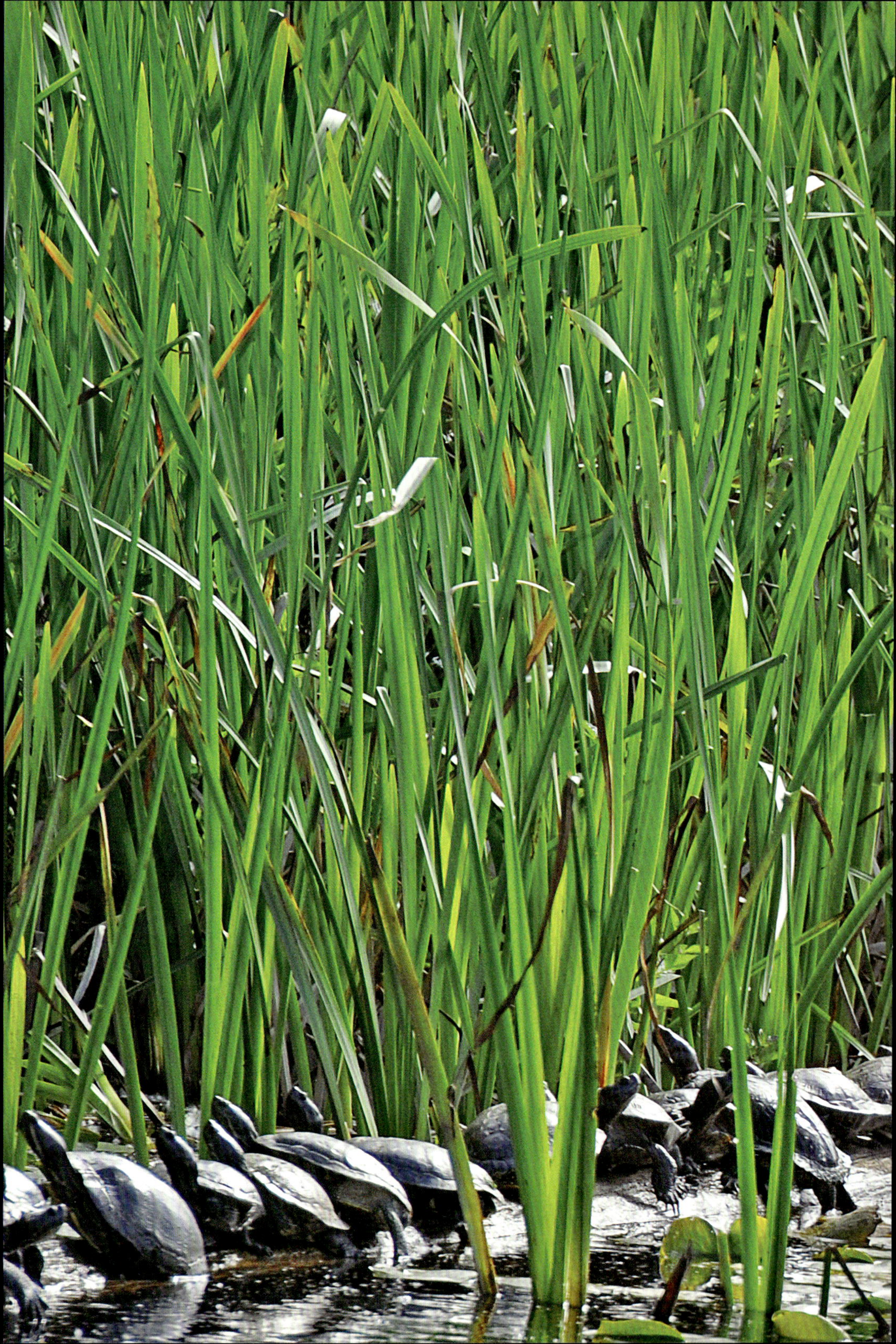

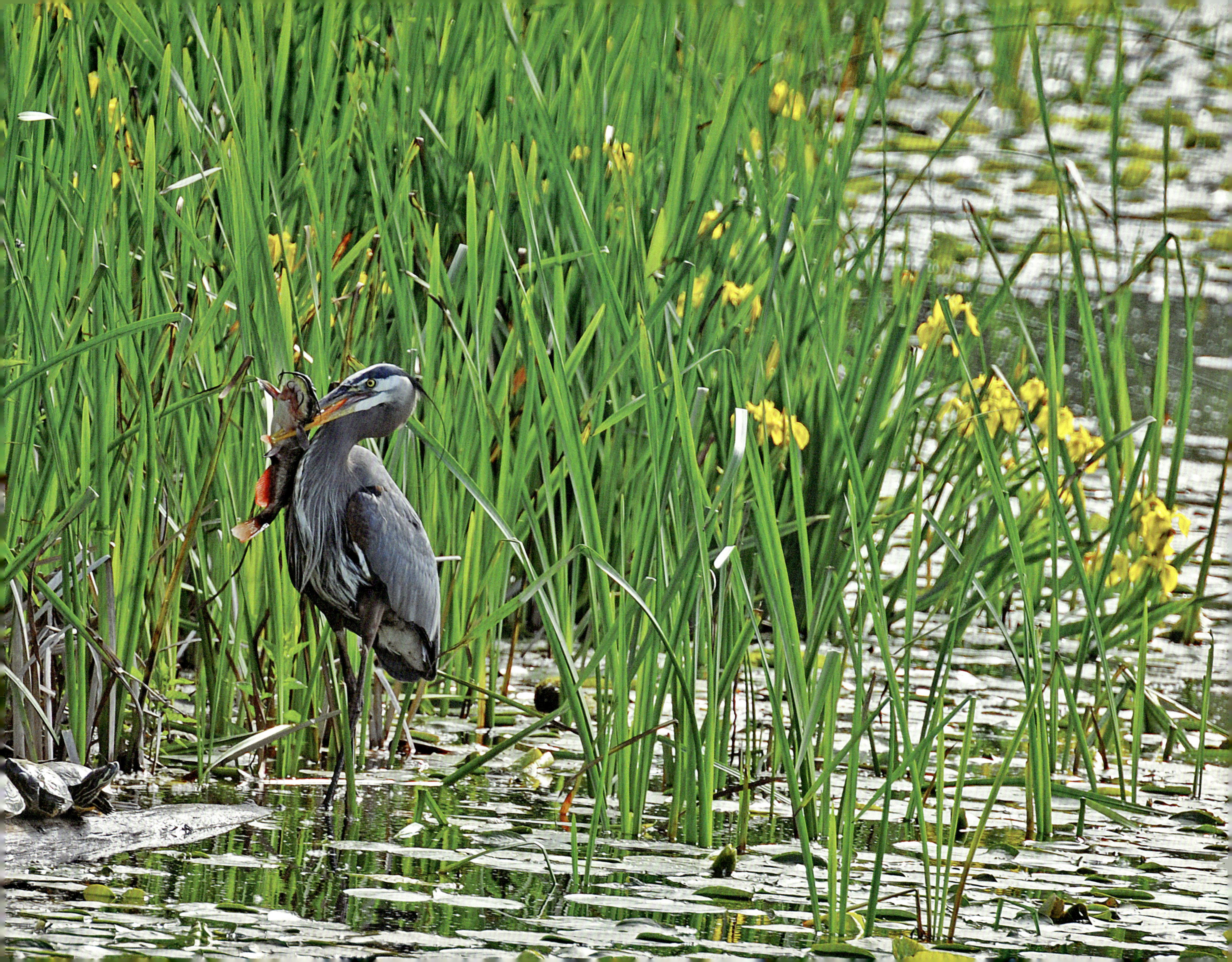

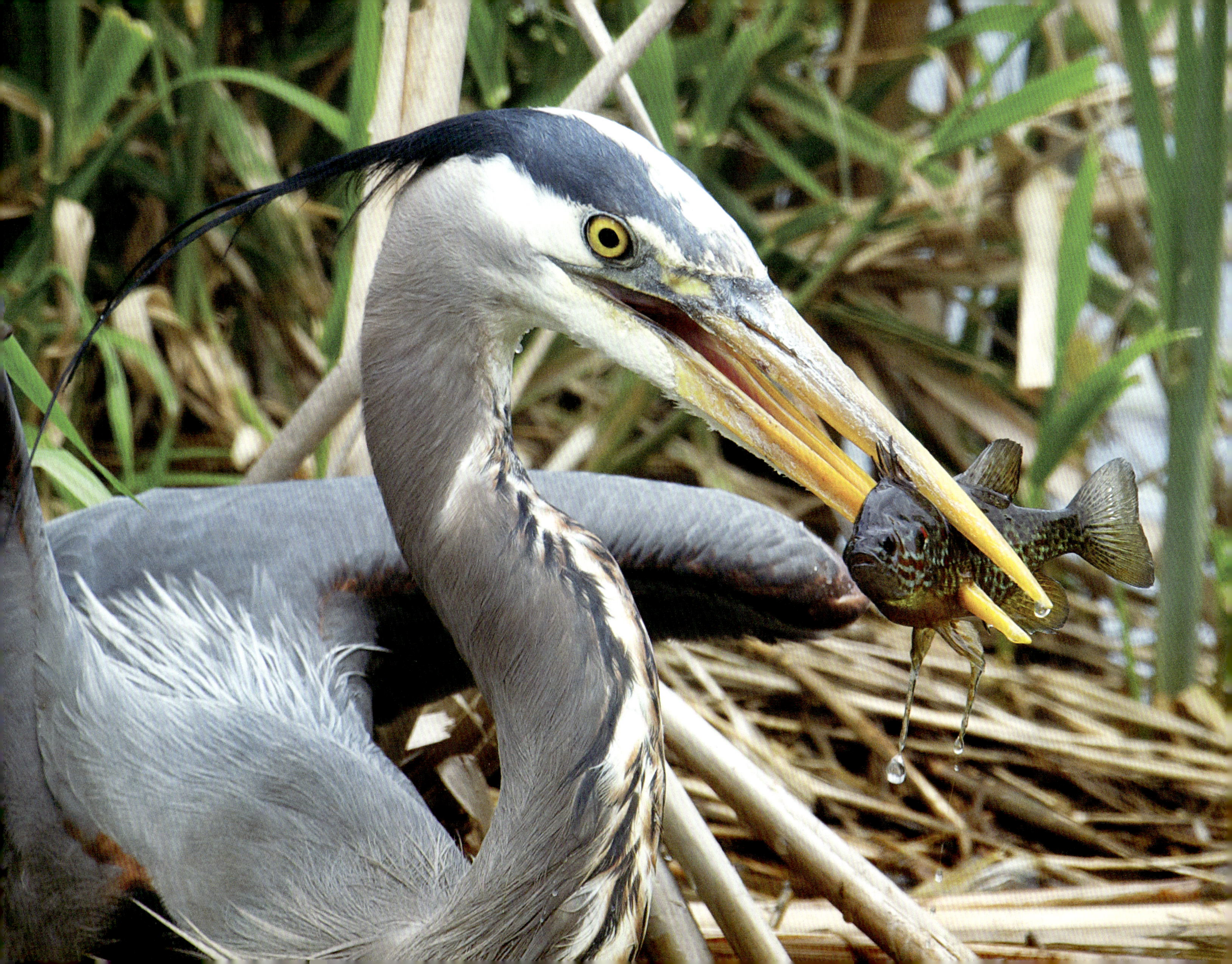

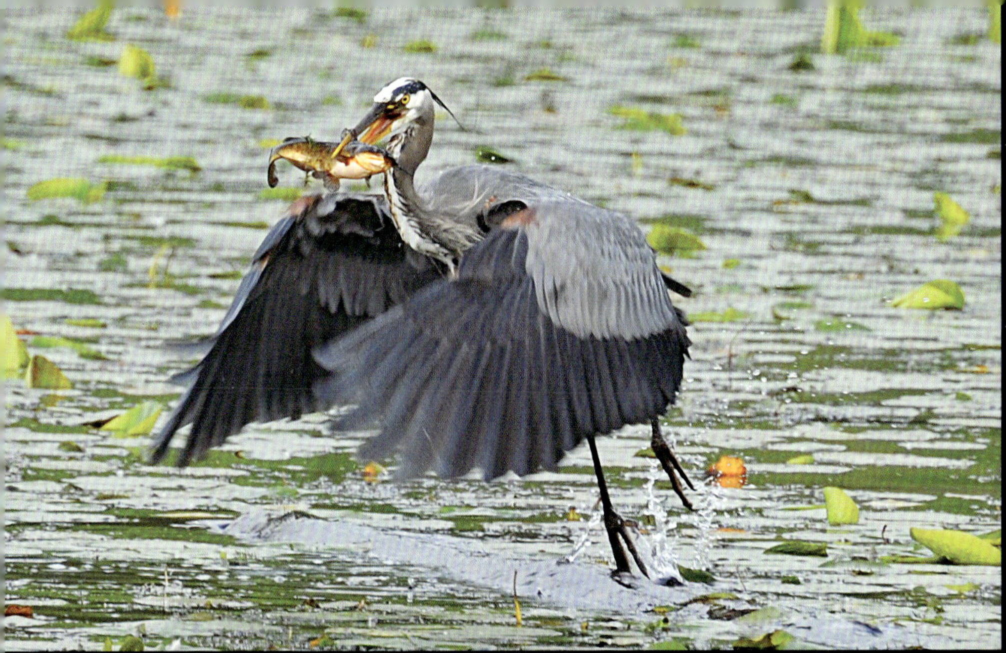

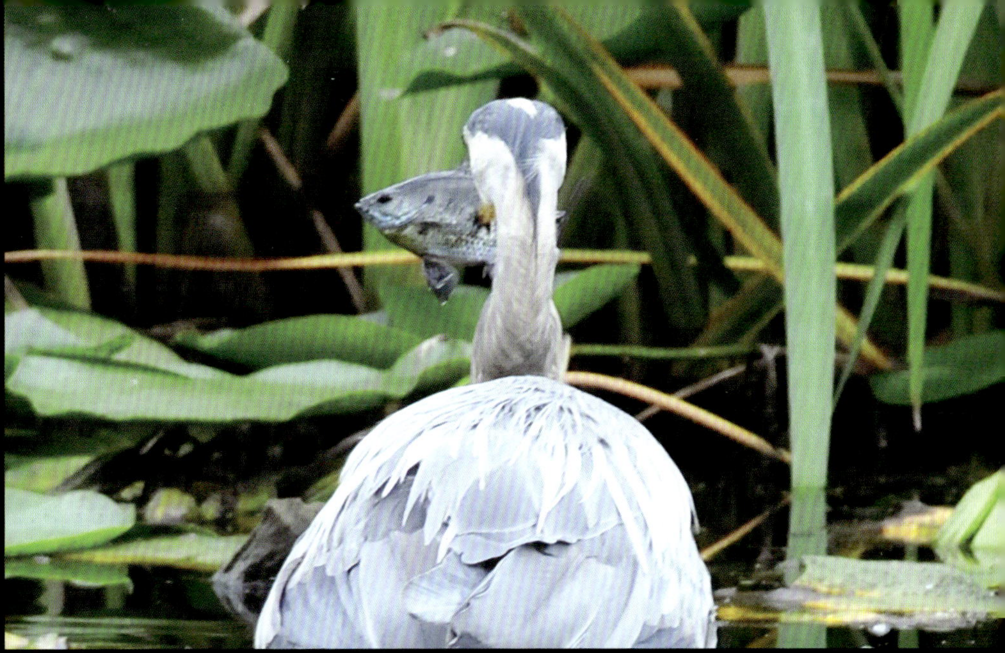

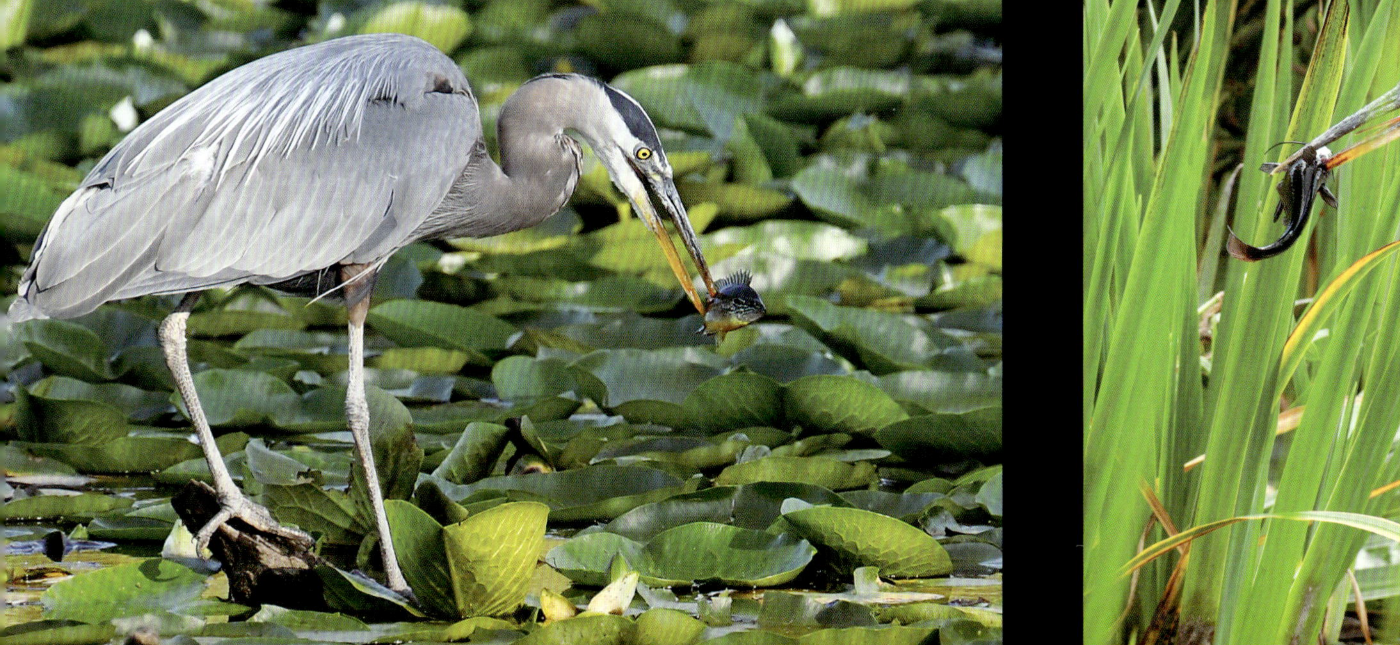

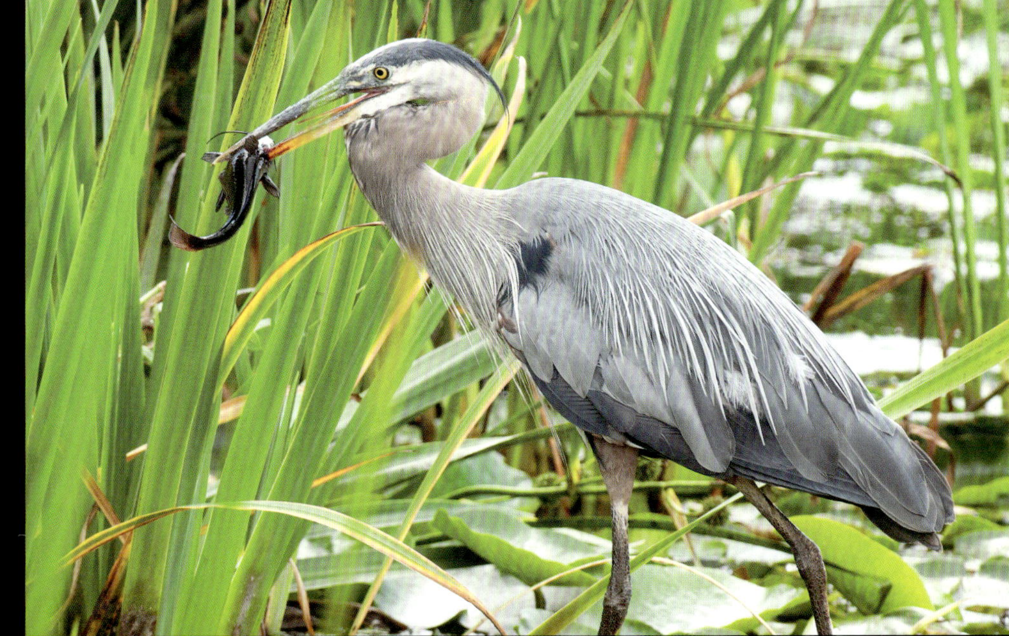

I have photographed great blue herons spearing an amazing variety of fish, reptiles, and even mice. After catching their meal, they usually walk or fly to a secluded spot where they swallow it whole.

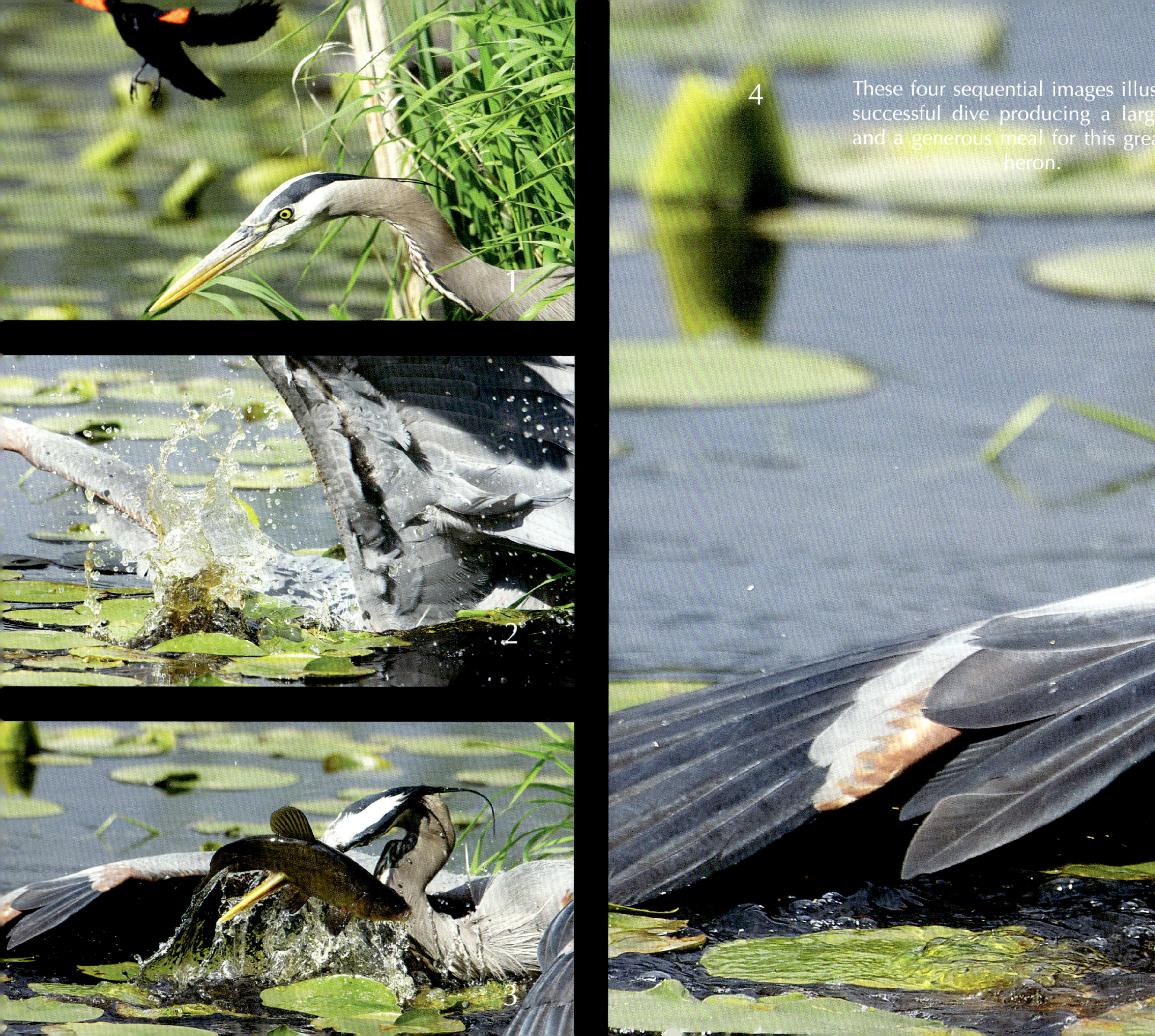

These four sequential images illustrate a successful dive producing a large carp and a generous meal for this great blue heron.

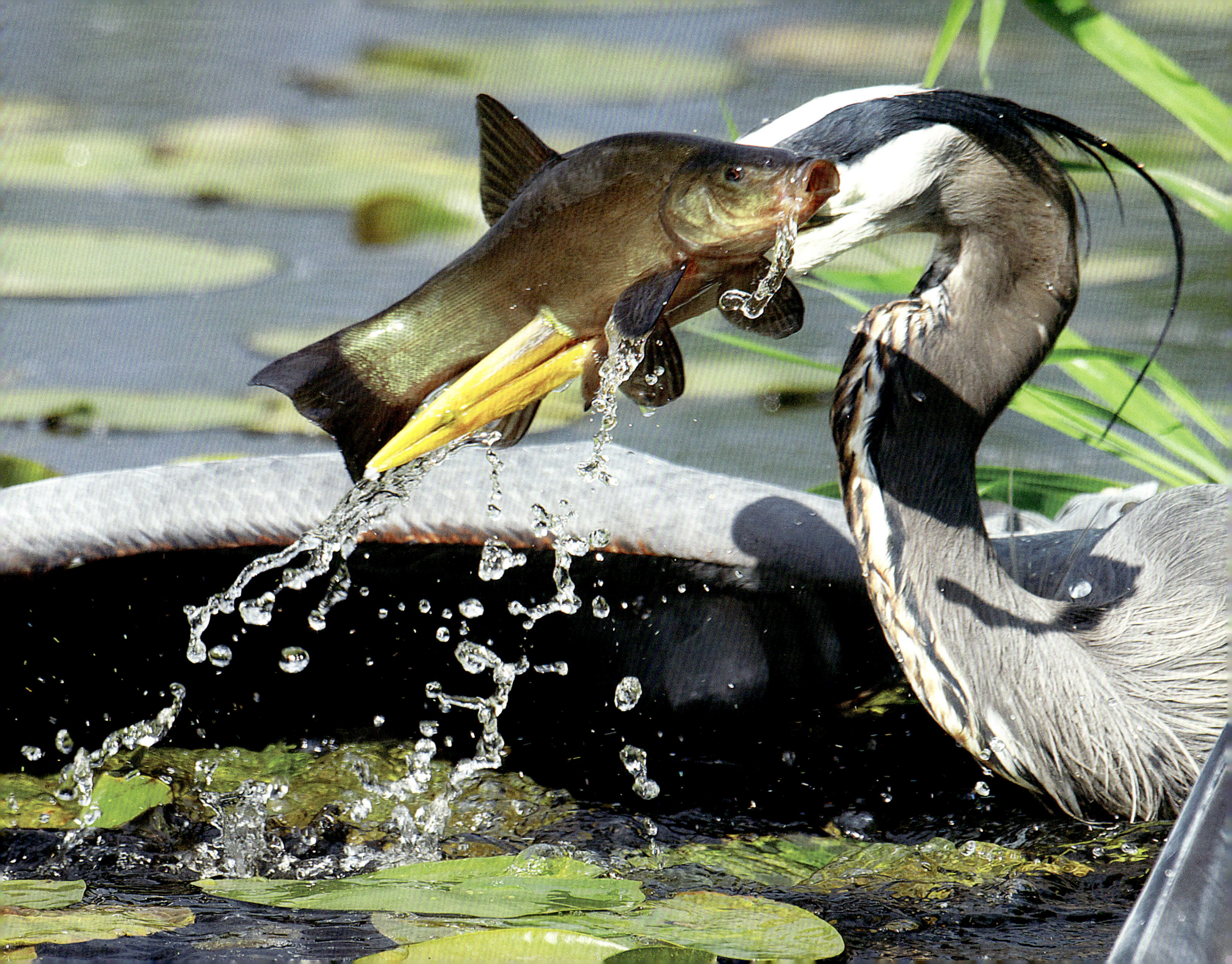

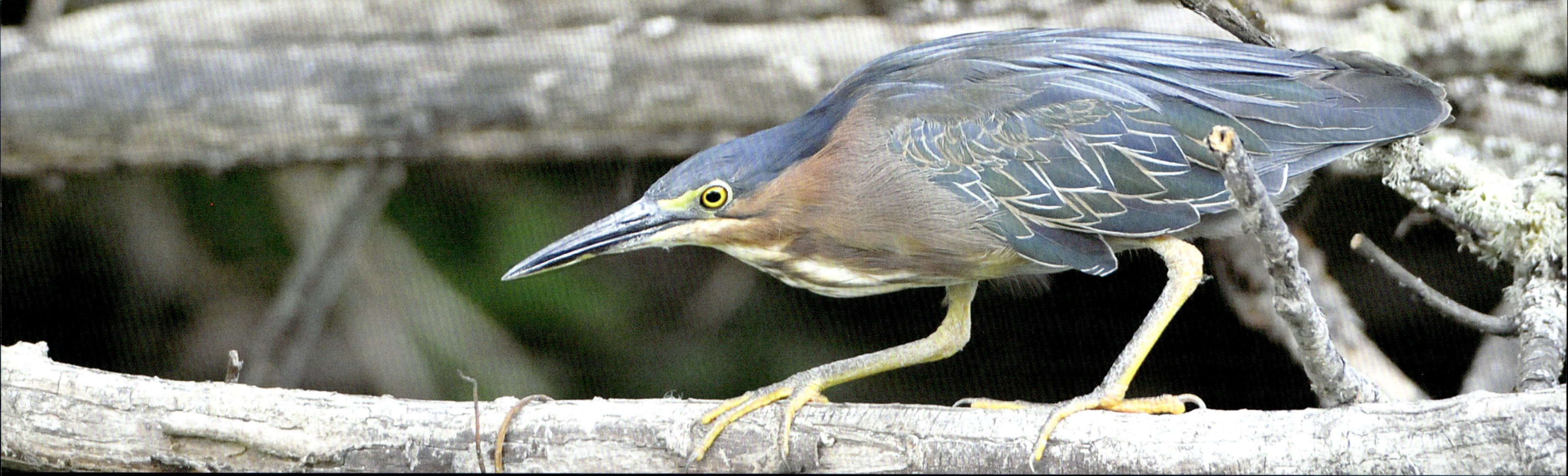

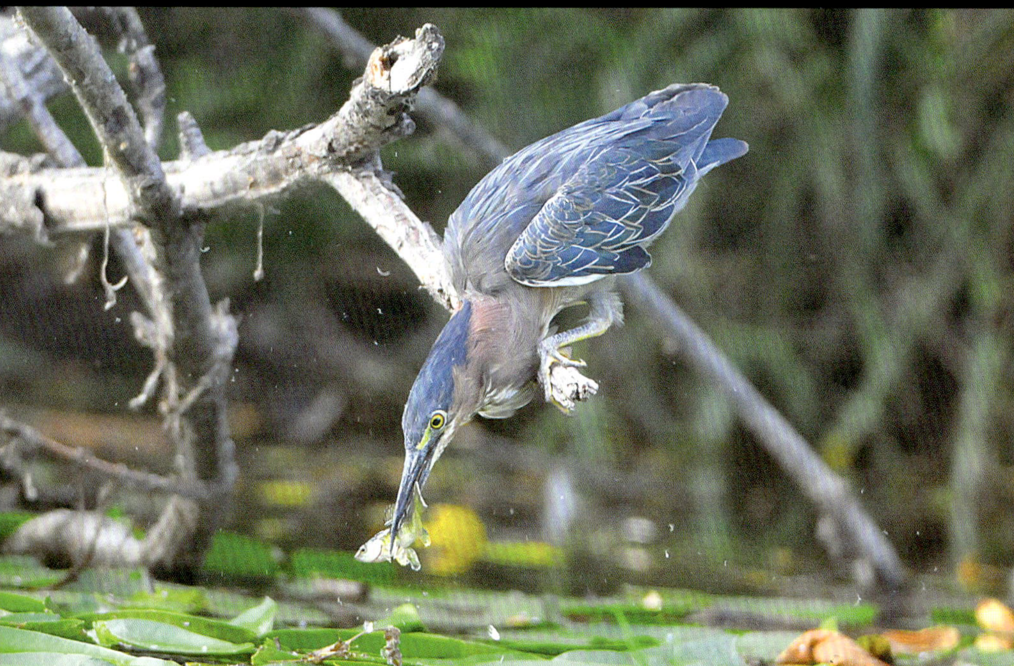

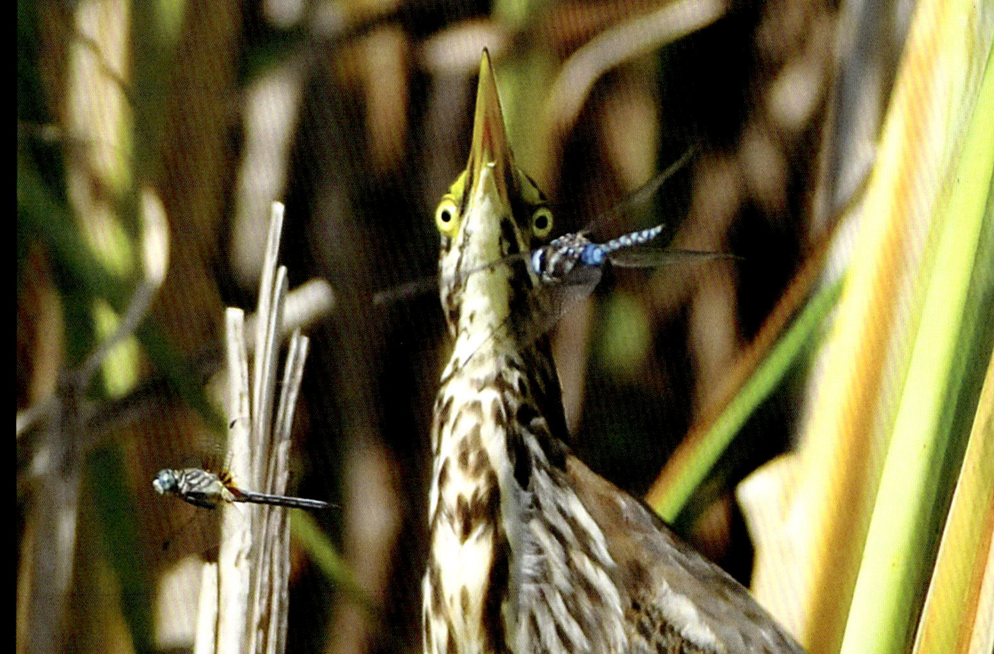

Top: Green herons occasionally drop small objects on the water's surface to attract fish to catch, making them one of the few known tool-using species in the world. Green herons are common near the Sammamish Slough at Marymoor Park. _Bottom Left_: A green heron snatches a fish. _Bottom Right_: This hunting juvenile green heron prepares to snatch one of two dragonflies.

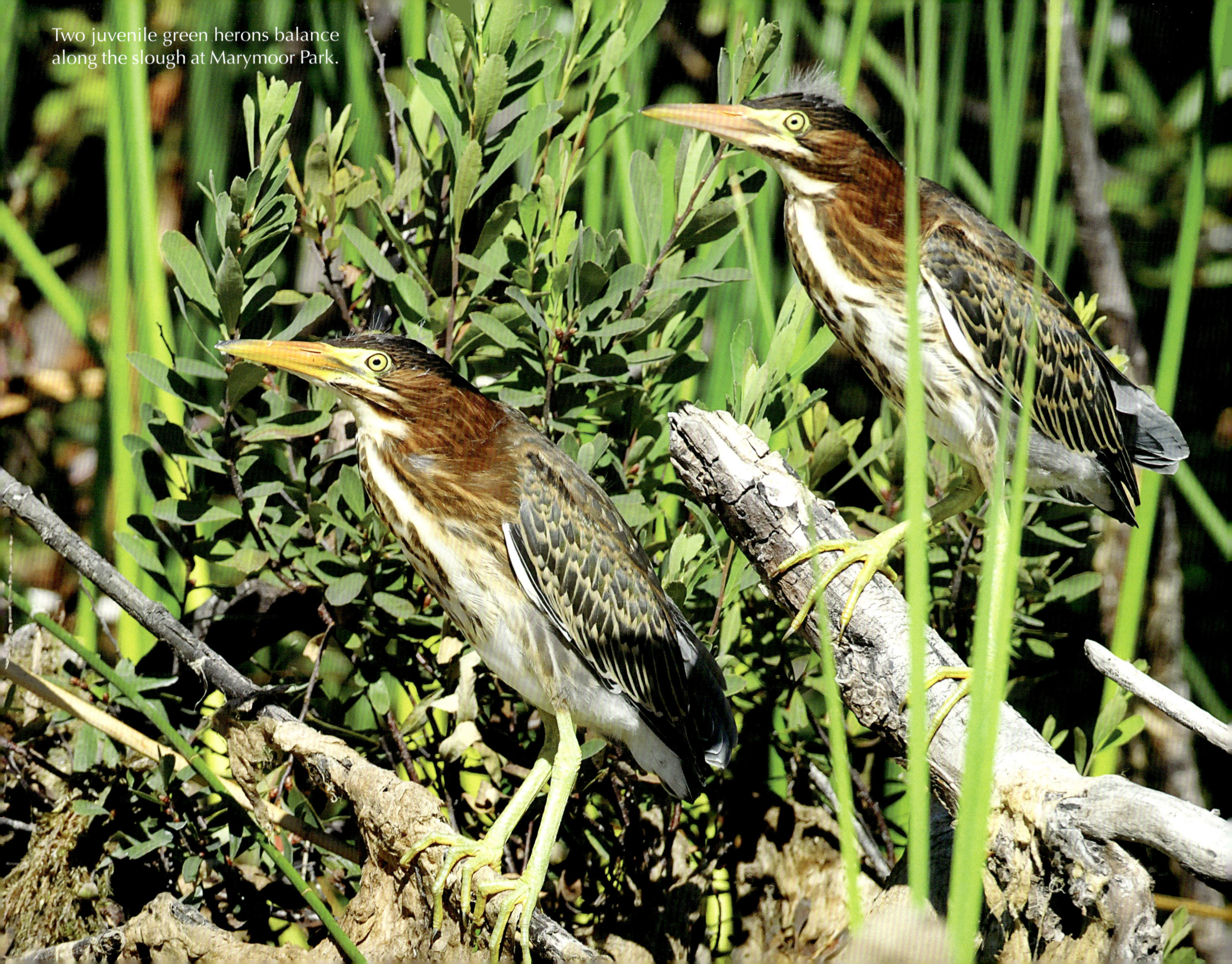

Two juvenile green herons balance along the slough at Marymoor Park.

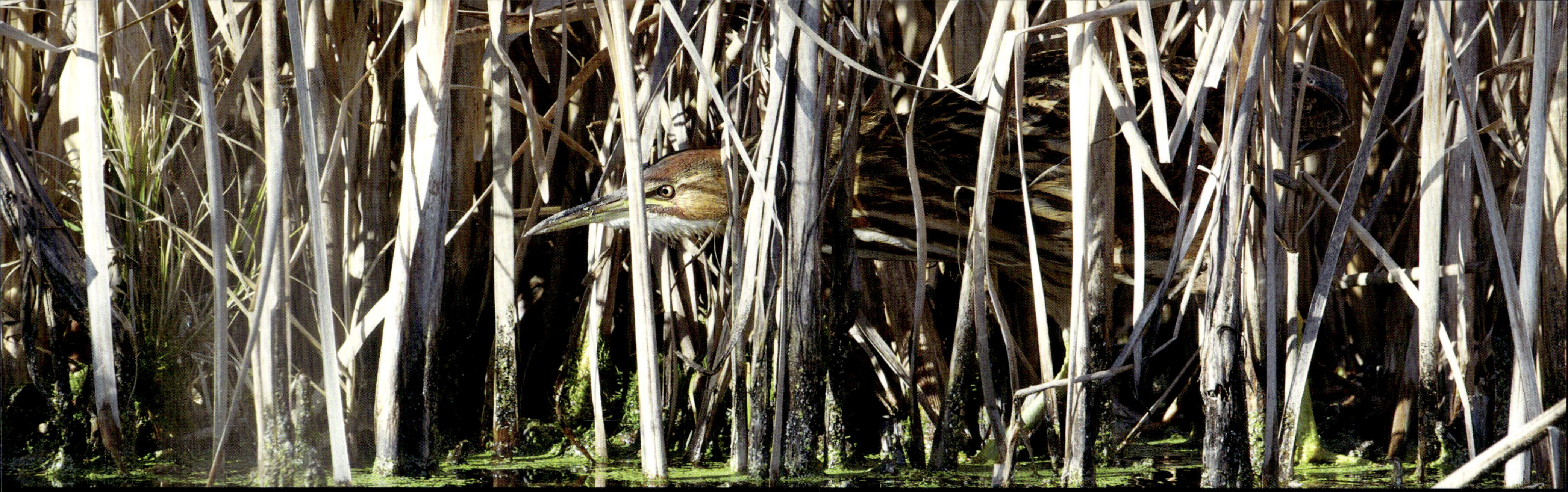

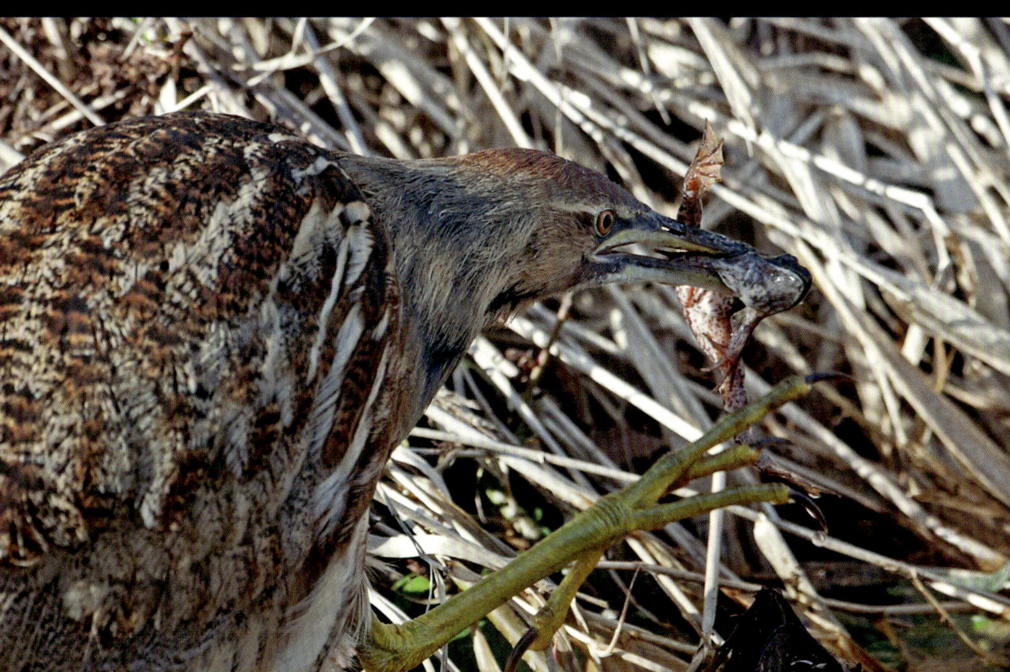

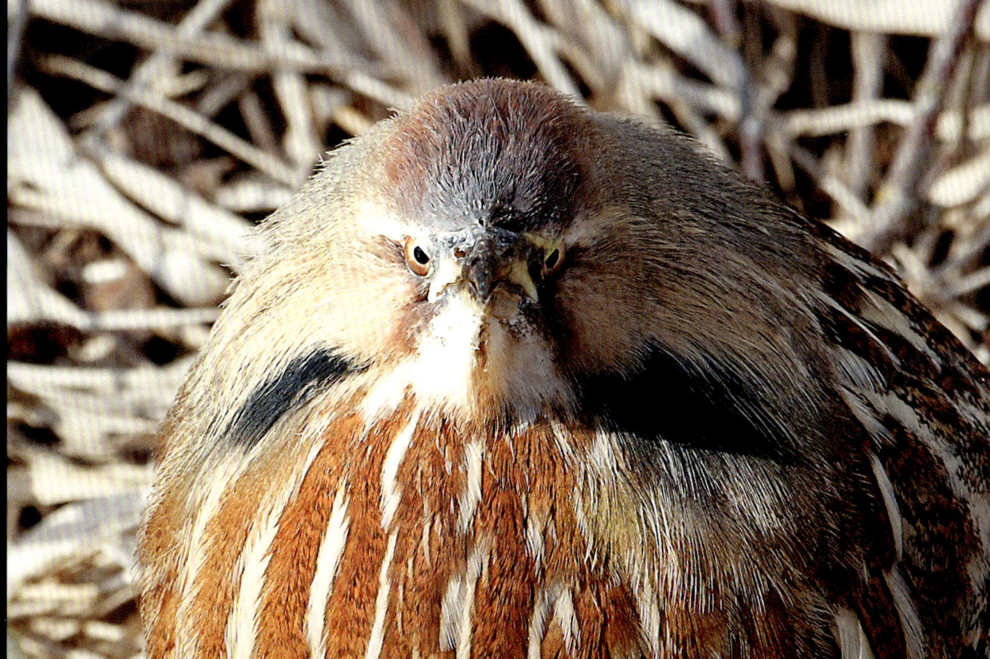

Top: The American bittern is a secretive heron-like bird that blends very well into its environment. *Bottom Left*: A frog in early spring makes a great snack for this bittern. *Bottom Right*: When startled, bitterns often freeze rather than fly, then sway to blend in like reeds in the wind. *Facing Page*: At times bitterns can be almost impossible to distinguish from their surroundings.

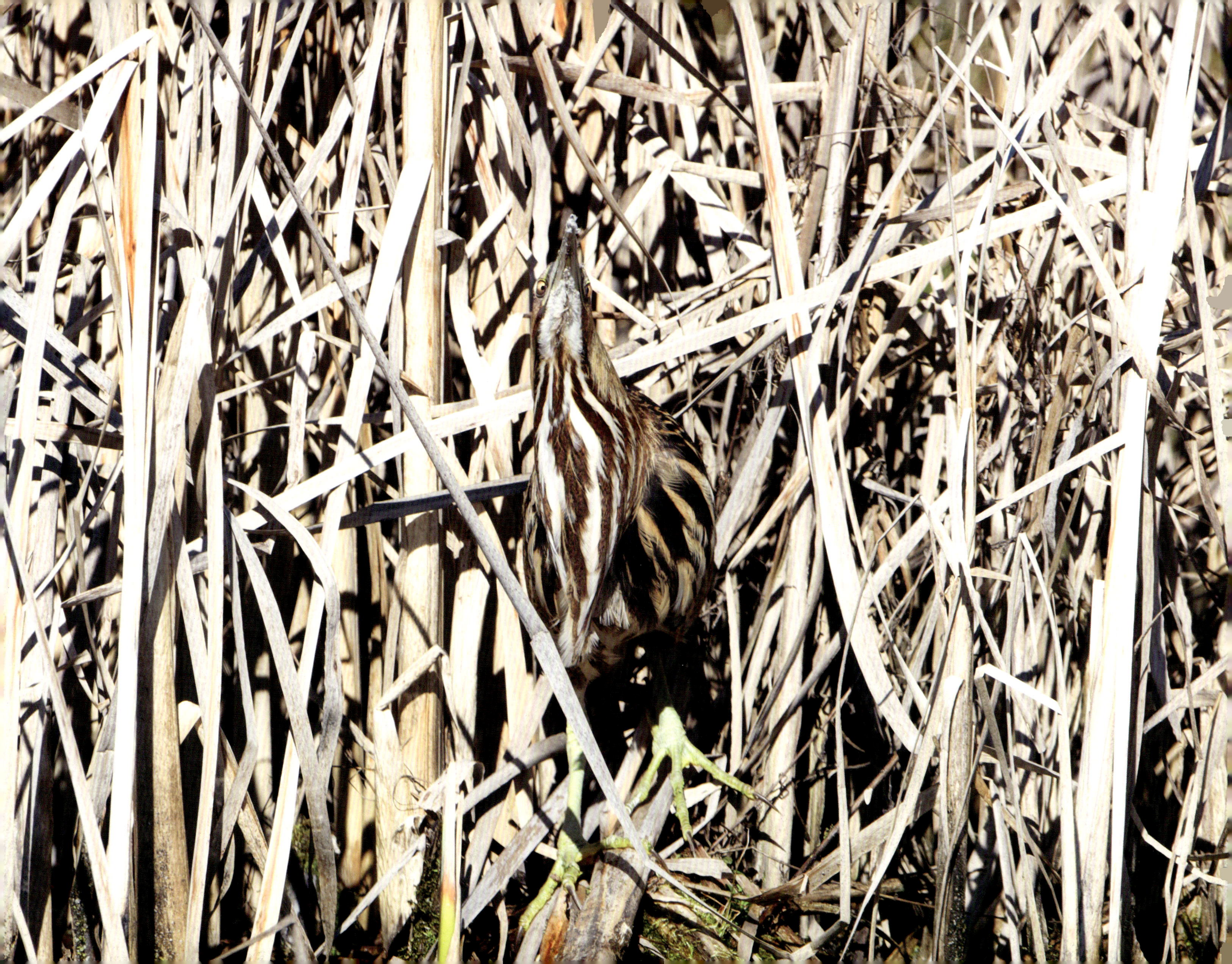

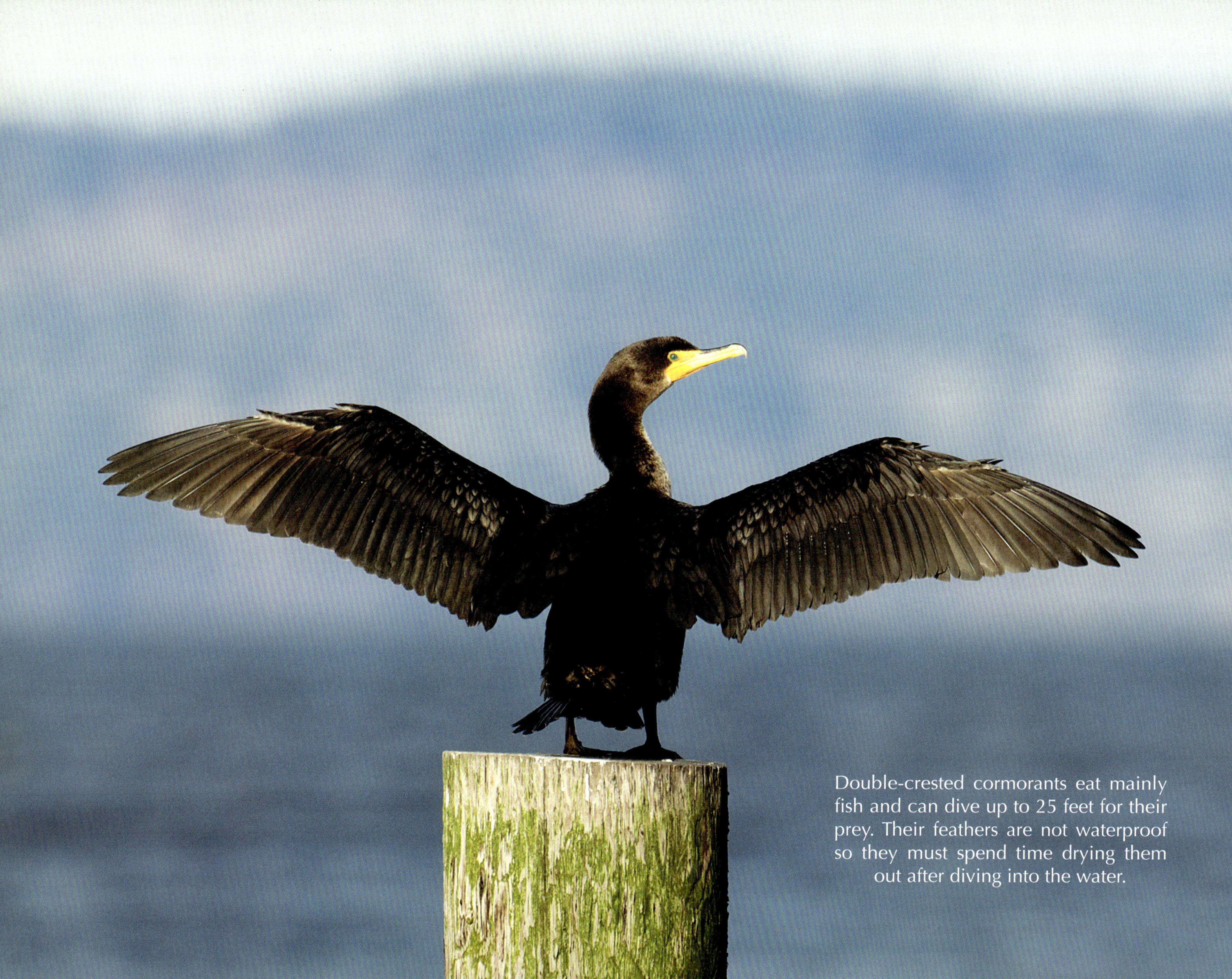

Double-crested cormorants eat mainly fish and can dive up to 25 feet for their prey. Their feathers are not waterproof so they must spend time drying them out after diving into the water.

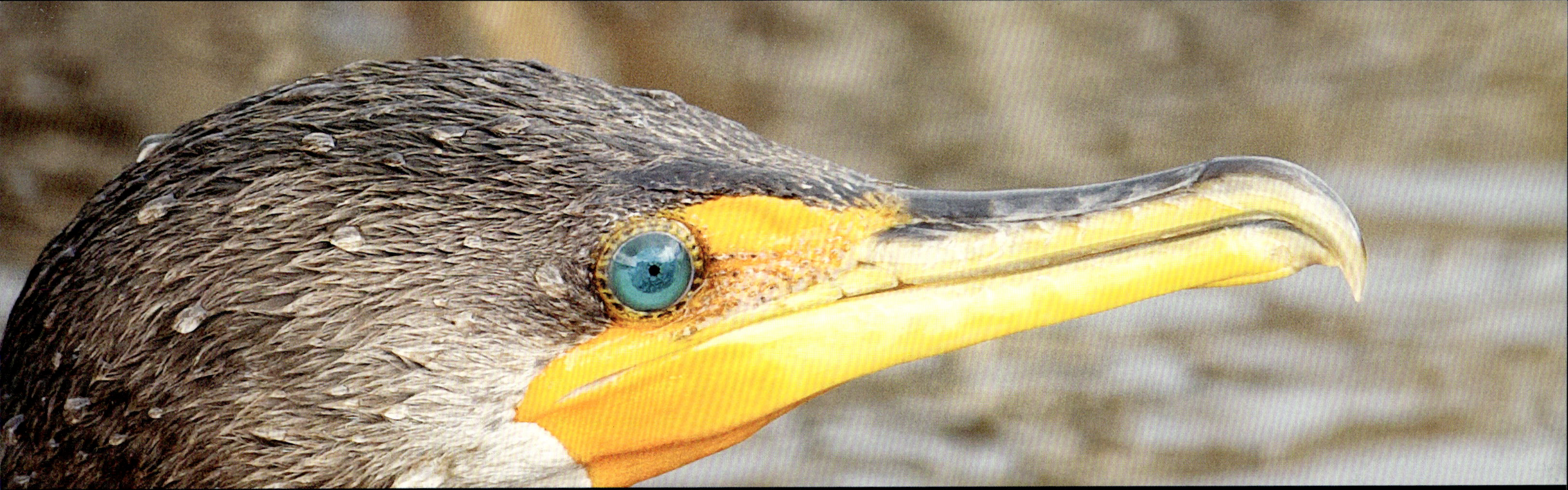

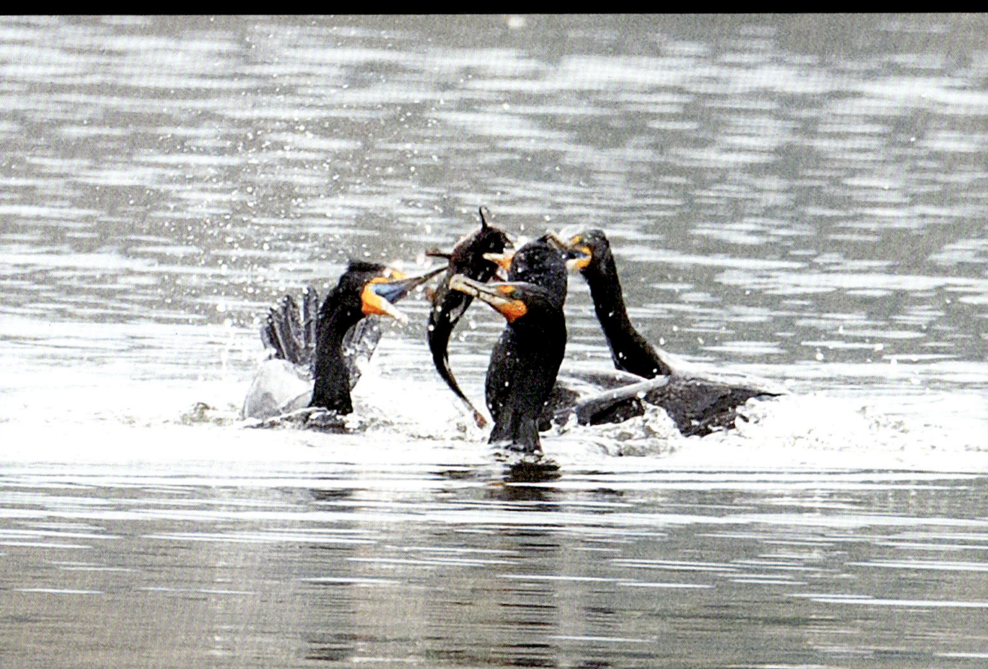

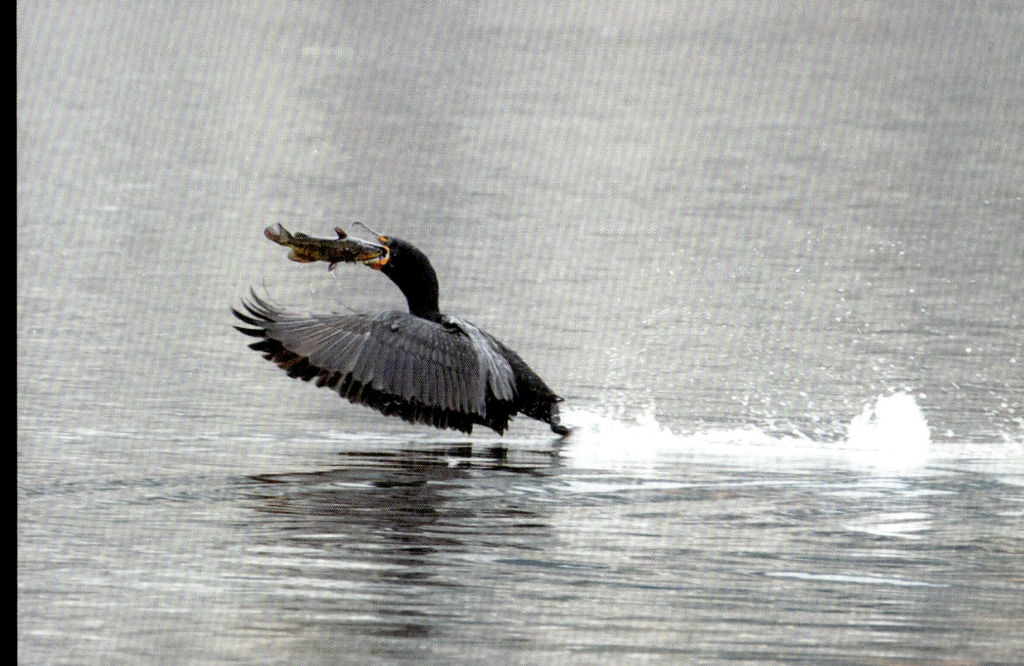

Top: Juvenile double-crested cormorants have lighter colored feathers. *Bottom Left*: Occasionally, cormorants catch very large fish which attract other birds and result in a tug of war or chase for the meal. *Bottom Right*: The tug of war winner takes the prize.

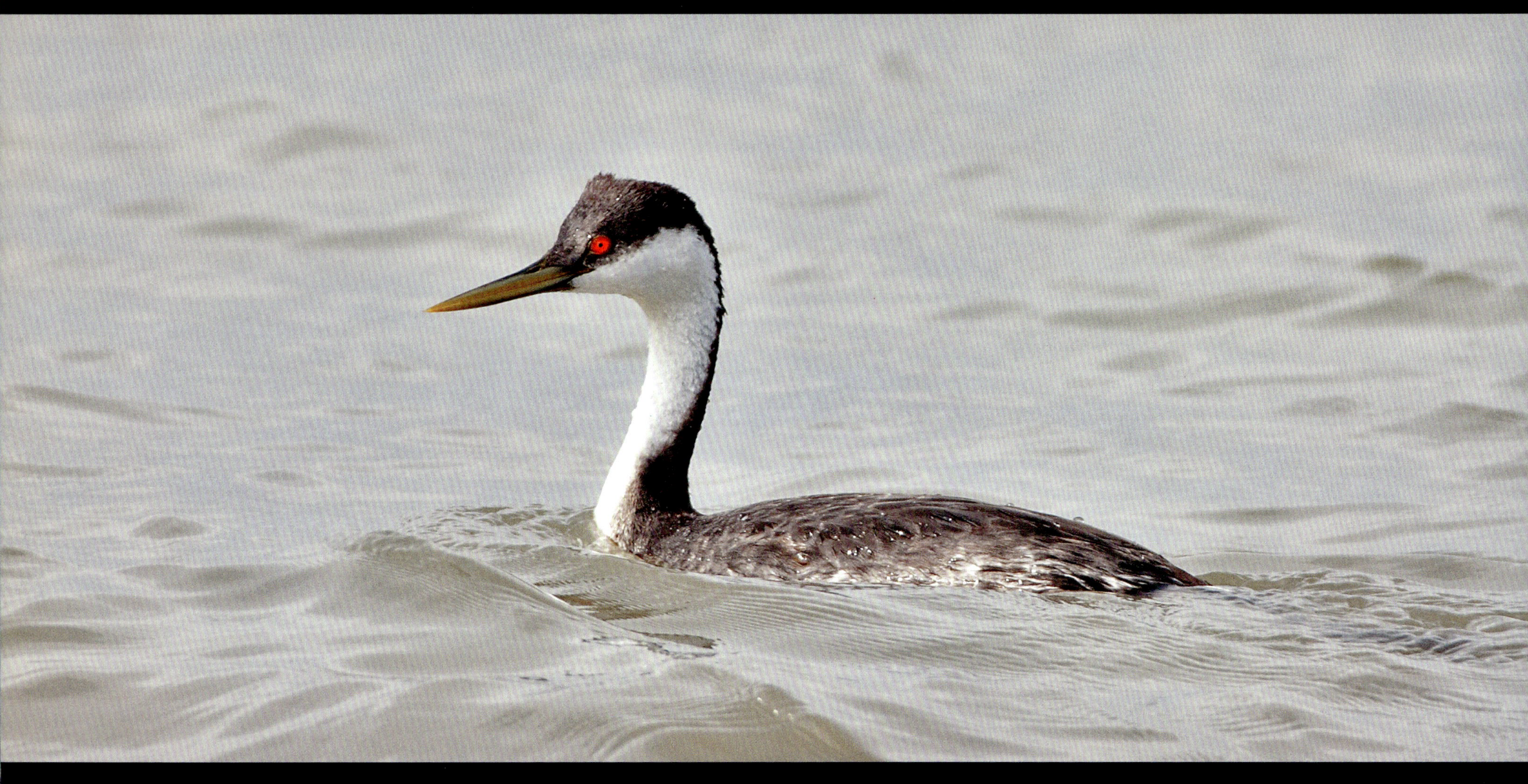

Above: A good place to look for western grebes, like this one, is on the water as you cross the 520 bridge.

Facing Page: I see red-breasted mergansers most commonly on saltwater. Occasionally I am surprised with a view of one on Lake Washington, so keep your eyes peeled for this gorgeous bird.

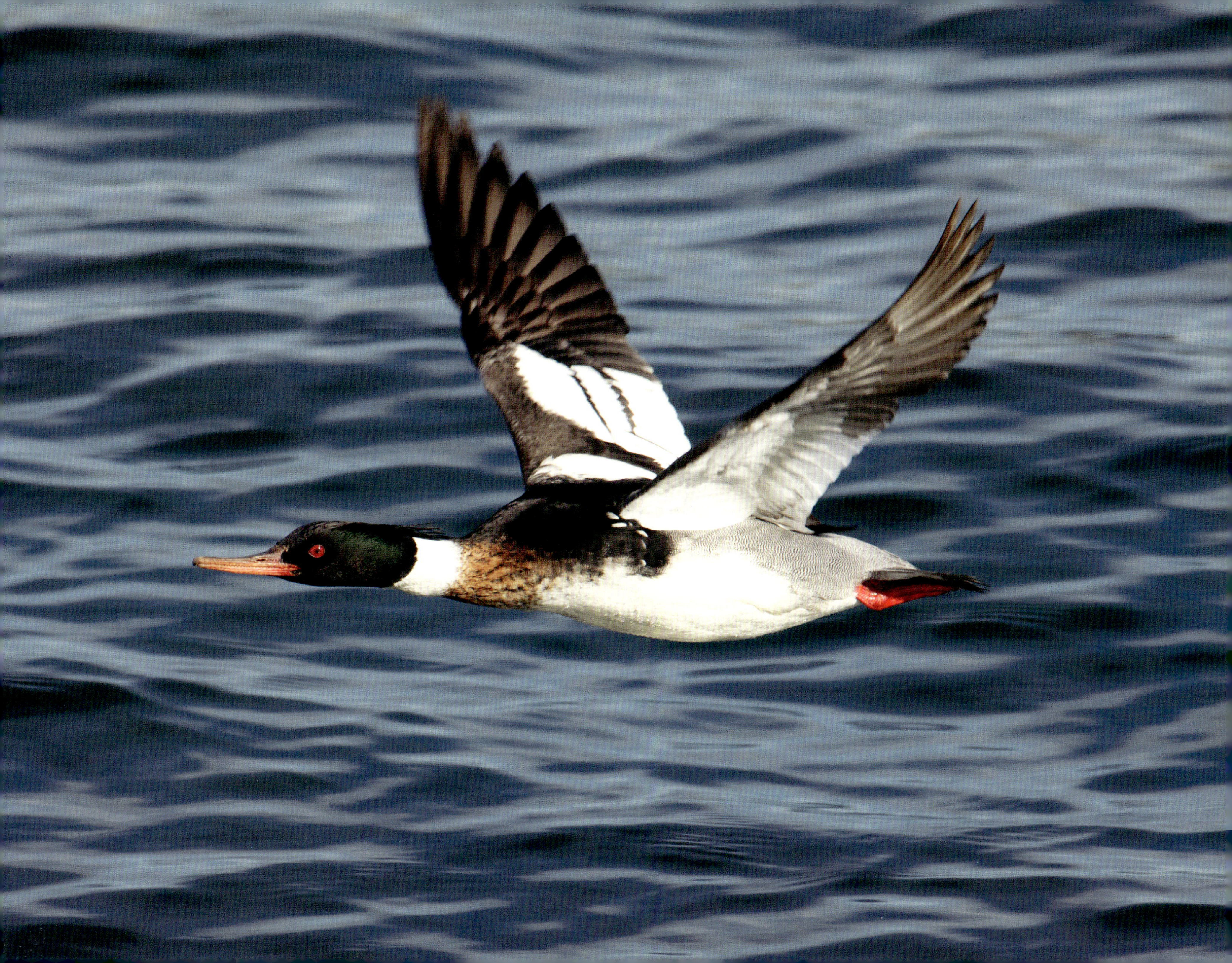

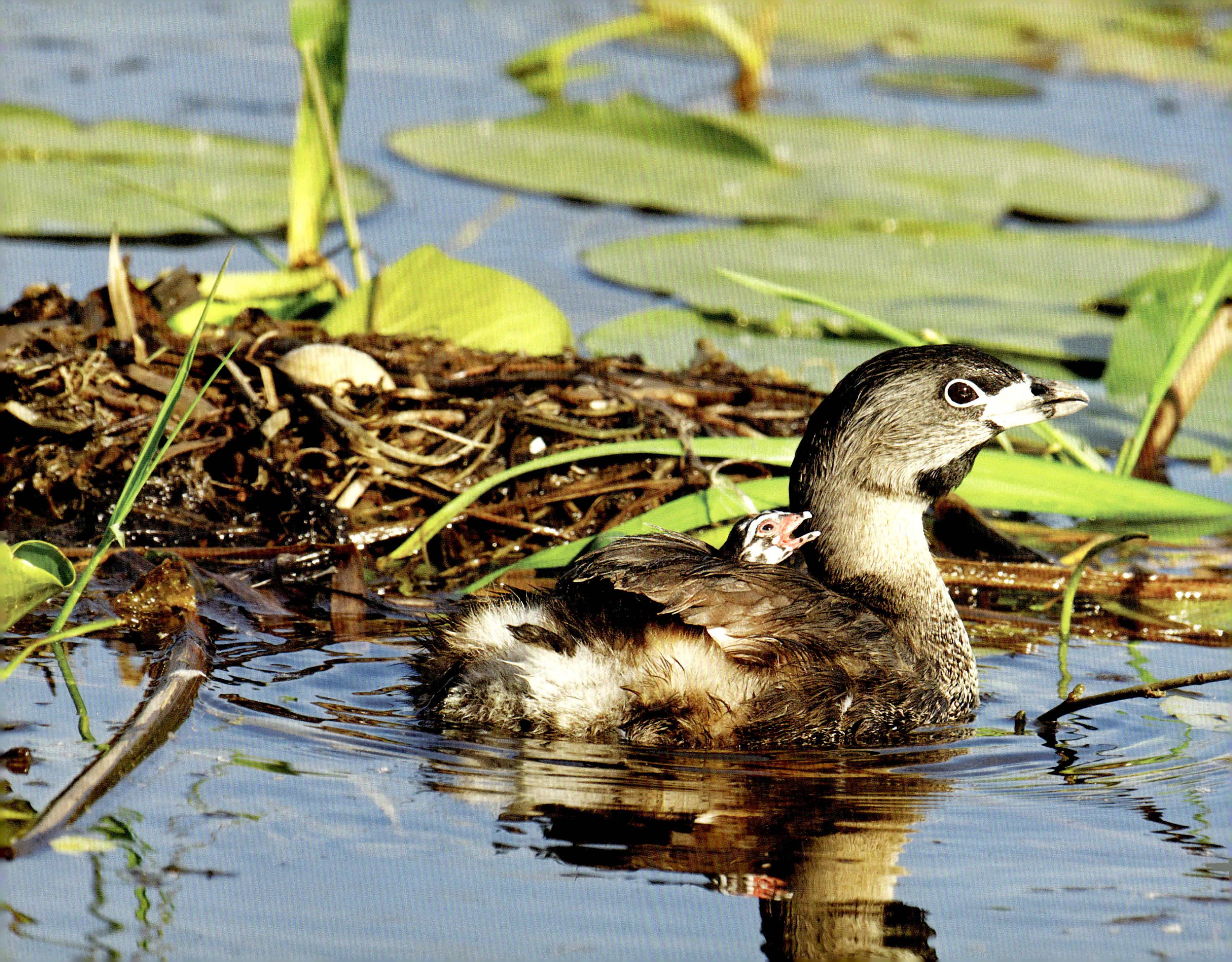

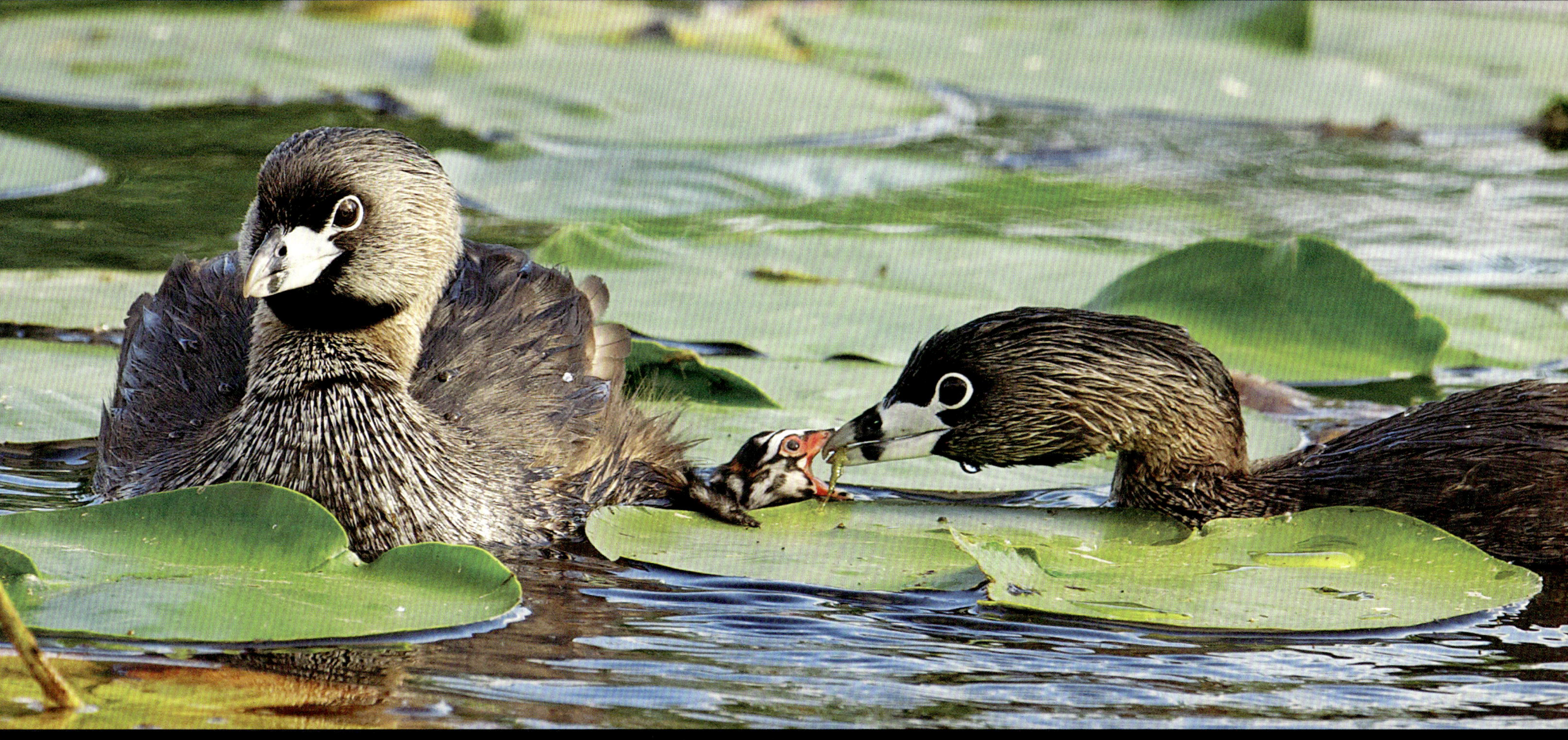

Facing Page: Pied-billed grebes build floating nests on water. When the babies hatch they jump on the parents' back for refuge until they grow into stronger swimmers.

Above: Less than 1/4 mile from Husky Stadium in Union Bay, these pied-billed grebe parents work together to feed their newborn a tender morsel.

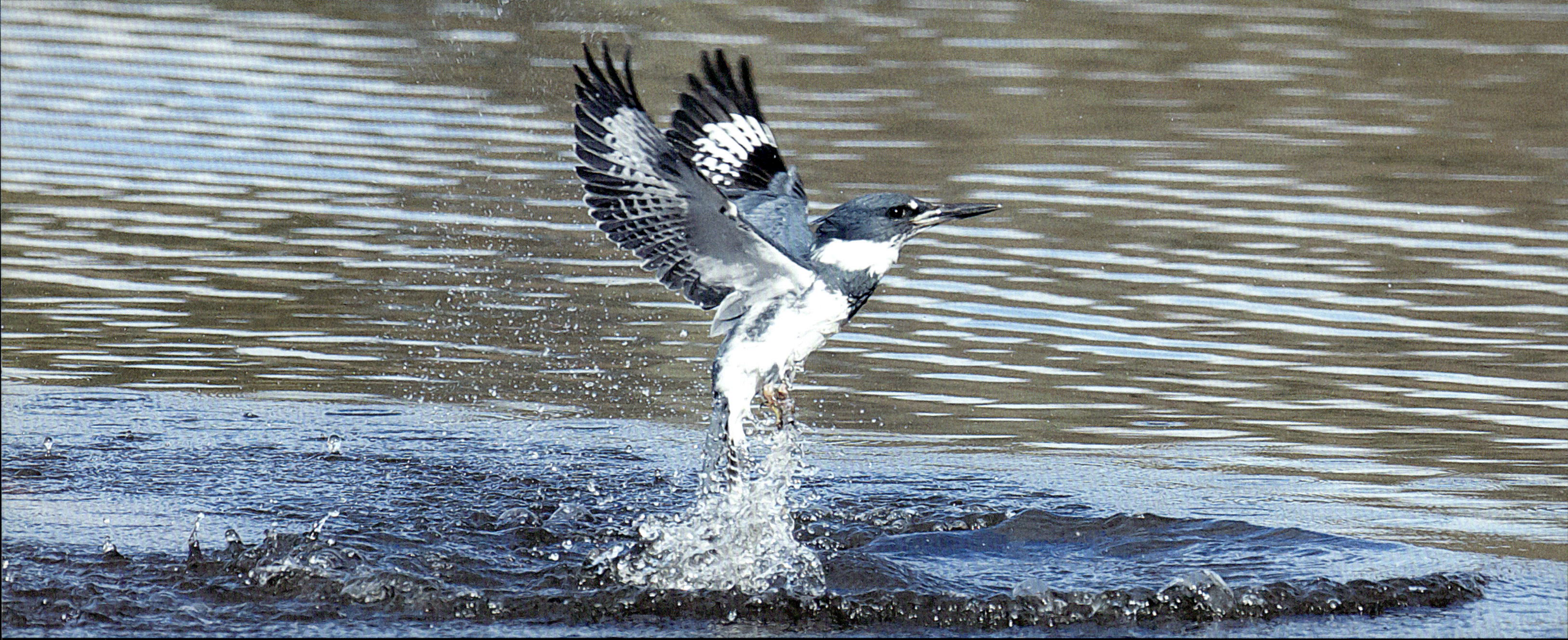

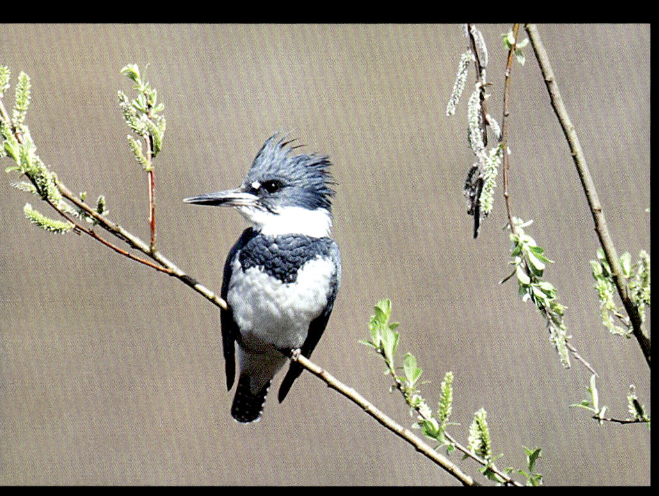

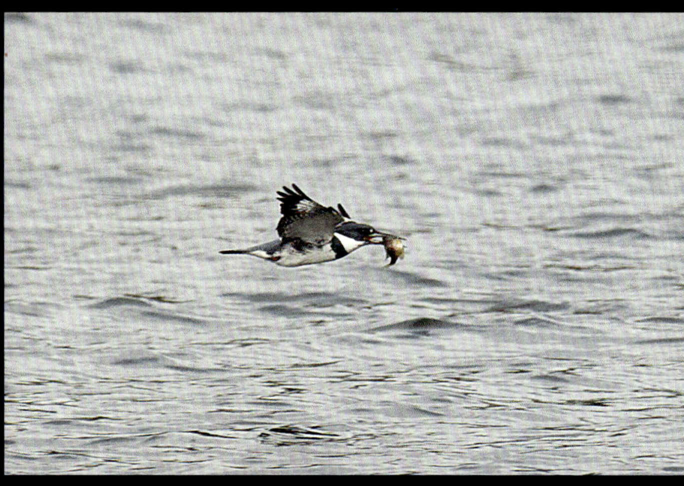

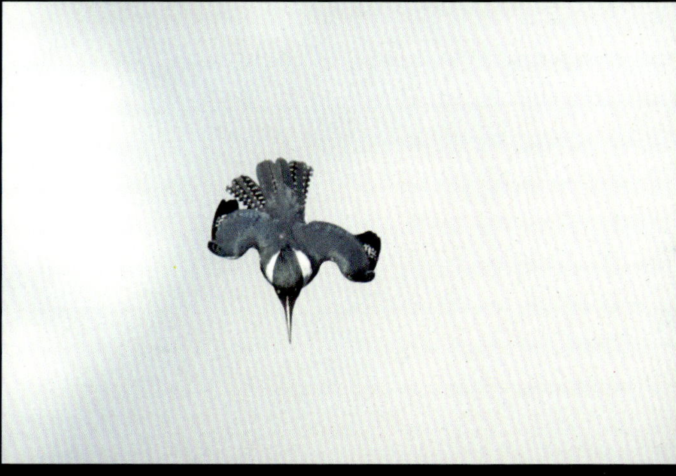

Above: The belted kingfisher is often seen perched on trees, posts, or other suitable "watchpoints" close to water before plunging in head first after its prey. They eat fish, amphibians, small crustaceans, insects, small mammals and reptiles. I love to watch their elaborate mating ritual which includes vocal chattering and the male offering fish to the female.

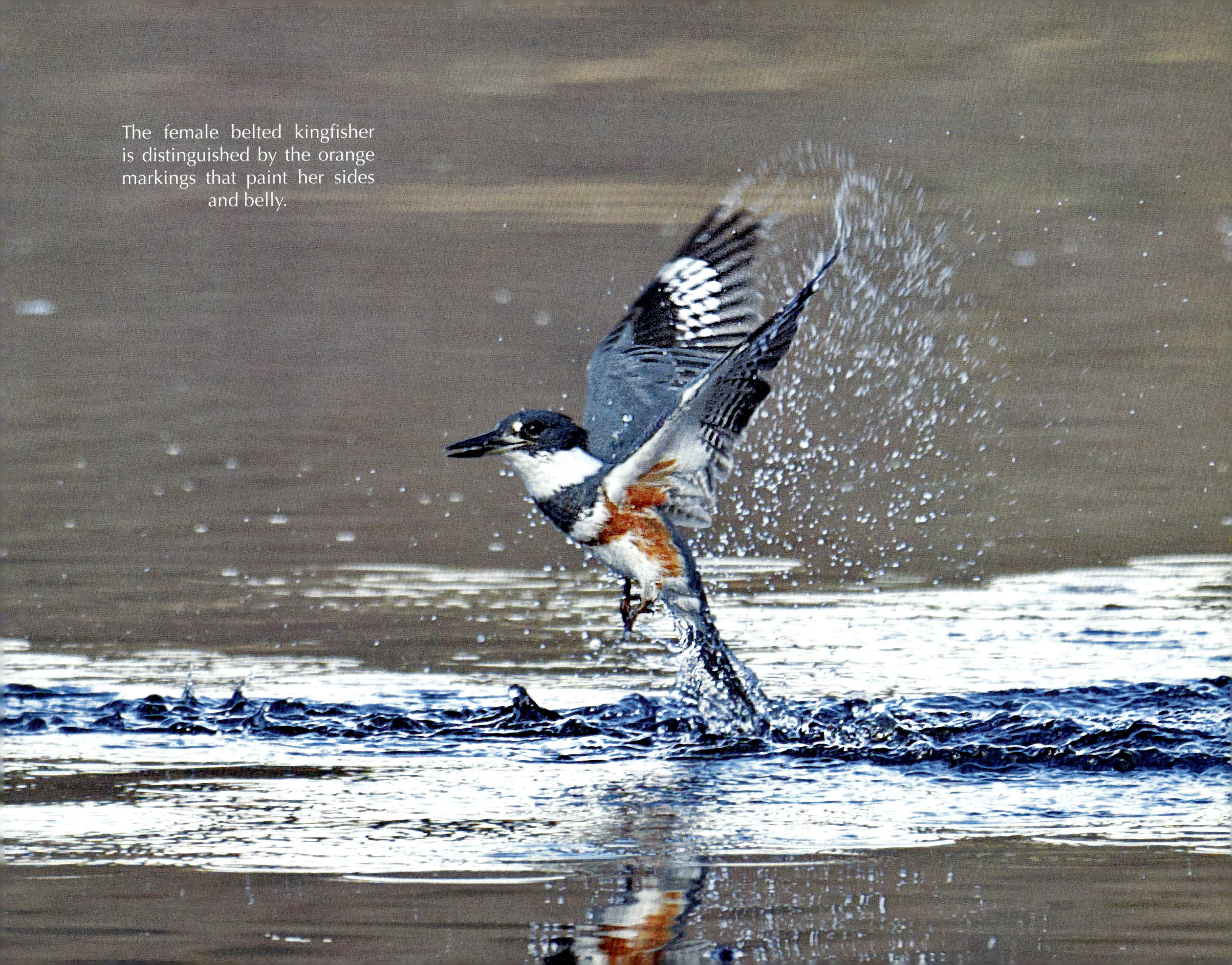

The female belted kingfisher is distinguished by the orange markings that paint her sides and belly.

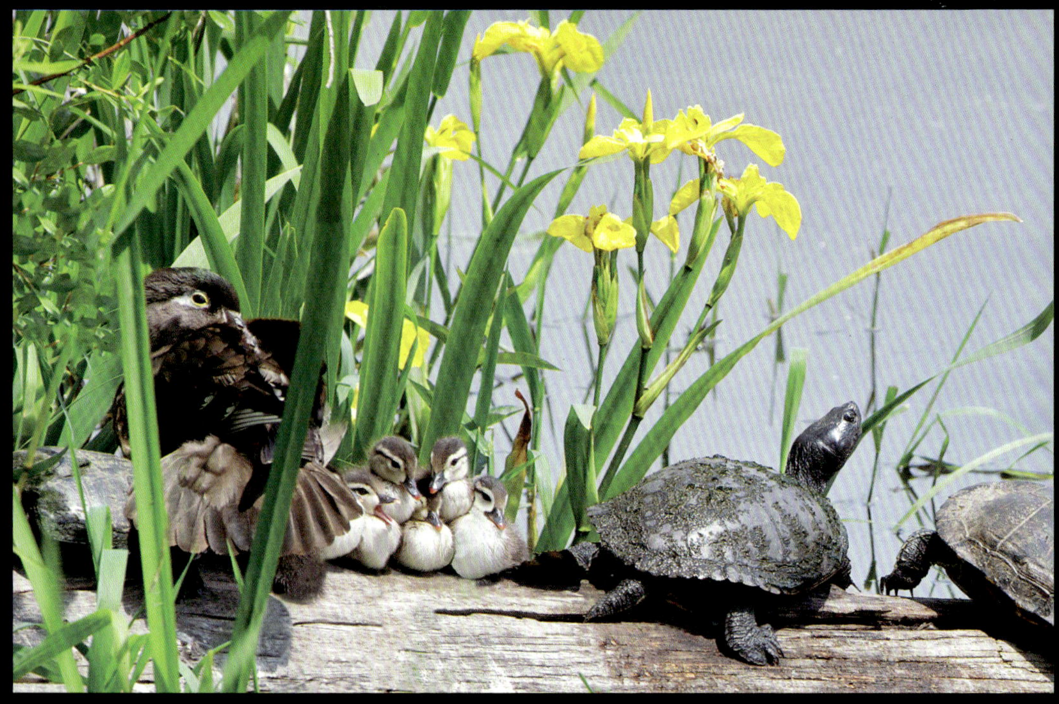

Above: Newly hatched baby wood ducks huddle together next to their mother to stay warm making for a wonderful spring composition. The late spring and early summer are excellent times to observe newborn baby ducks at any park near water.

Right: Wood ducks are among the most colorful and beautiful ducks in the world. It is strange and sad to think that these birds were almost hunted to extinction in the late 19th century. After being federally protected under a migratory bird treaty act their populations have rebounded and can now be found on Lake Washington and its surrounding lakes and ponds.

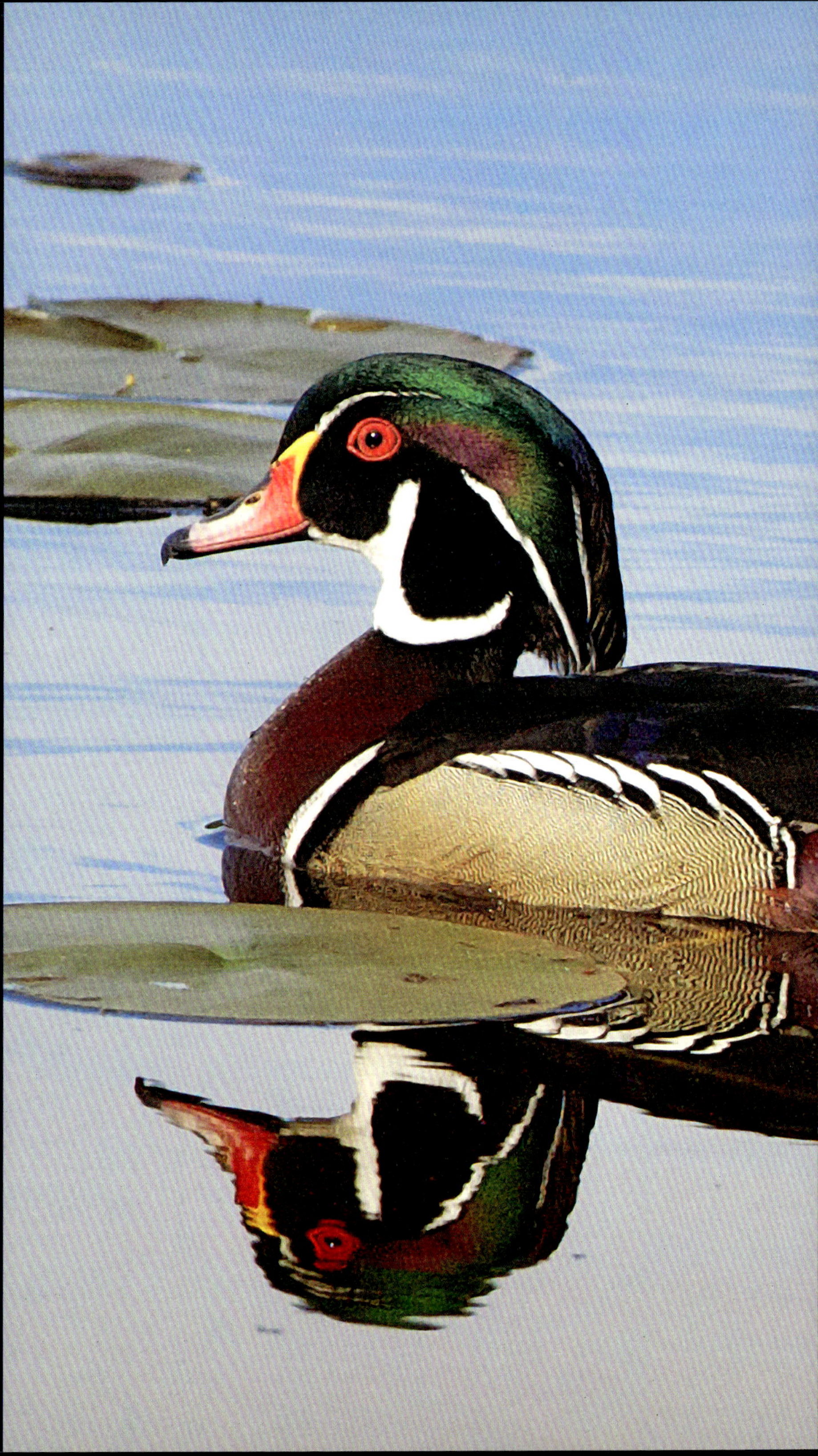

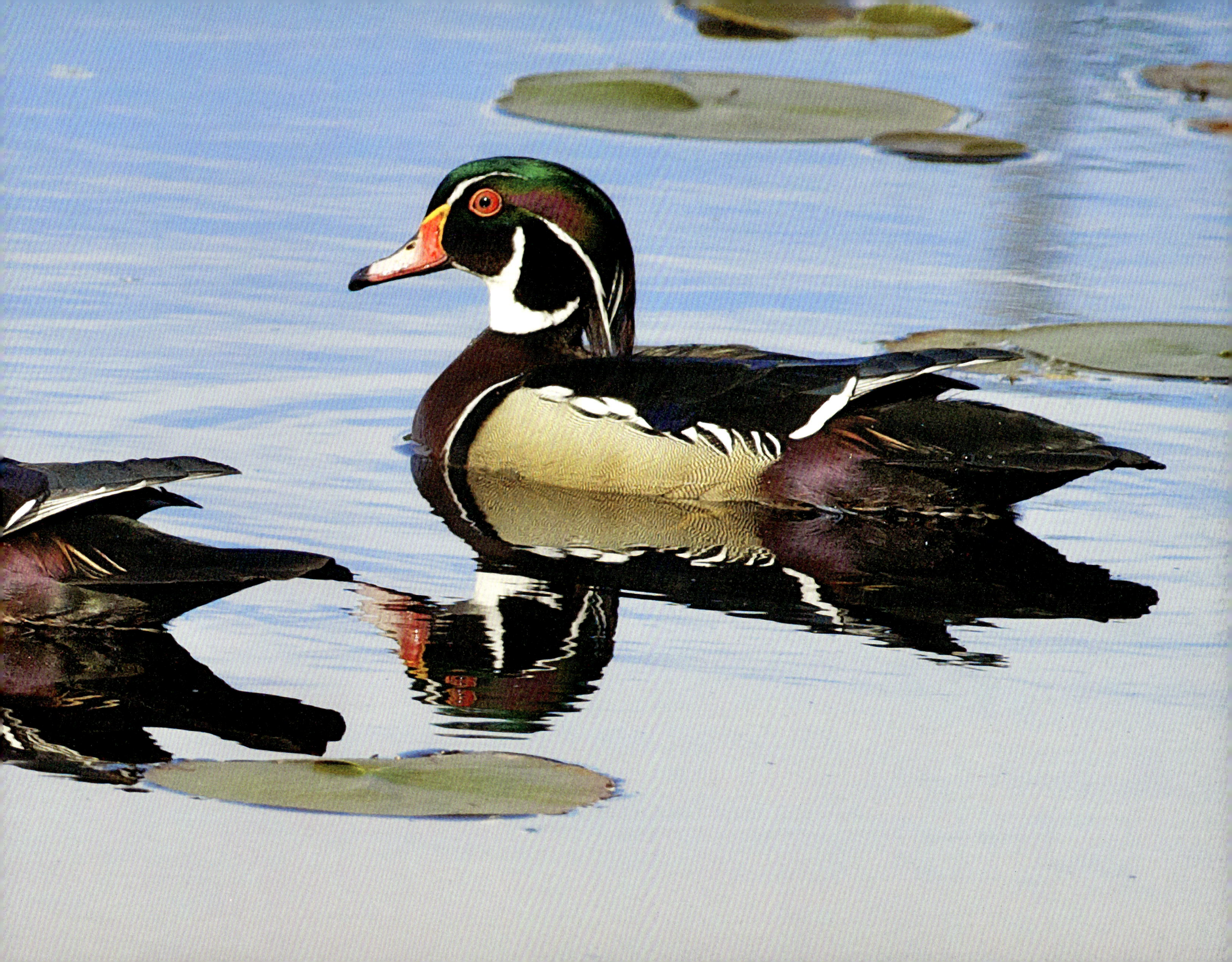

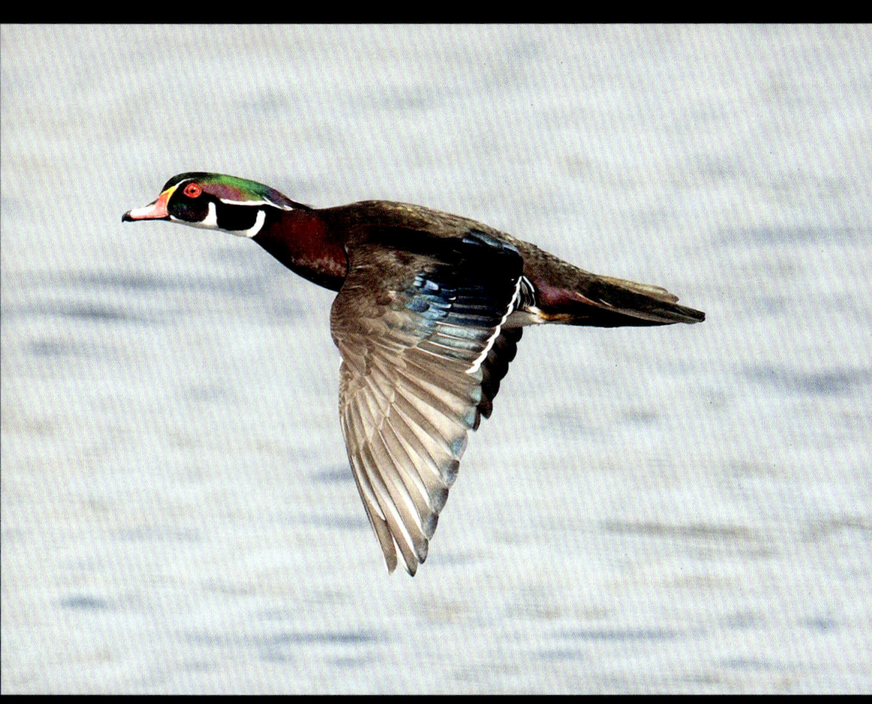

Above: A male wood duck's feathers shimmer in the sun mid-flight over Juanita Bay.

Right: Wood ducks nest inside holes in trees or in man-made nest boxes. After hatching they stay very close to their mother following her every command to avoid danger.

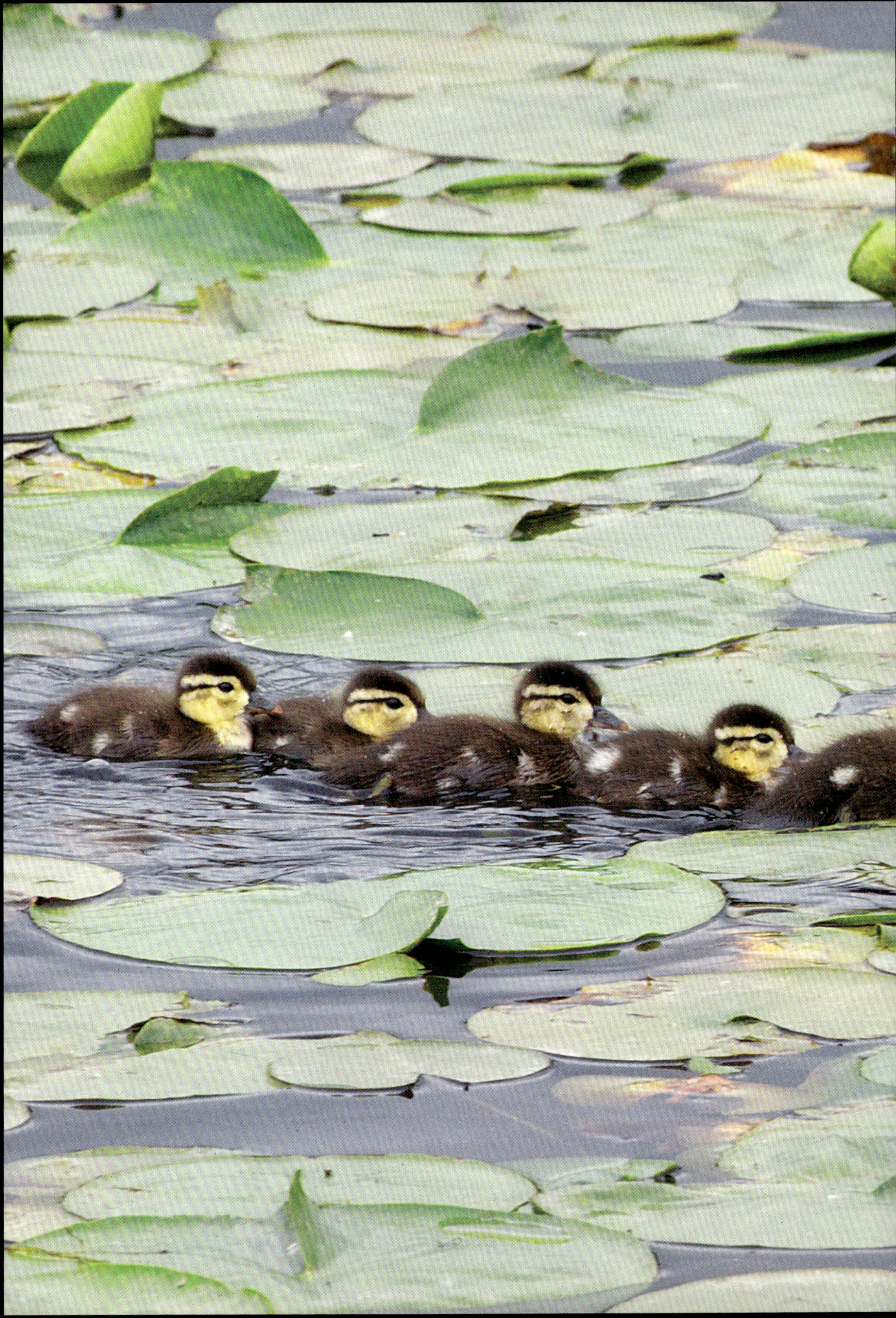

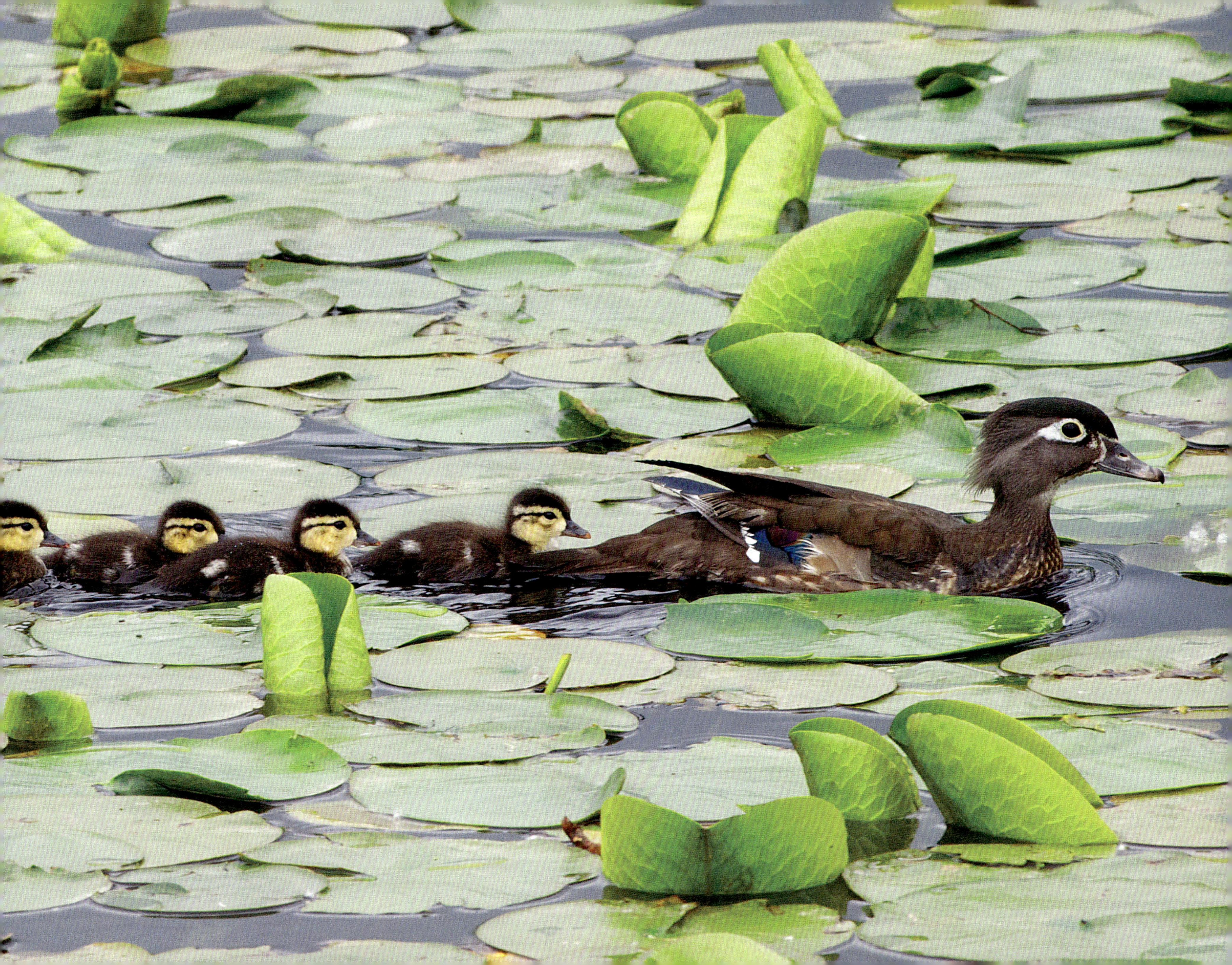

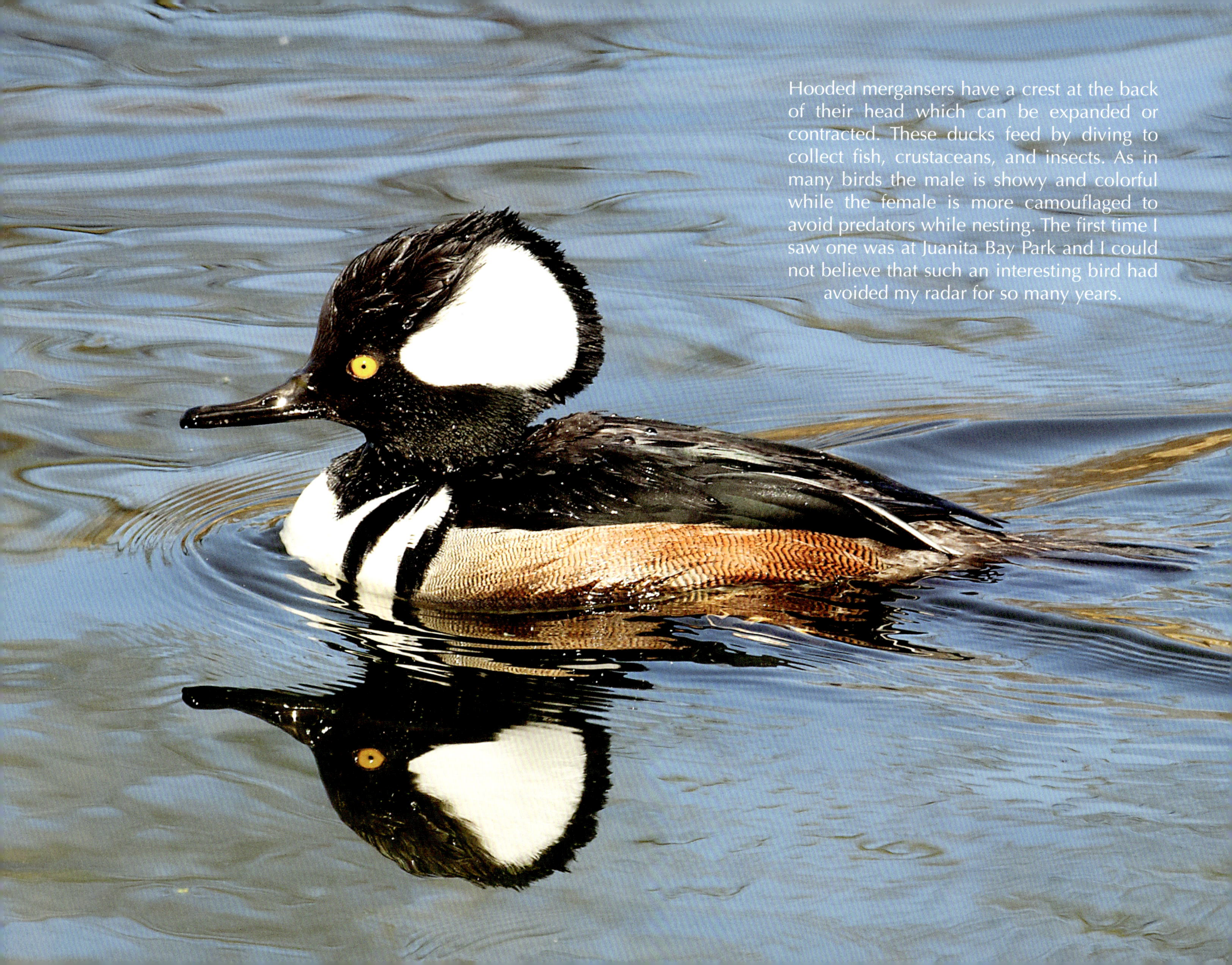

Hooded mergansers have a crest at the back of their head which can be expanded or contracted. These ducks feed by diving to collect fish, crustaceans, and insects. As in many birds the male is showy and colorful while the female is more camouflaged to avoid predators while nesting. The first time I saw one was at Juanita Bay Park and I could not believe that such an interesting bird had avoided my radar for so many years.

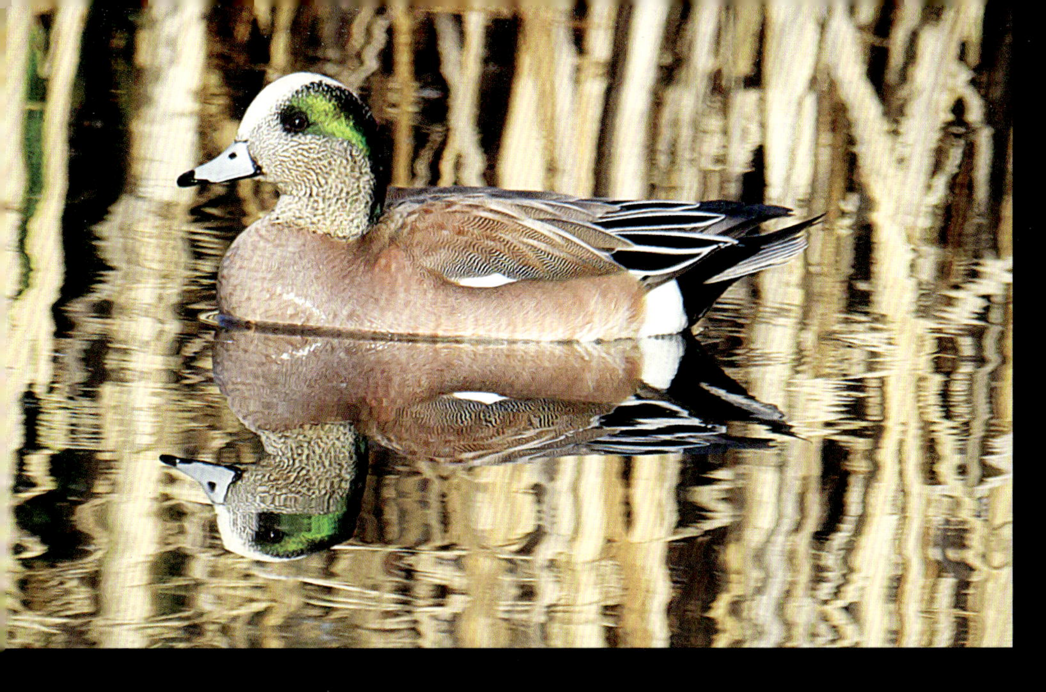
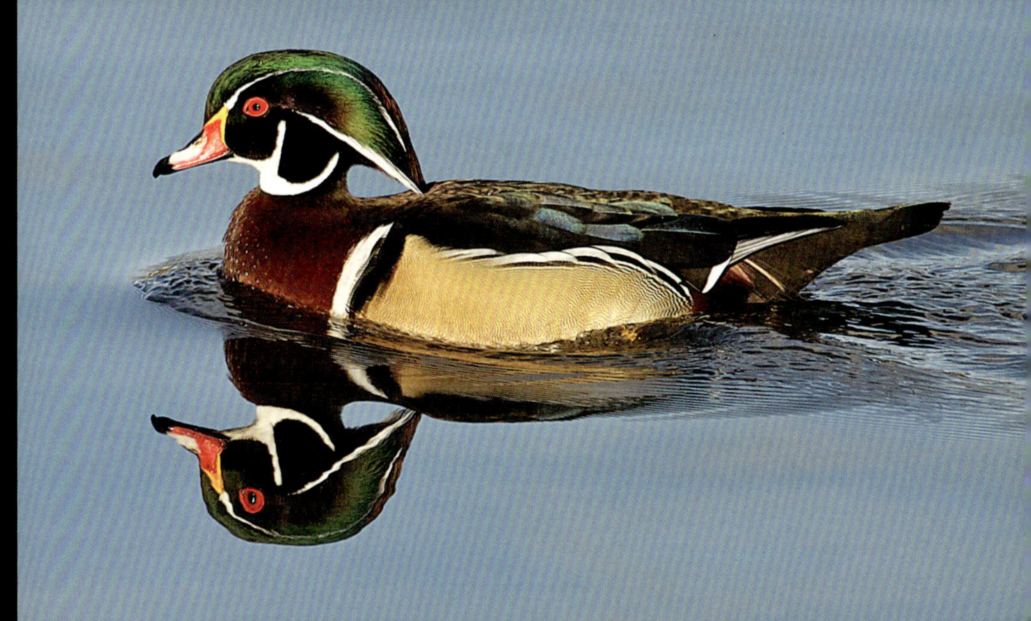
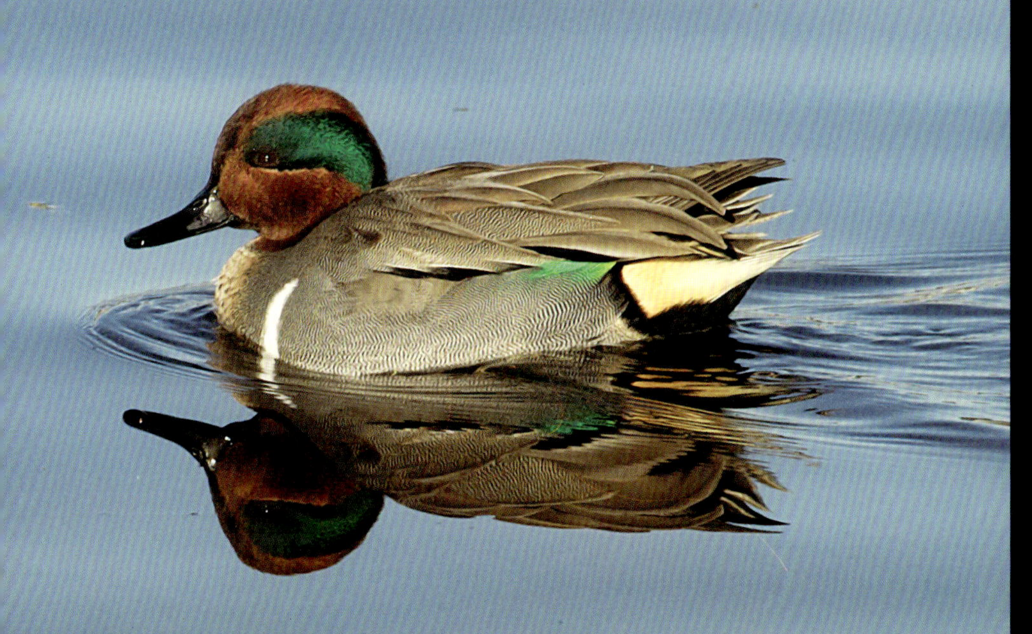
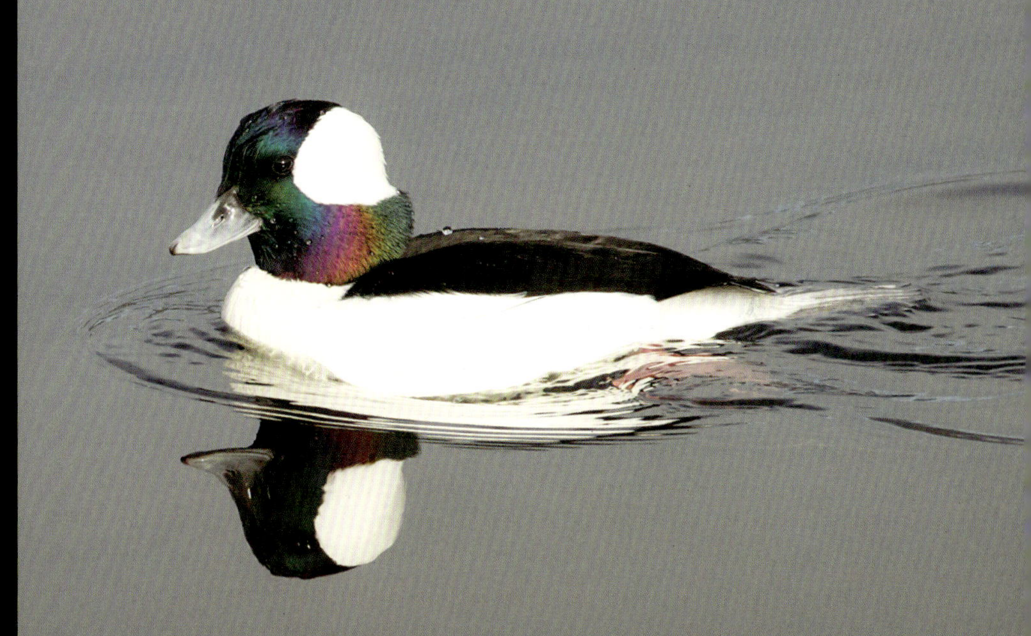

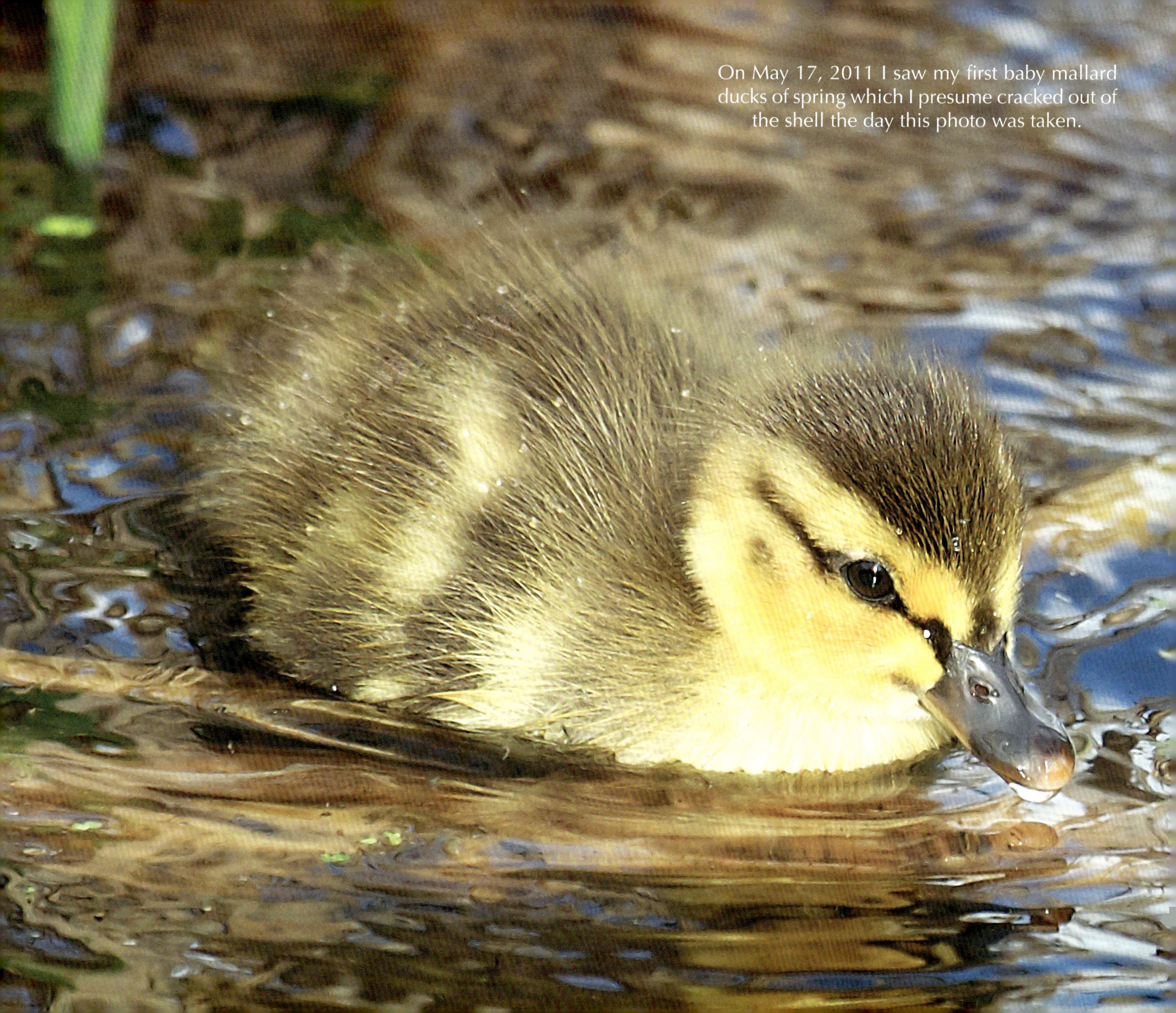

On May 17, 2011 I saw my first baby mallard ducks of spring which I presume cracked out of the shell the day this photo was taken.

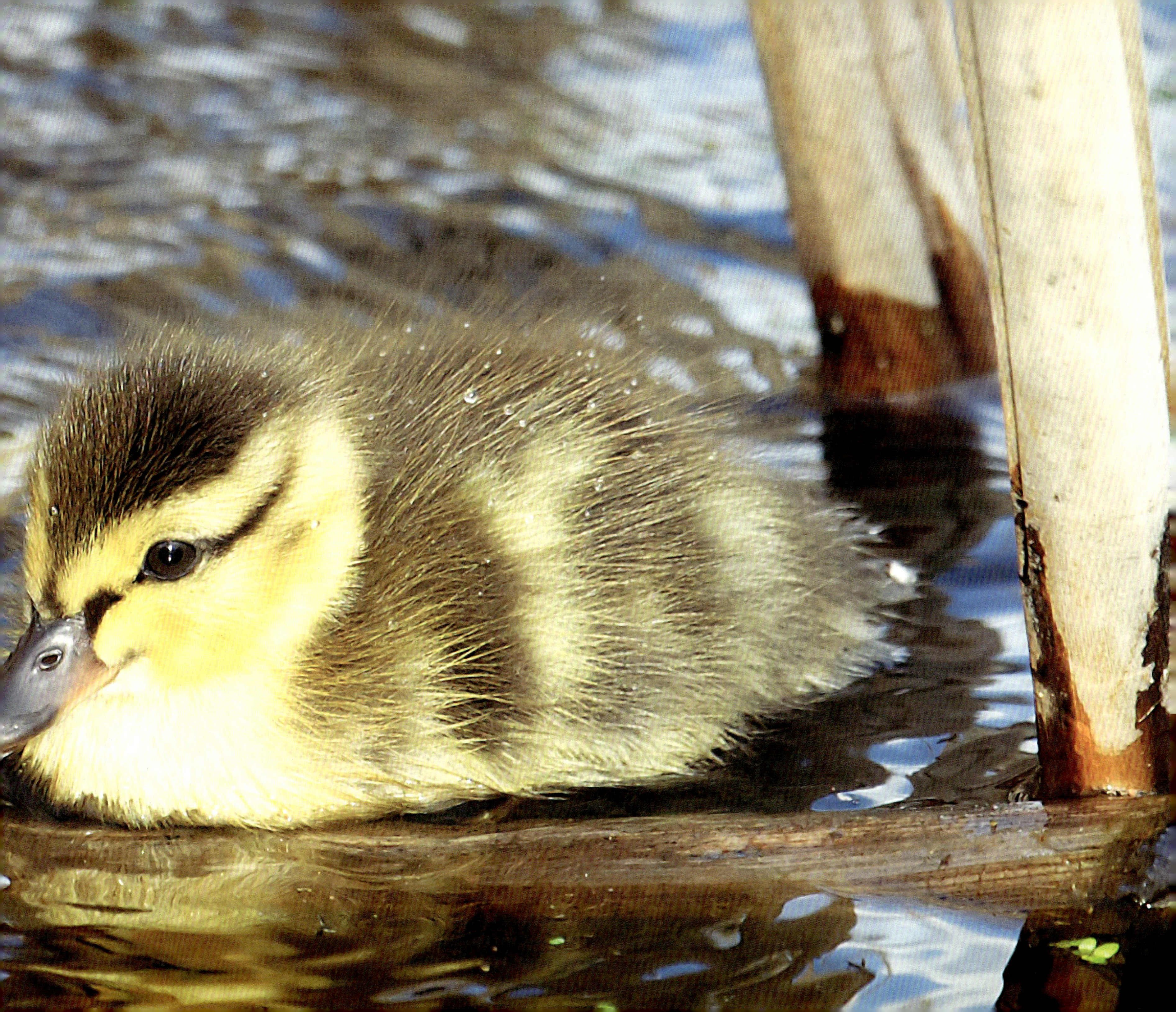

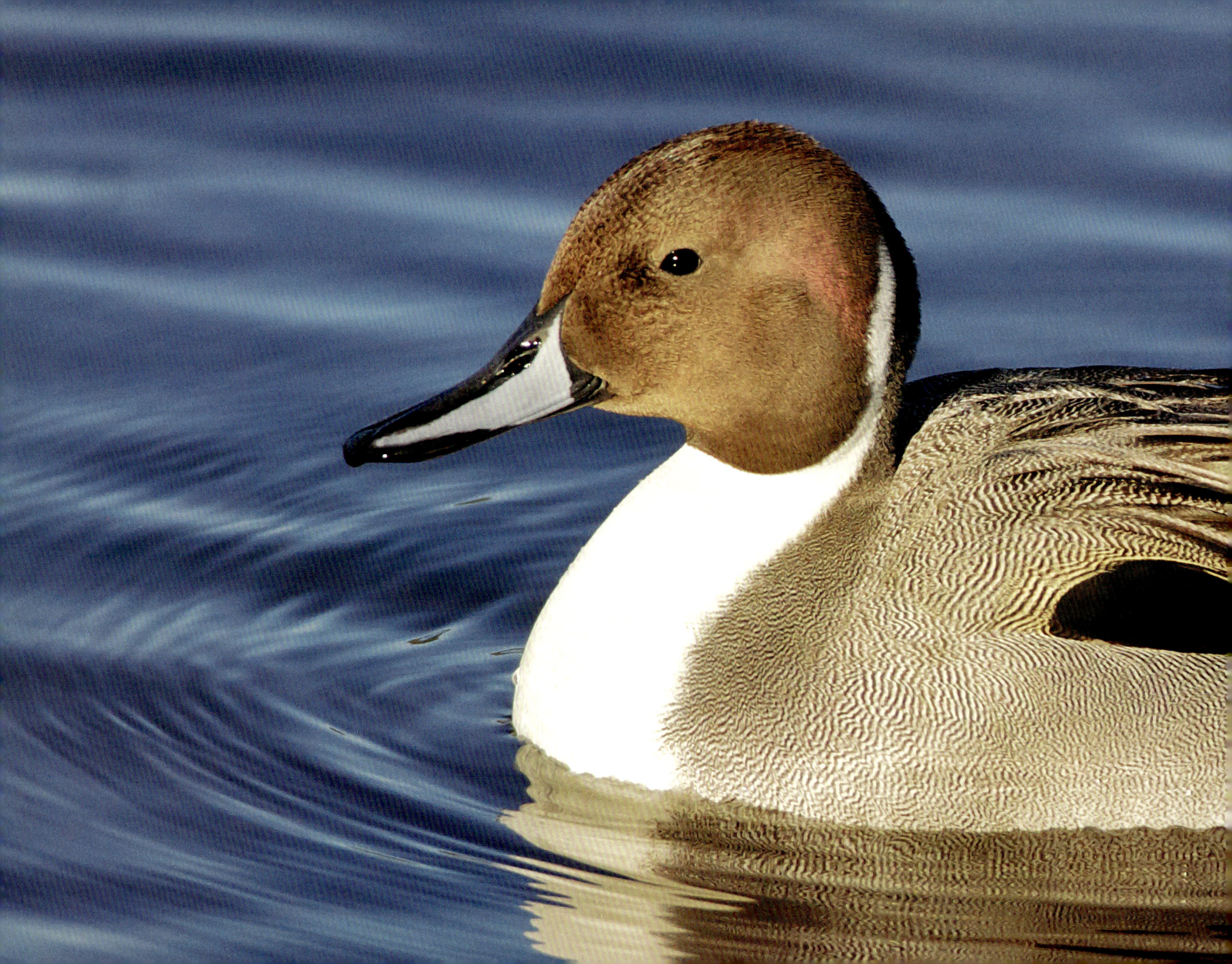

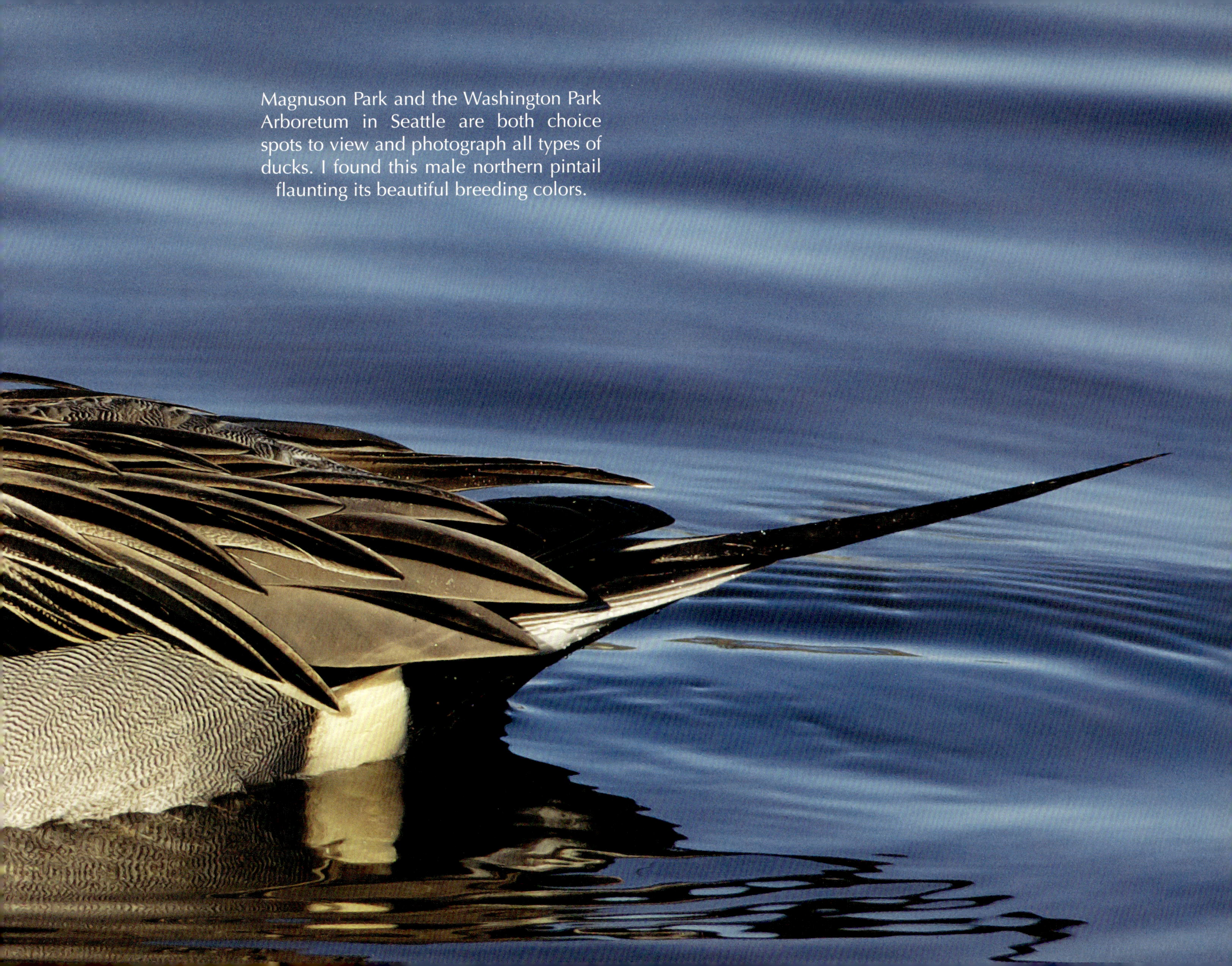

Magnuson Park and the Washington Park Arboretum in Seattle are both choice spots to view and photograph all types of ducks. I found this male northern pintail flaunting its beautiful breeding colors.

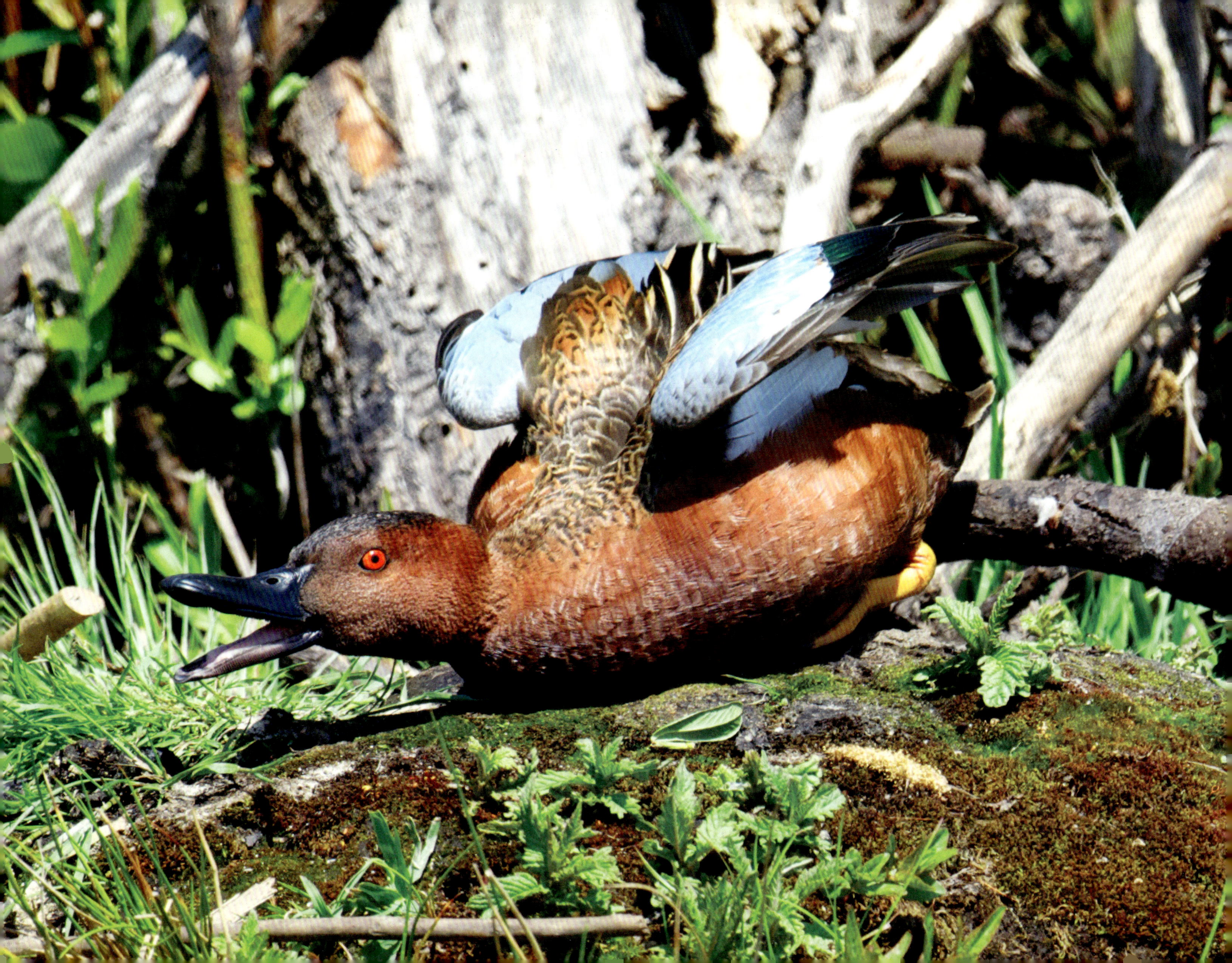

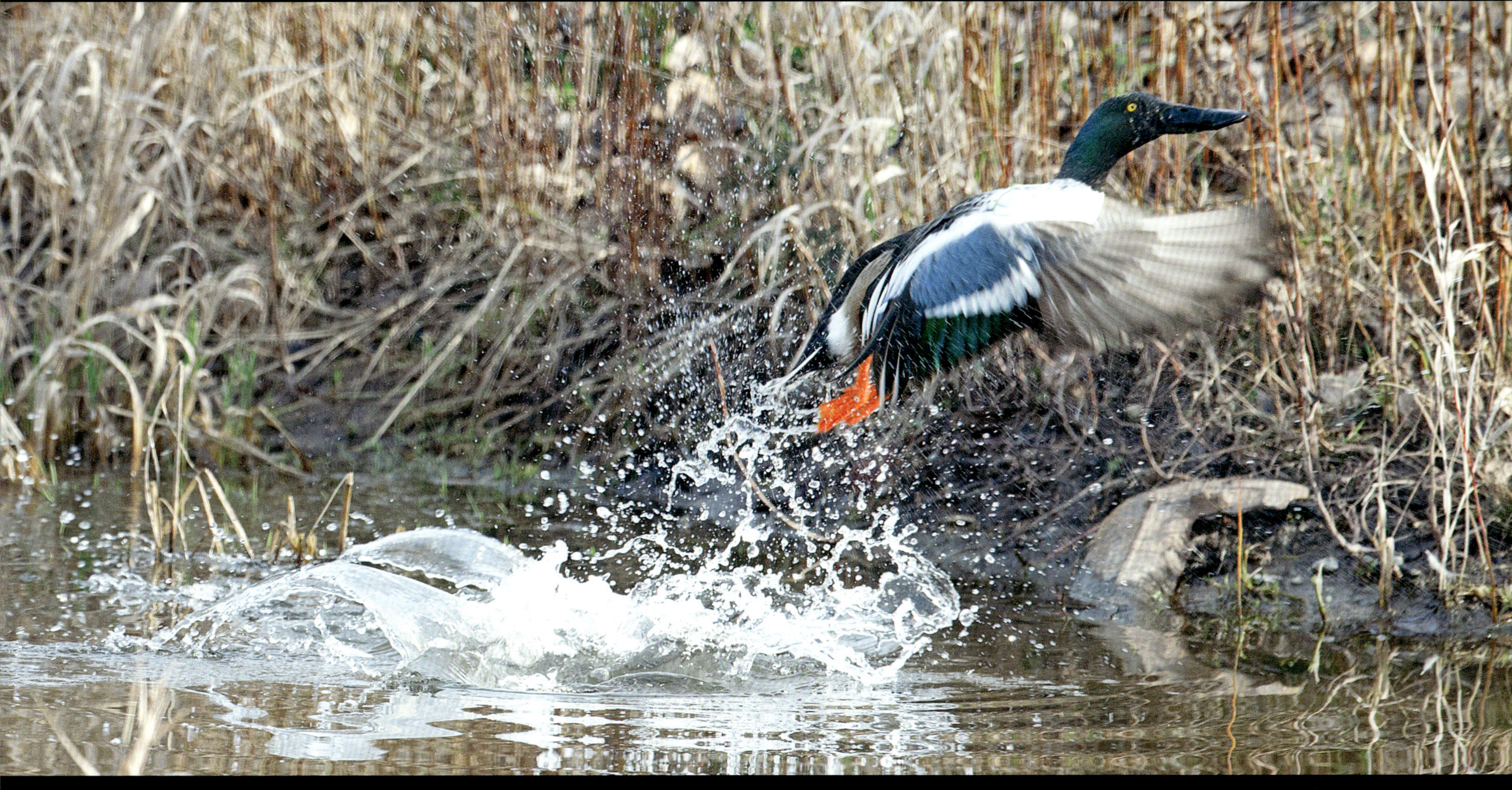

Facing Page: Cinnamon teals winter in Mexico and Central America but are a pleasant visitor in Washington during their spring migration north. Look for them at the Montlake Fill.

Above: A northern shoveler takes to the wing out of a pond in Magnuson Park.

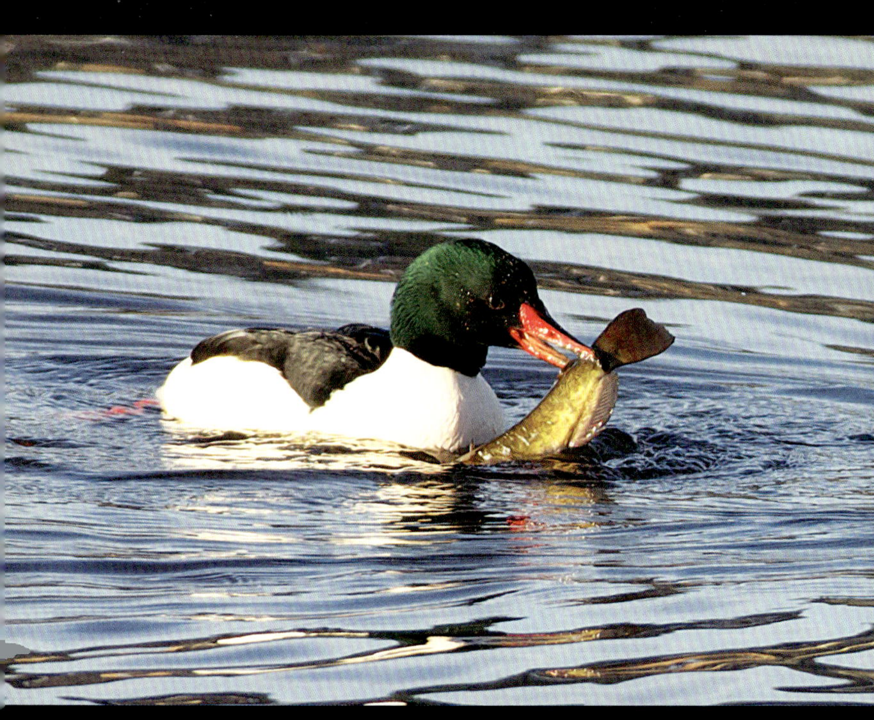

Above: A male common merganser emerges from a dive with a large fish. Shortly after, the catch was stolen by a seagull. Finally, a bald eagle made off with the spoils which made for an interesting scene.

Facing Page: Two juvenile common mergansers hitch a lucky ride on mother's back.

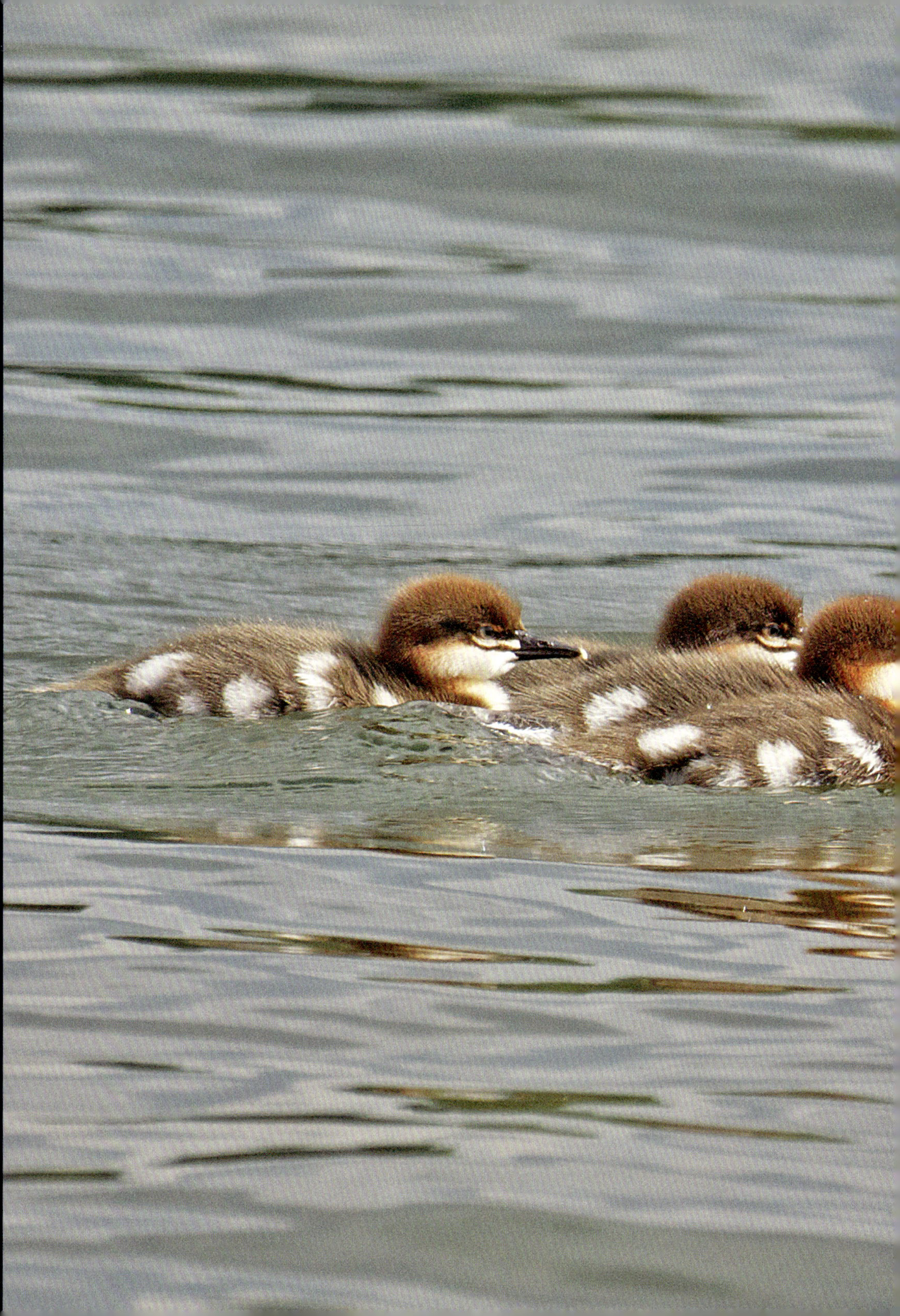

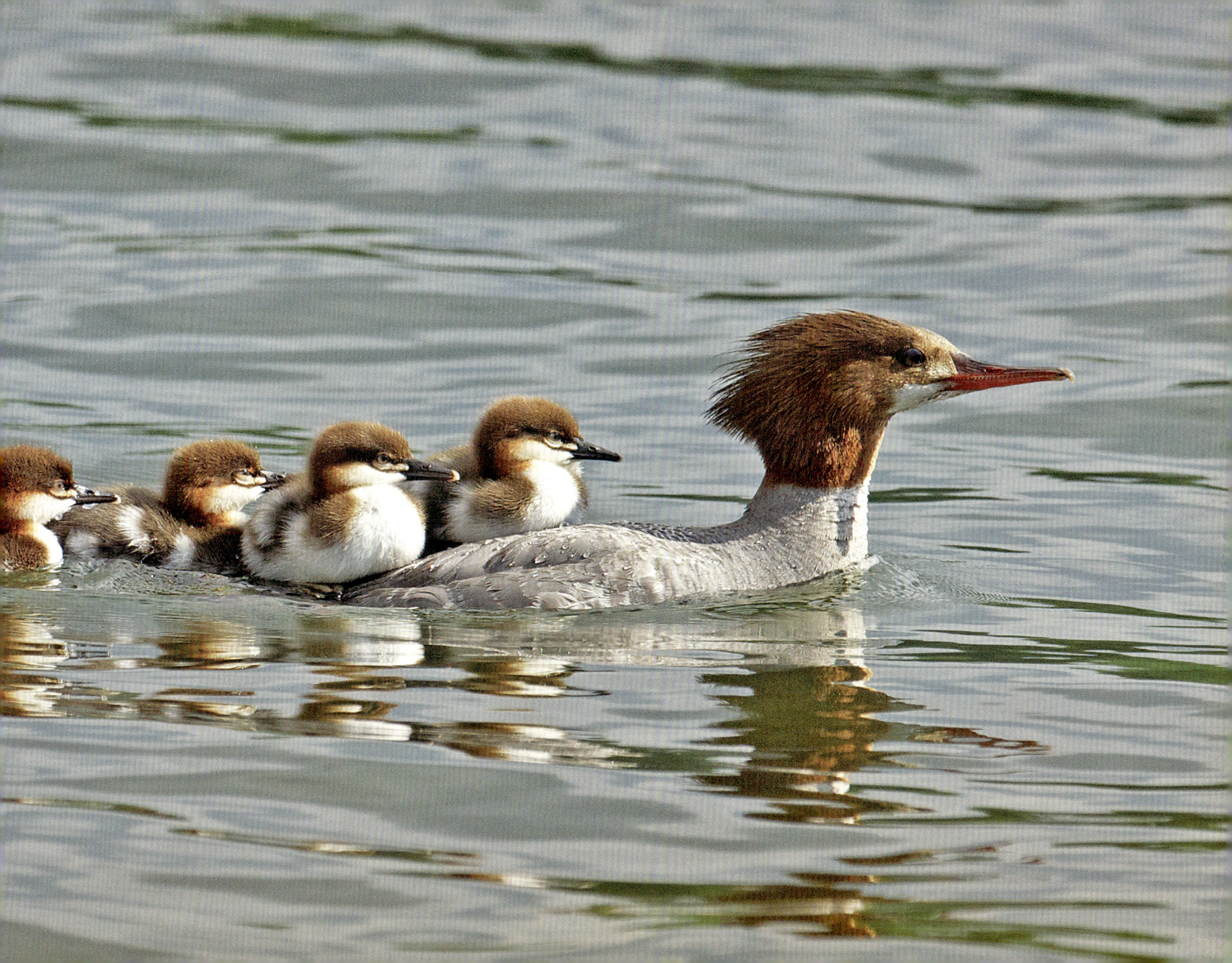

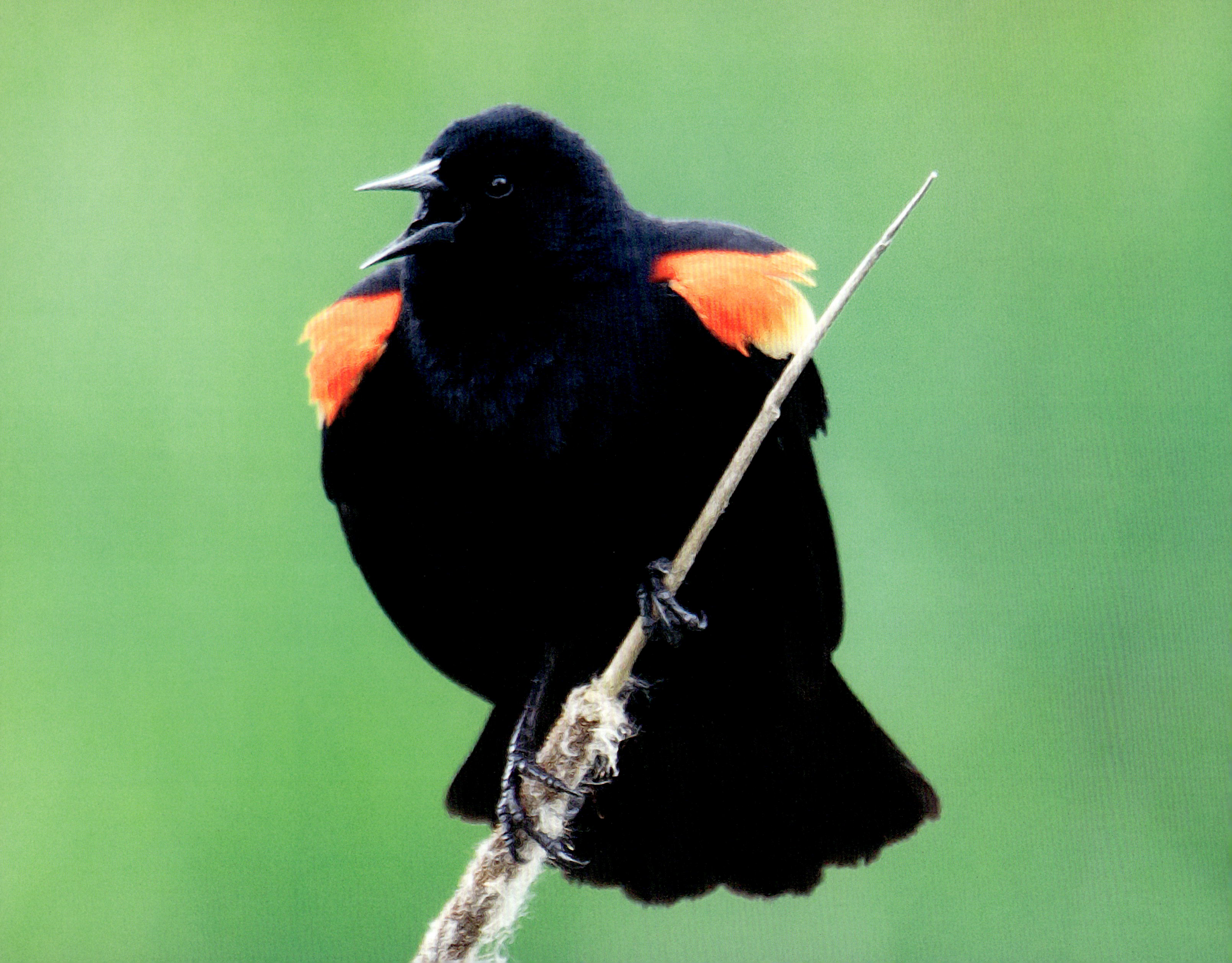

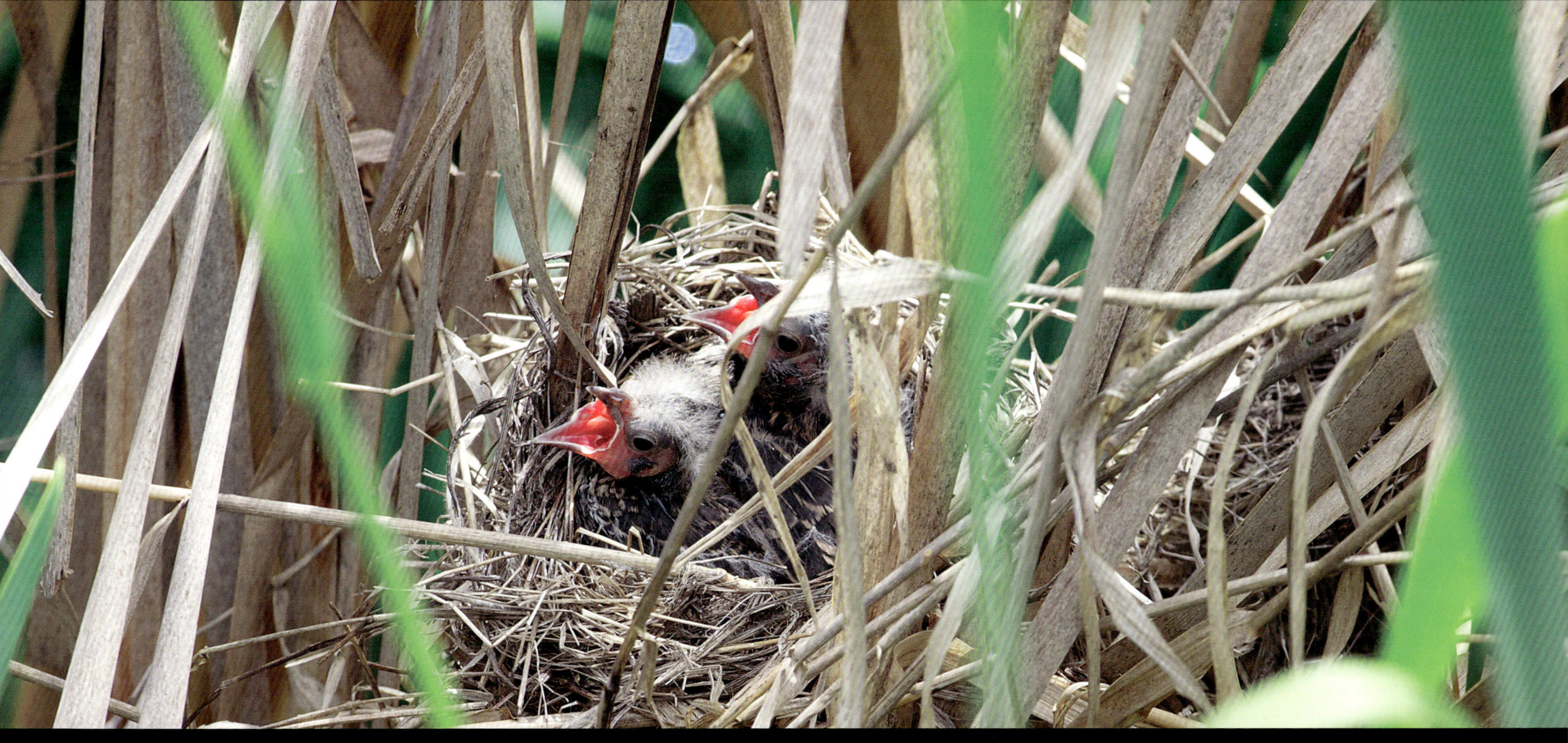

Facing Page: The red-winged blackbird is claimed to be the most abundant bird in North America. Their reddish-orange wing flaps are visible when flying or displaying to attract a female.

Above: Baby red-winged blackbirds beg for food.

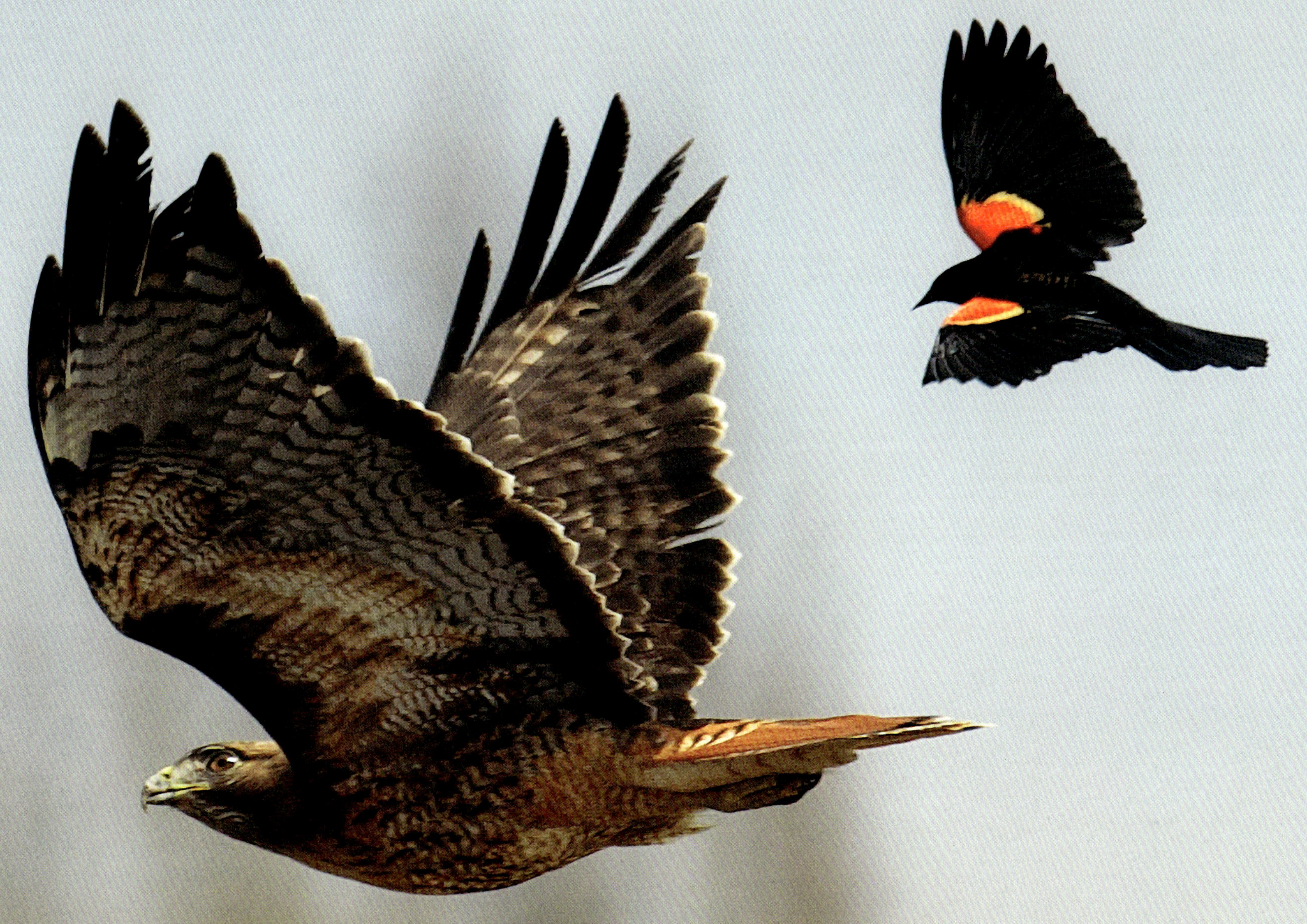

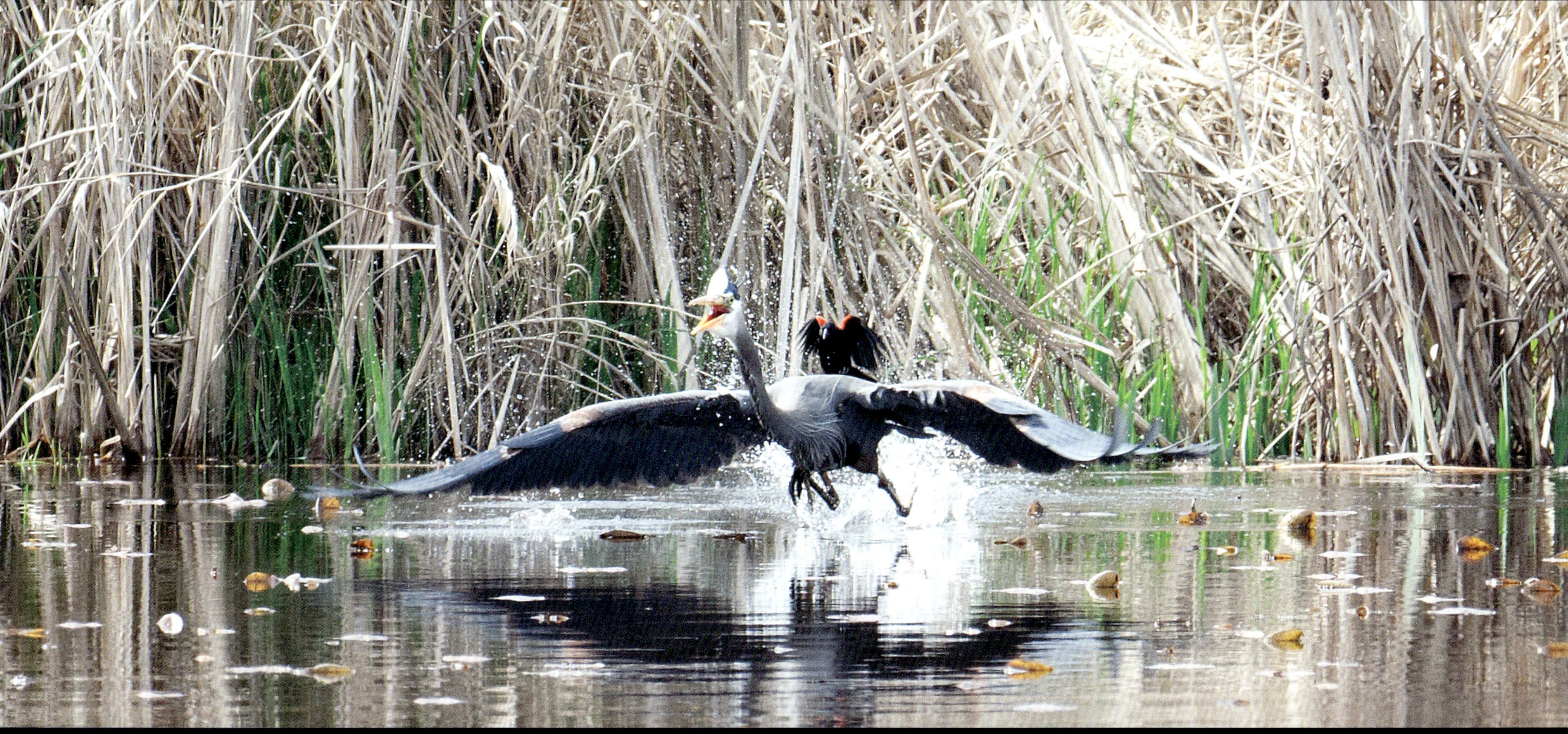

Facing Page: Red-winged blackbirds are very aggressive when defending their territory and are known to attack much larger birds like this red-tailed hawk.

Above: A red-winged blackbird chases a great blue heron out of its nesting territory.

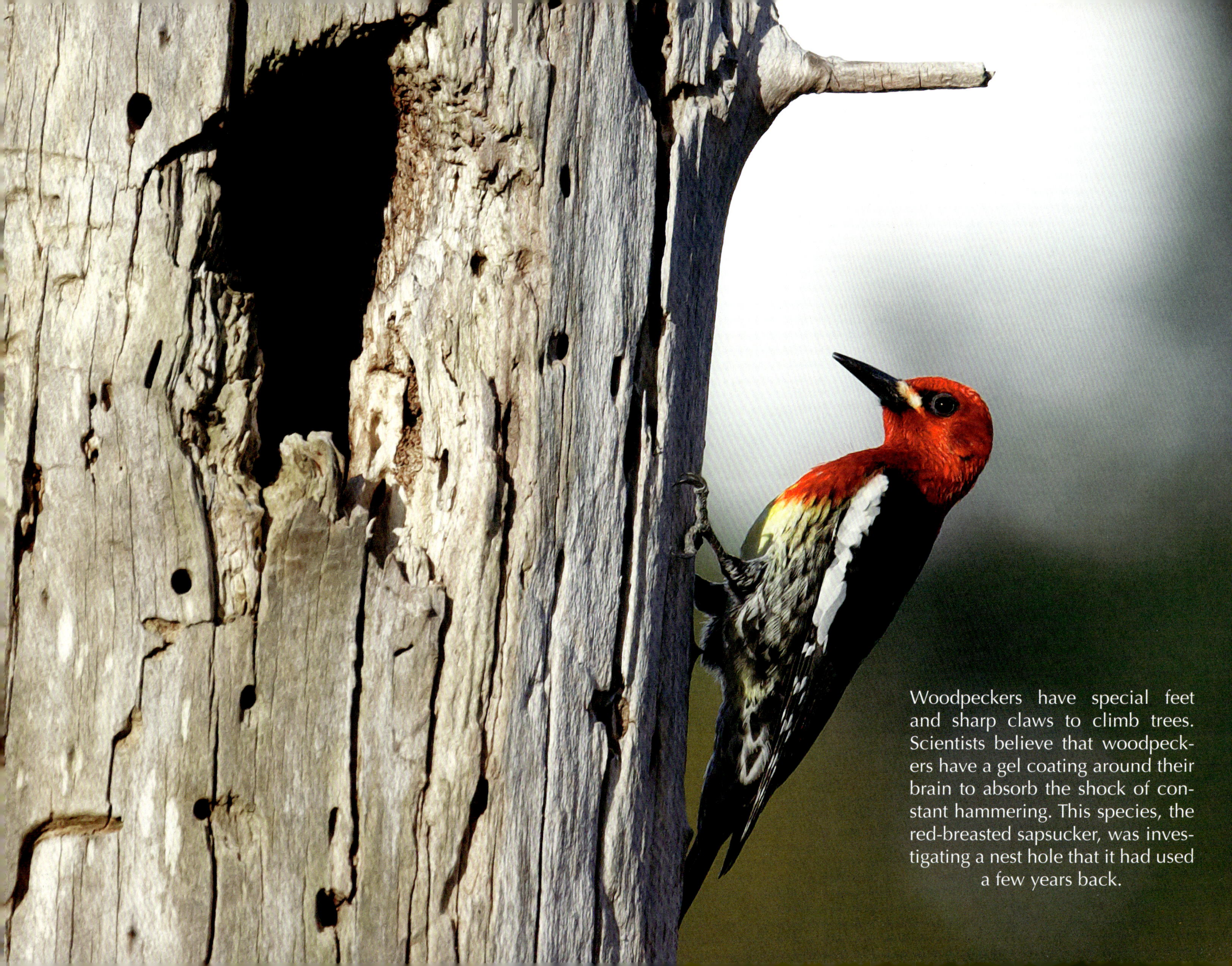

Woodpeckers have special feet and sharp claws to climb trees. Scientists believe that woodpeckers have a gel coating around their brain to absorb the shock of constant hammering. This species, the red-breasted sapsucker, was investigating a nest hole that it had used a few years back.

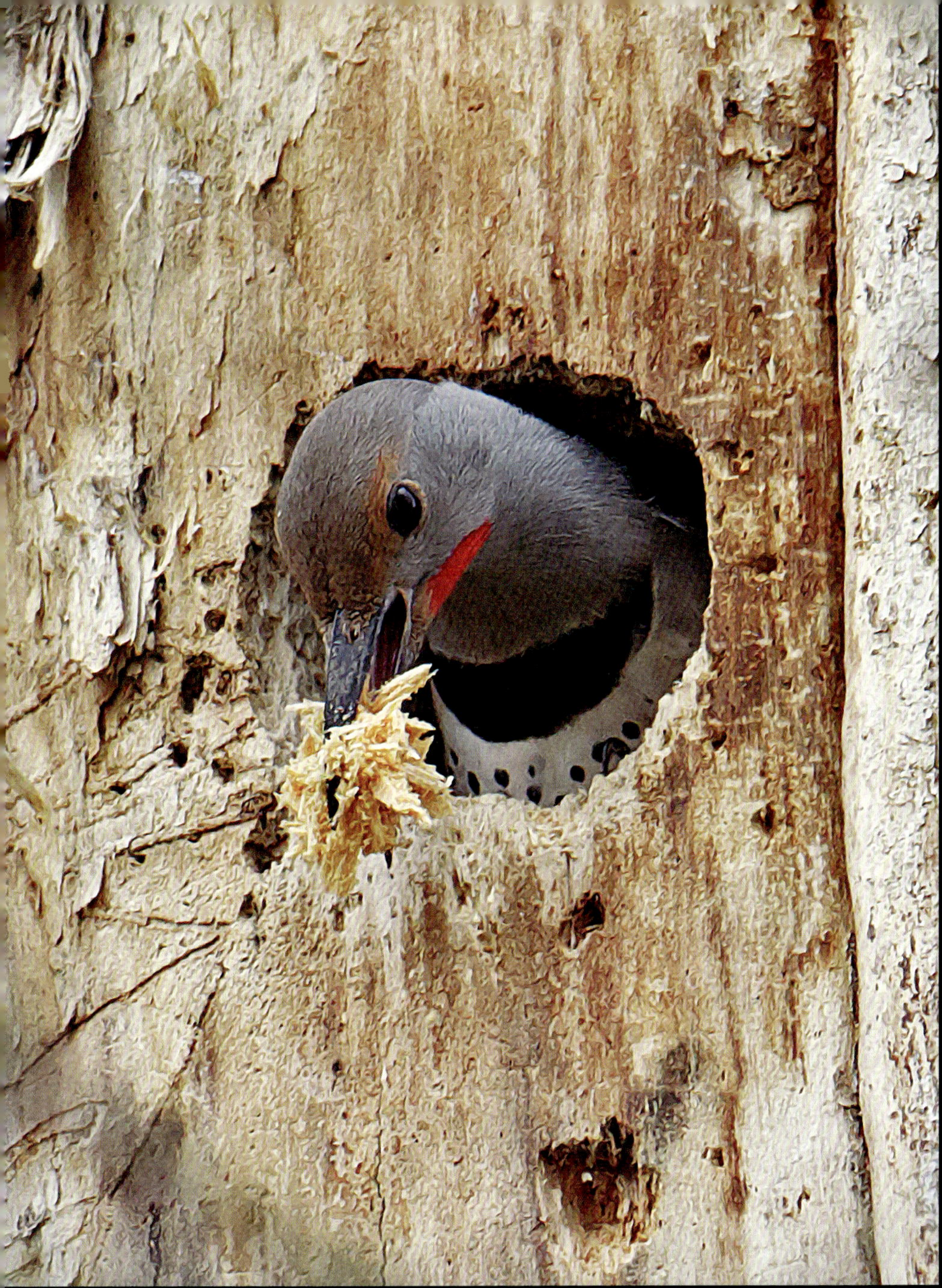

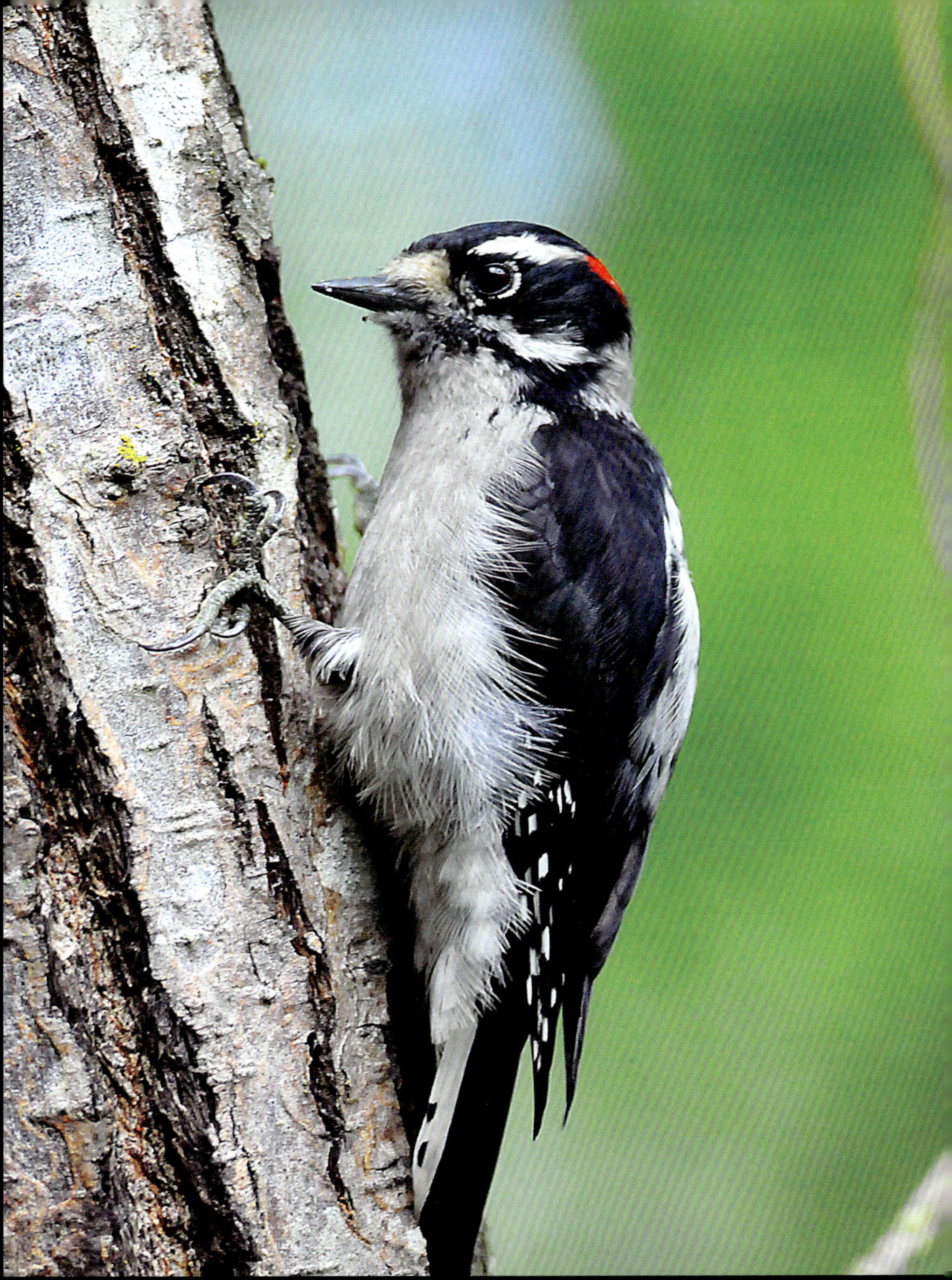

Above Left: A northern flicker excavates a nesting cavity.
Above Right: A downy woodpecker clings to a tree with its backwards toes designed for climbing

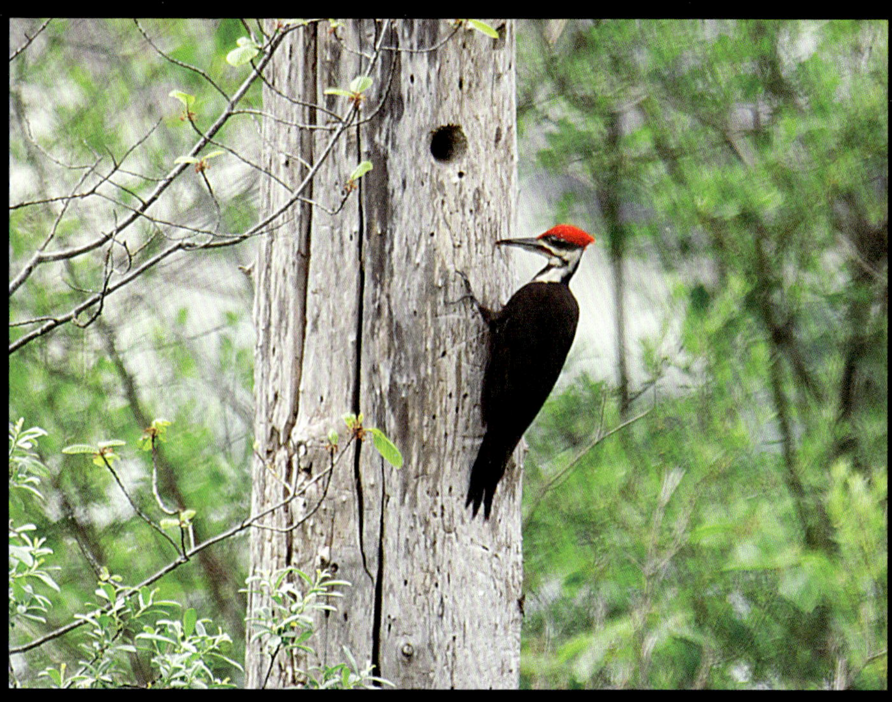

Above: A pileated woodpecker searches a dead tree for insects, its favorite food.

Facing Page: I found this pileated woodpecker hammering large rectangular holes in a fallen stump in search of food along the shore of the lake.

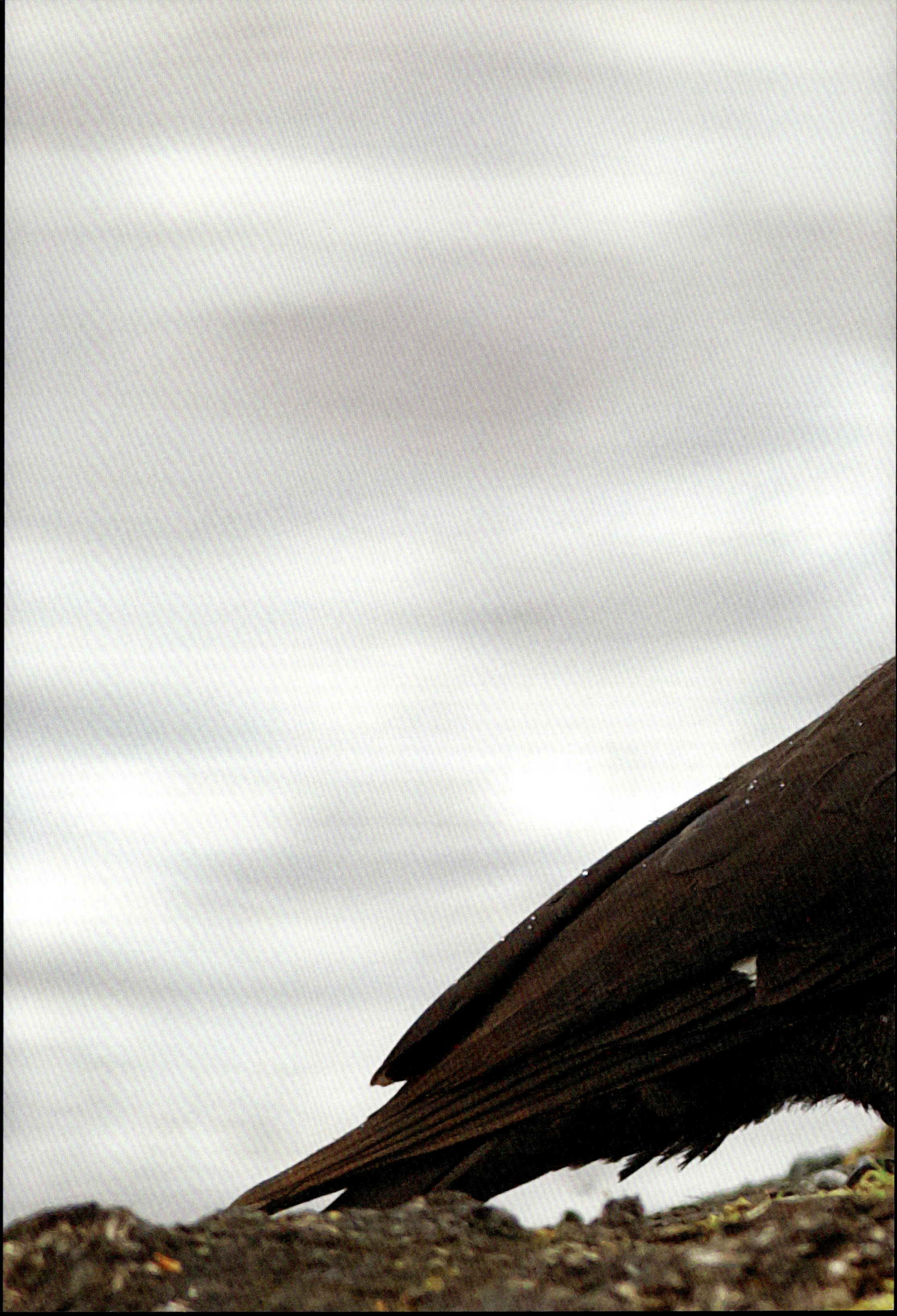

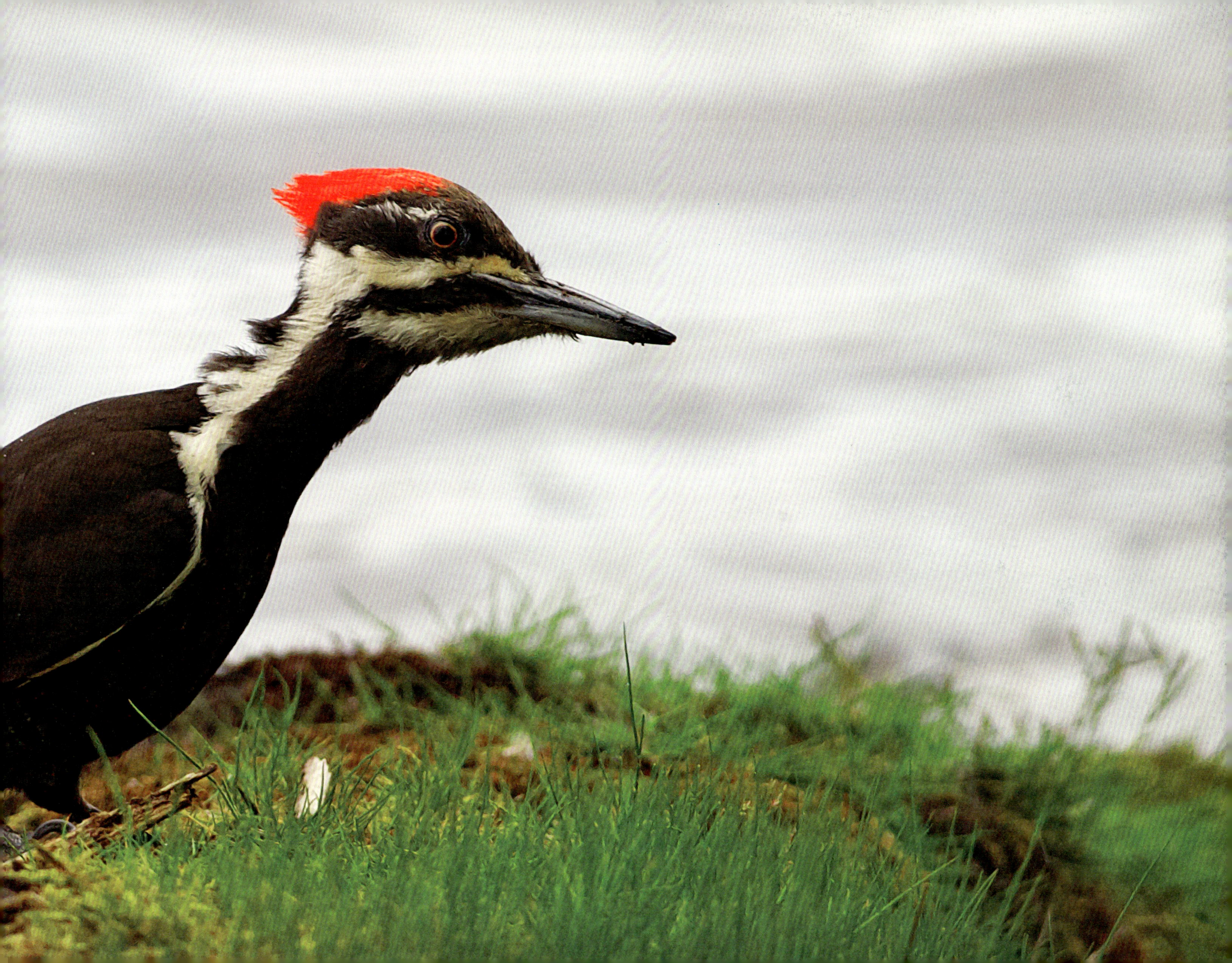

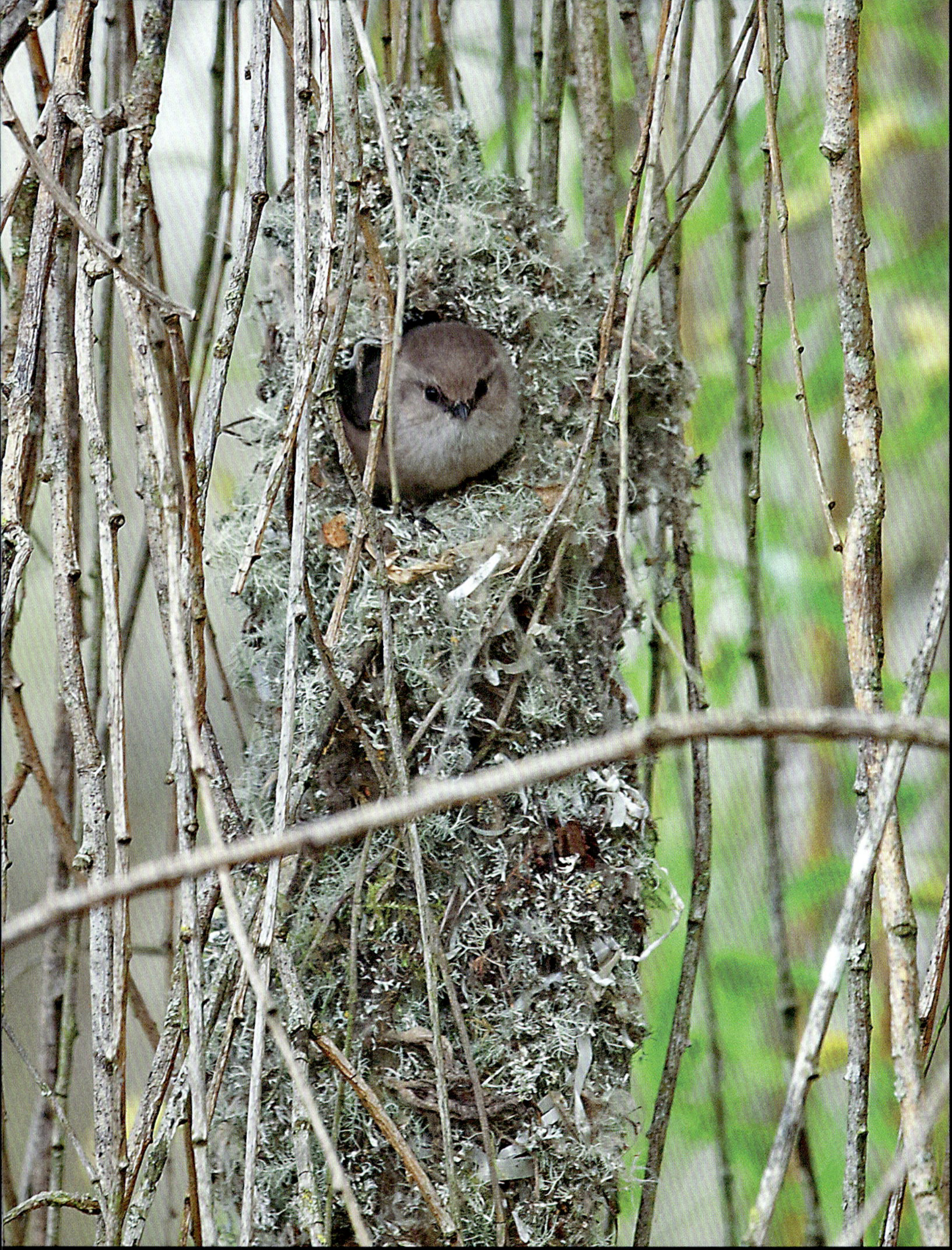

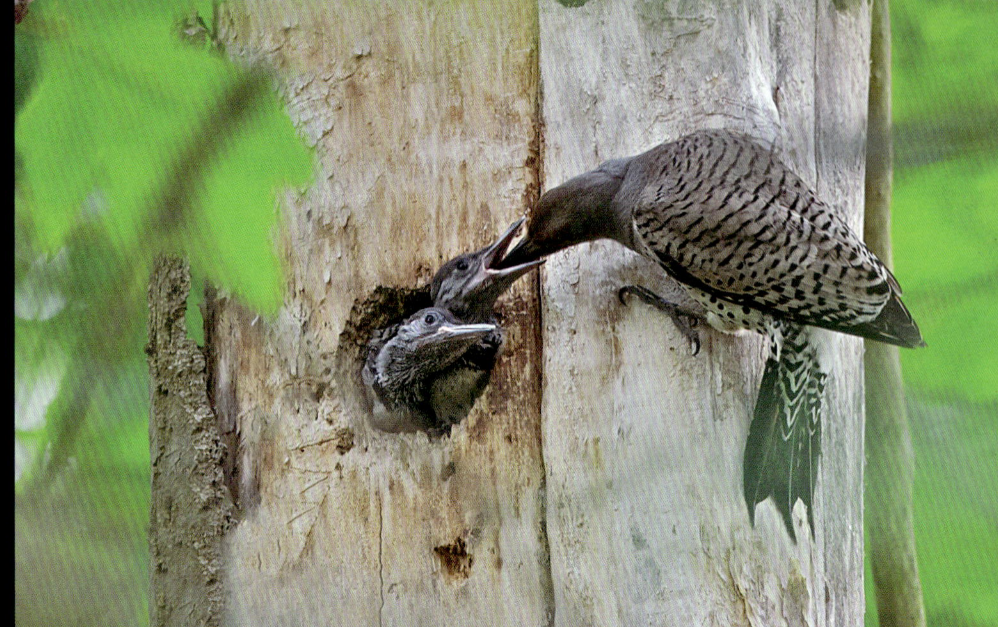

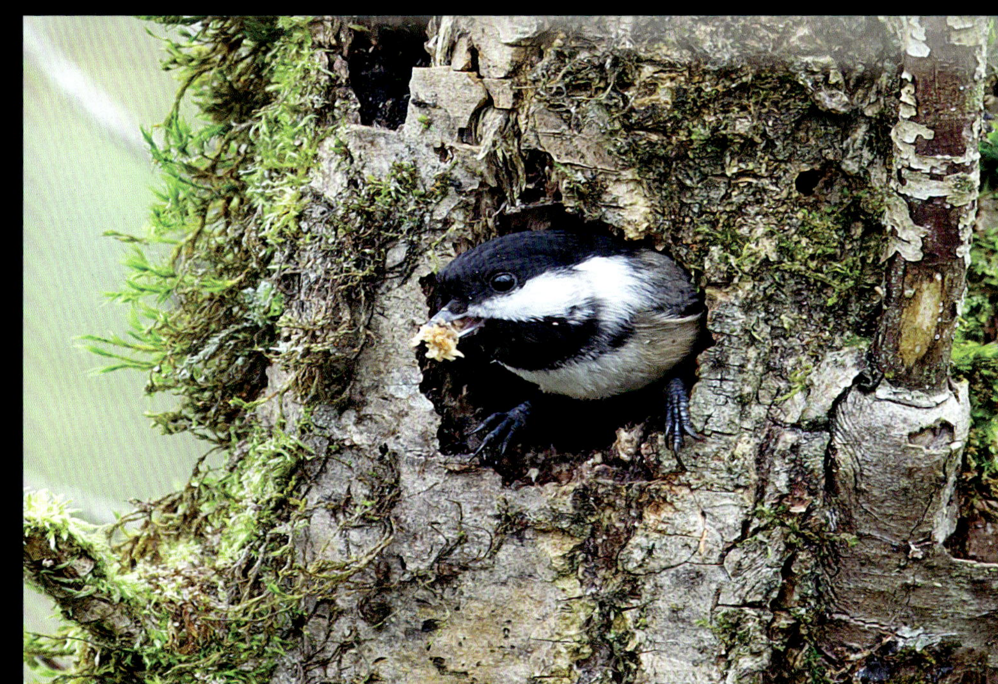

Above Left: Bushtits build hanging nests made of spider webs, moss, grass, and lichen. *Top Right*: A northern flicker feeds its hungry and fast growing young. *Bottom Right*: A chickadee excavates a nesting cavity.

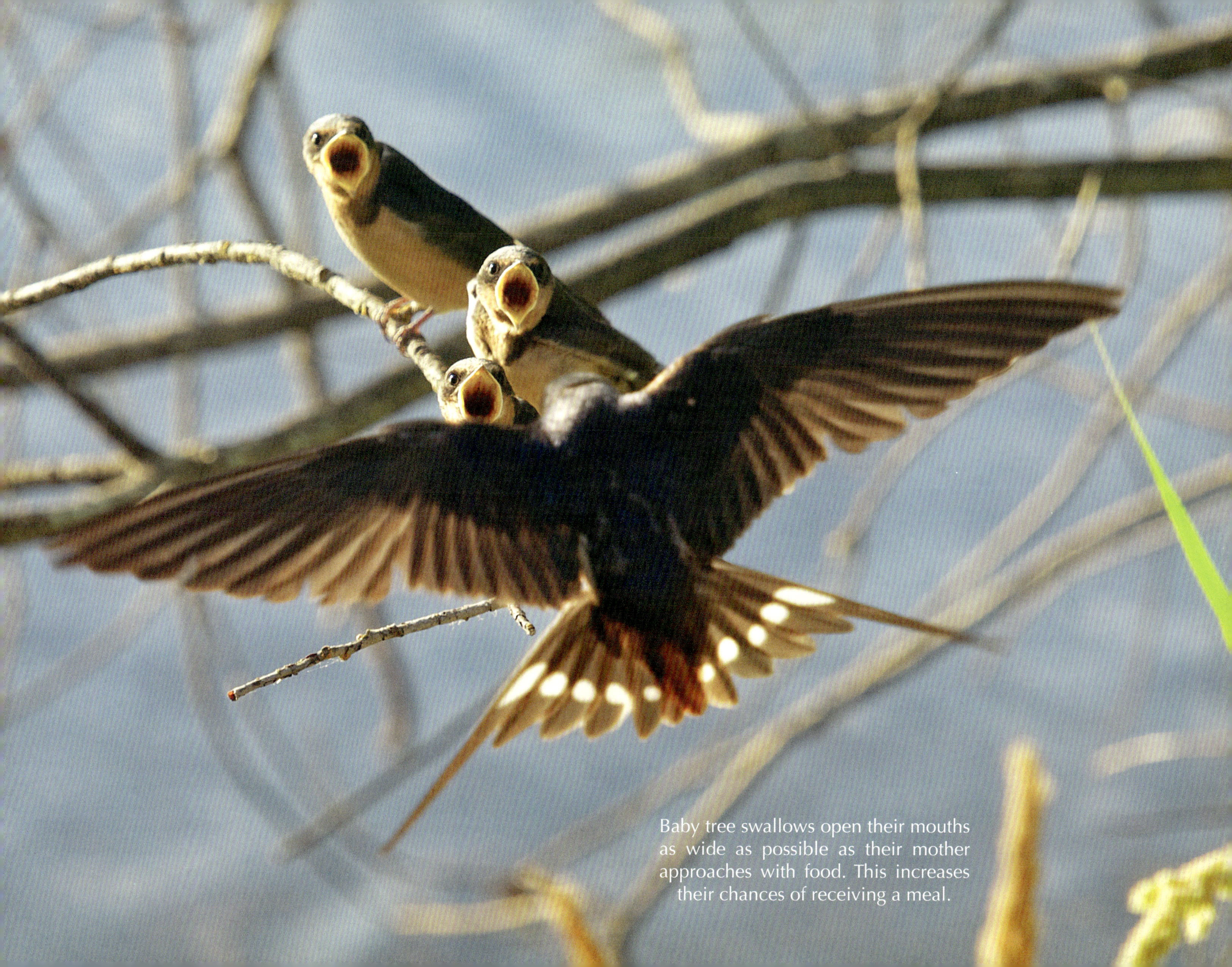

Baby tree swallows open their mouths as wide as possible as their mother approaches with food. This increases their chances of receiving a meal.

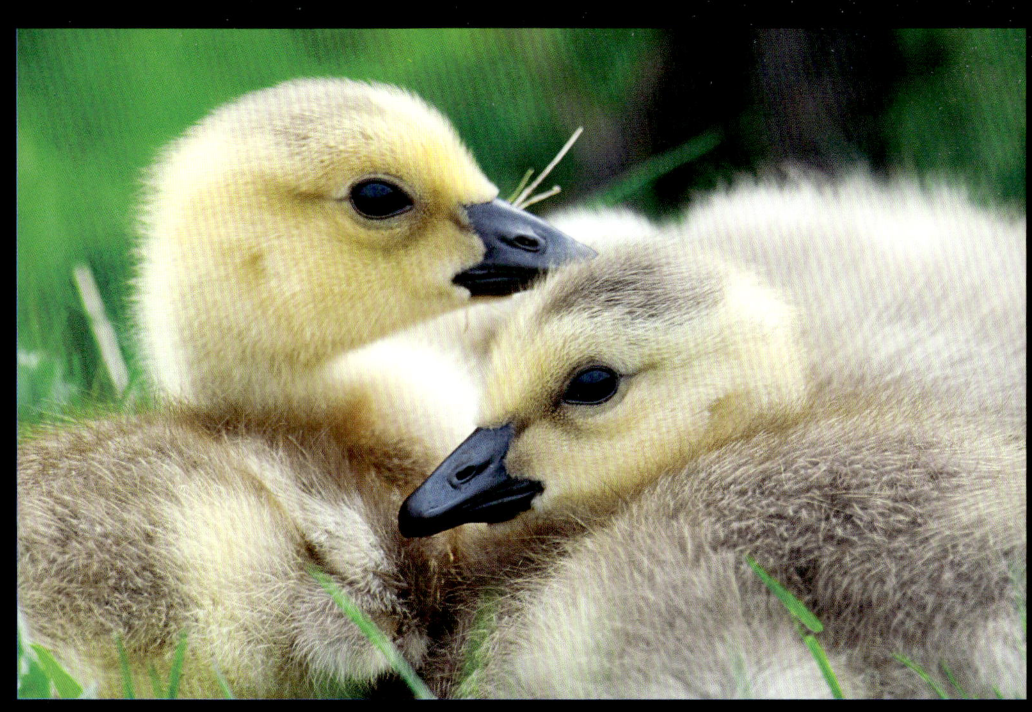

Above: Canada (not "Canadian") geese were once threatened but due to conservation efforts are now common throughout North America. I found these newly born Canada goose goslings huddled together to stay warm.

Facing Page: Mother and father Canada geese stand guard over their inexperienced and vulnerable goslings at the Montlake Fill.

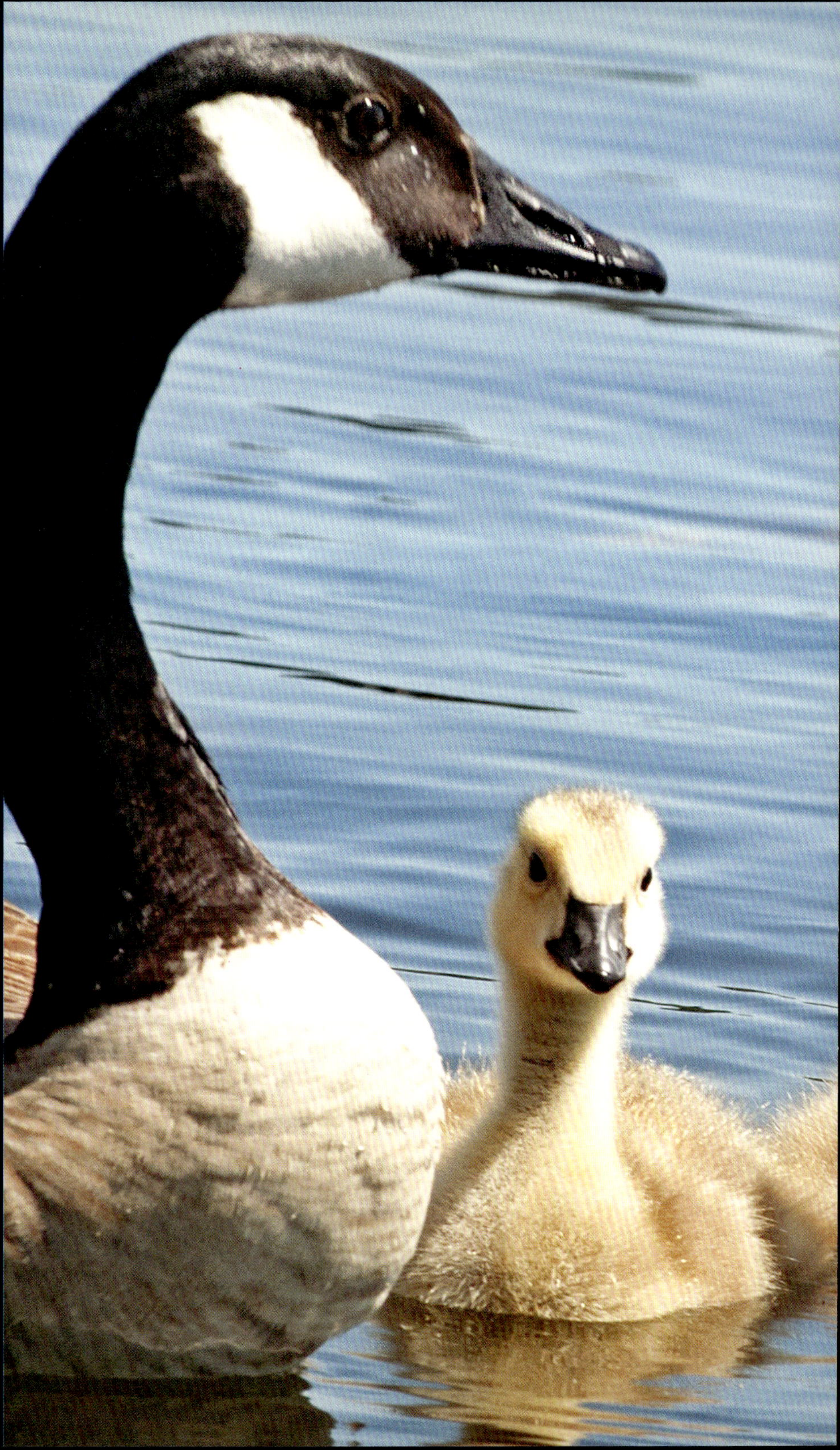

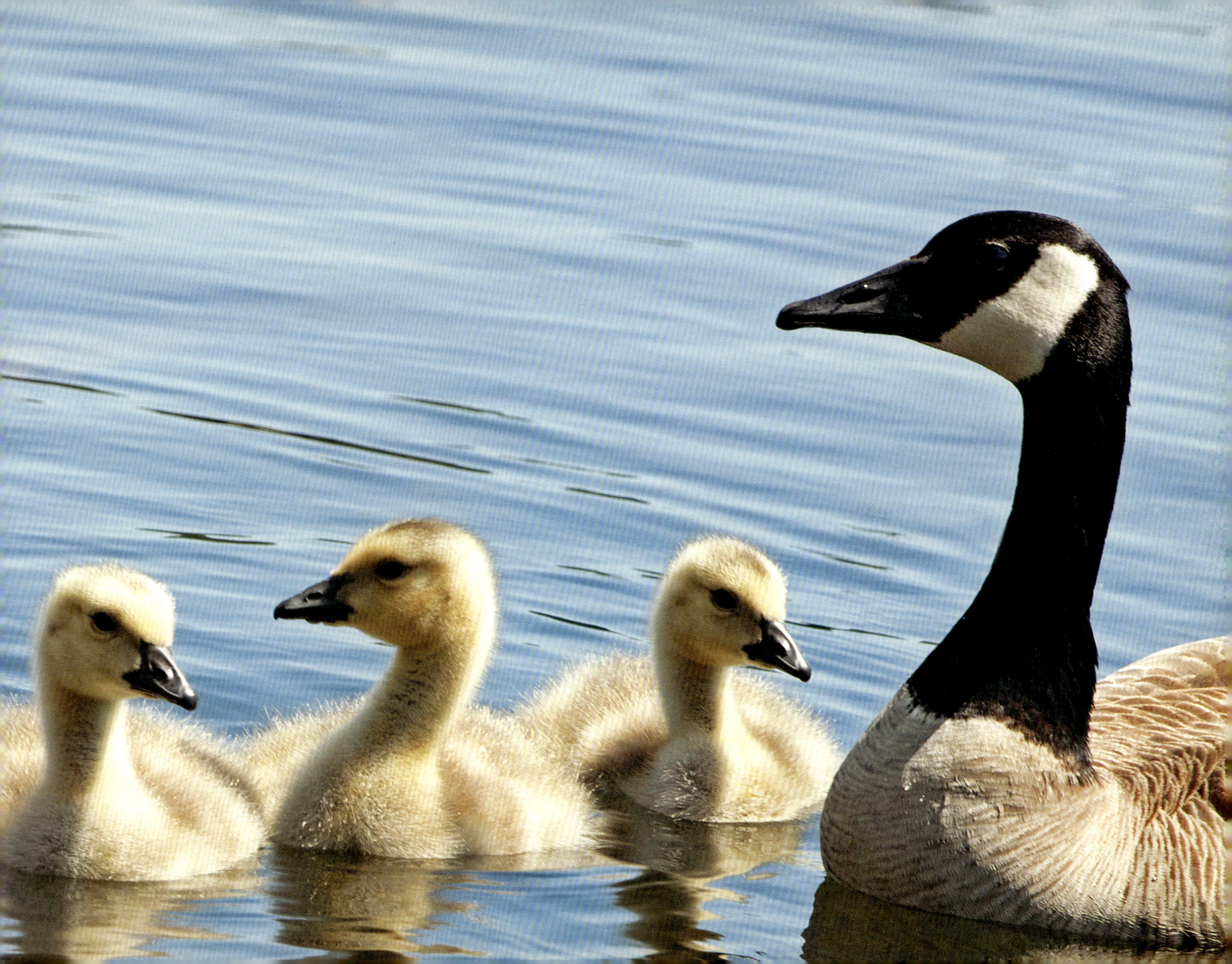

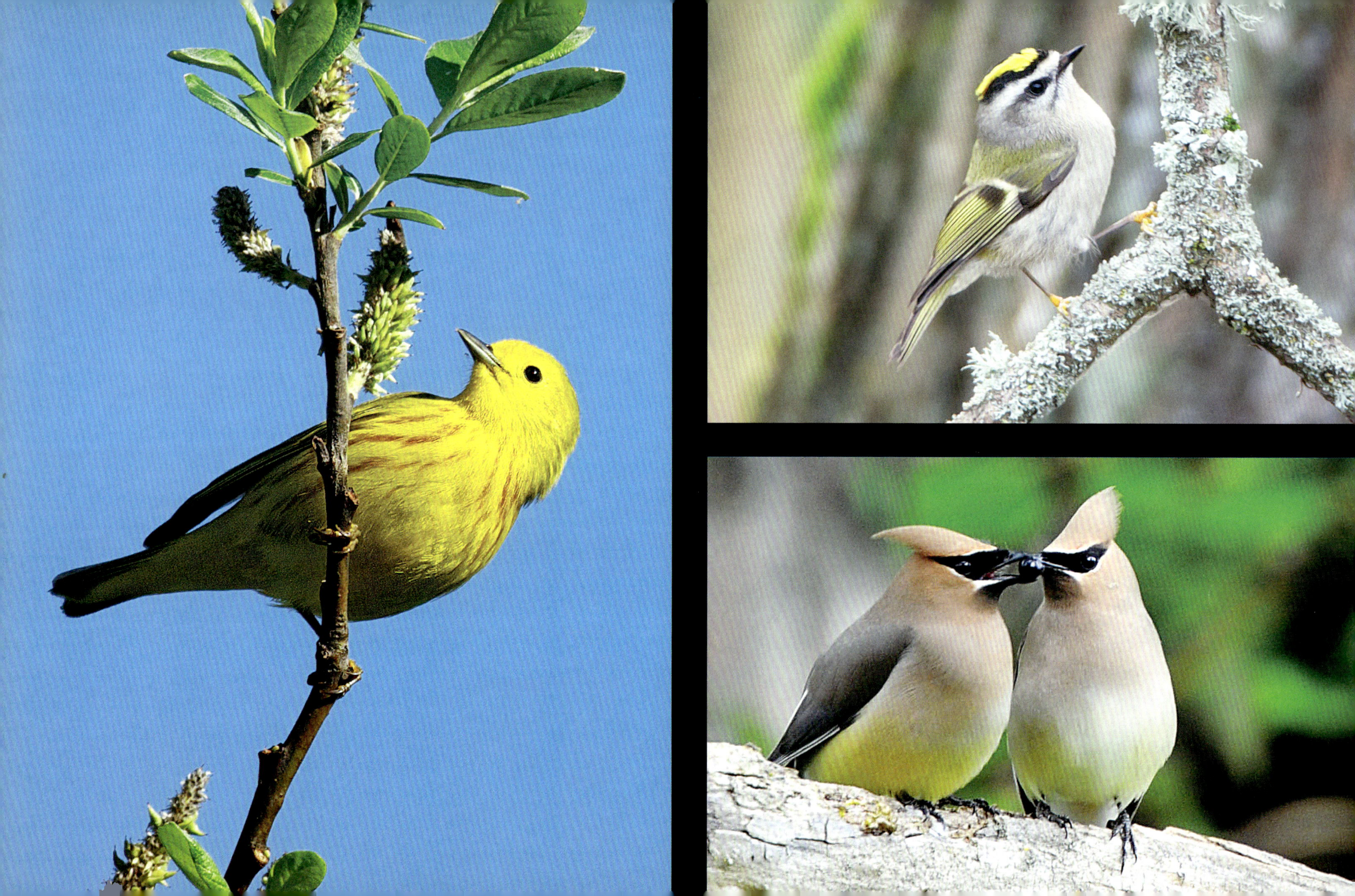

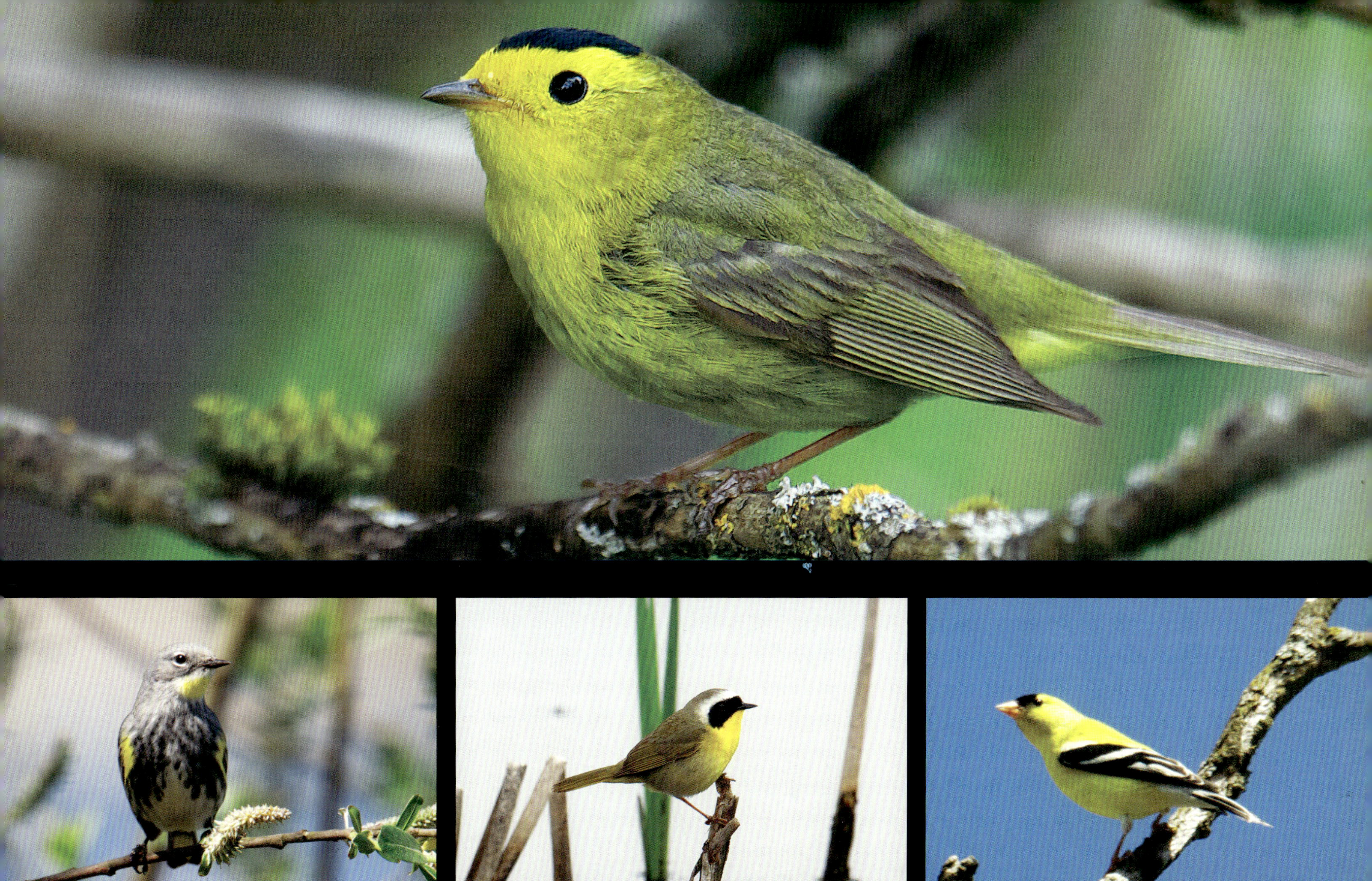

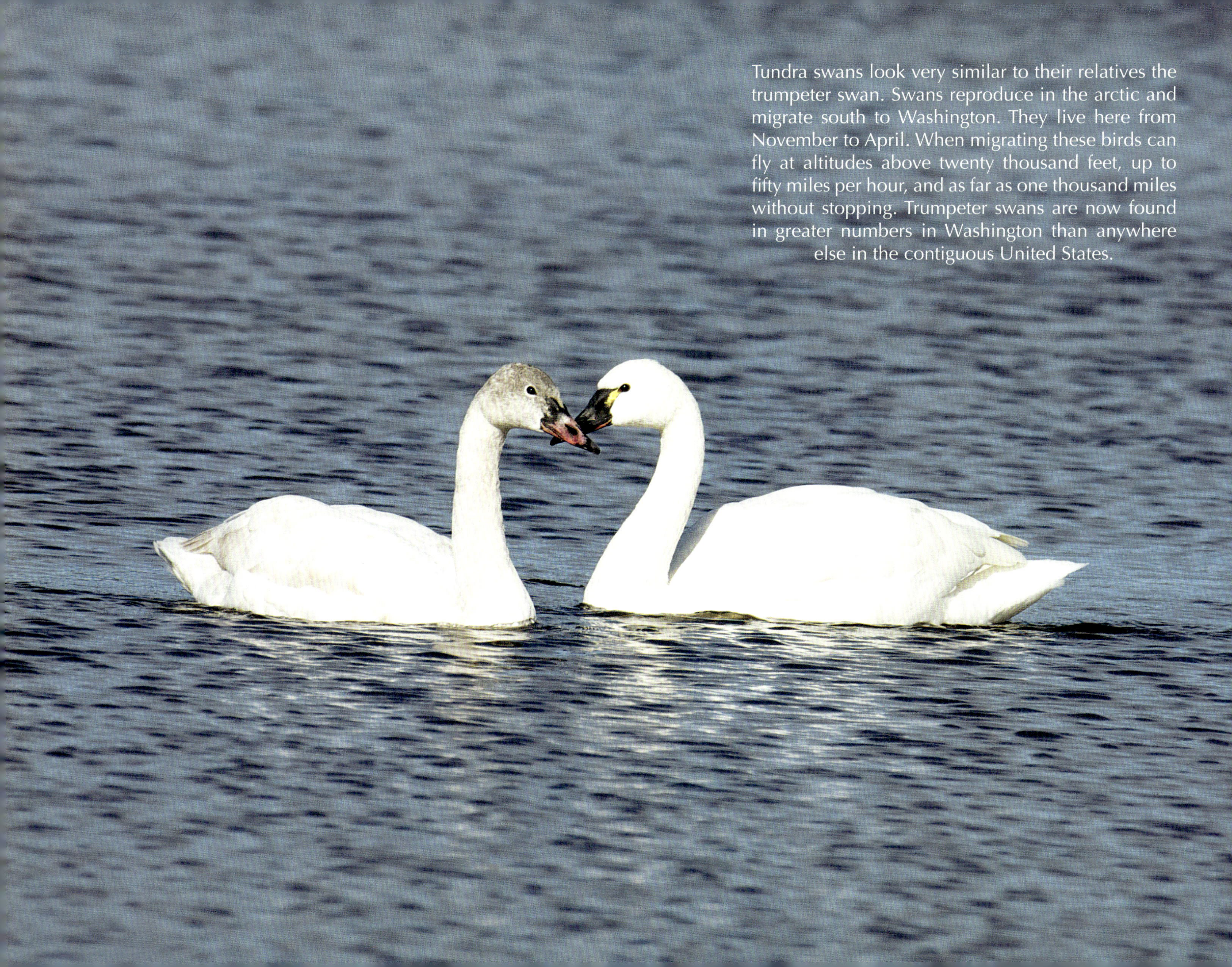

Tundra swans look very similar to their relatives the trumpeter swan. Swans reproduce in the arctic and migrate south to Washington. They live here from November to April. When migrating these birds can fly at altitudes above twenty thousand feet, up to fifty miles per hour, and as far as one thousand miles without stopping. Trumpeter swans are now found in greater numbers in Washington than anywhere else in the contiguous United States.

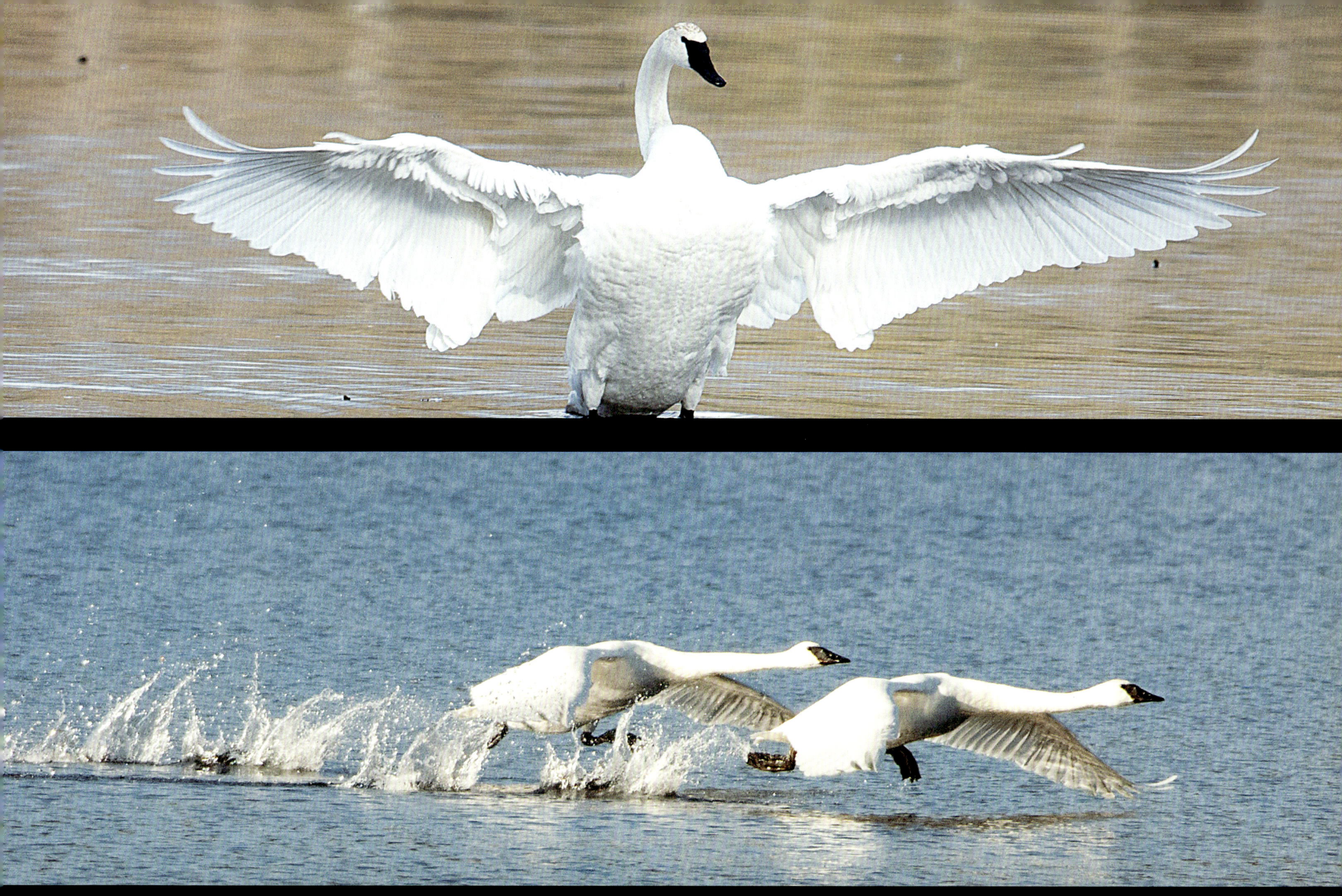

Top: Three flaps of its wings was enough to dry off after this trumpeter swan's bath.
Bottom: A pair of trumpeter swans dash off the water of Lake Washington into an elegant flight

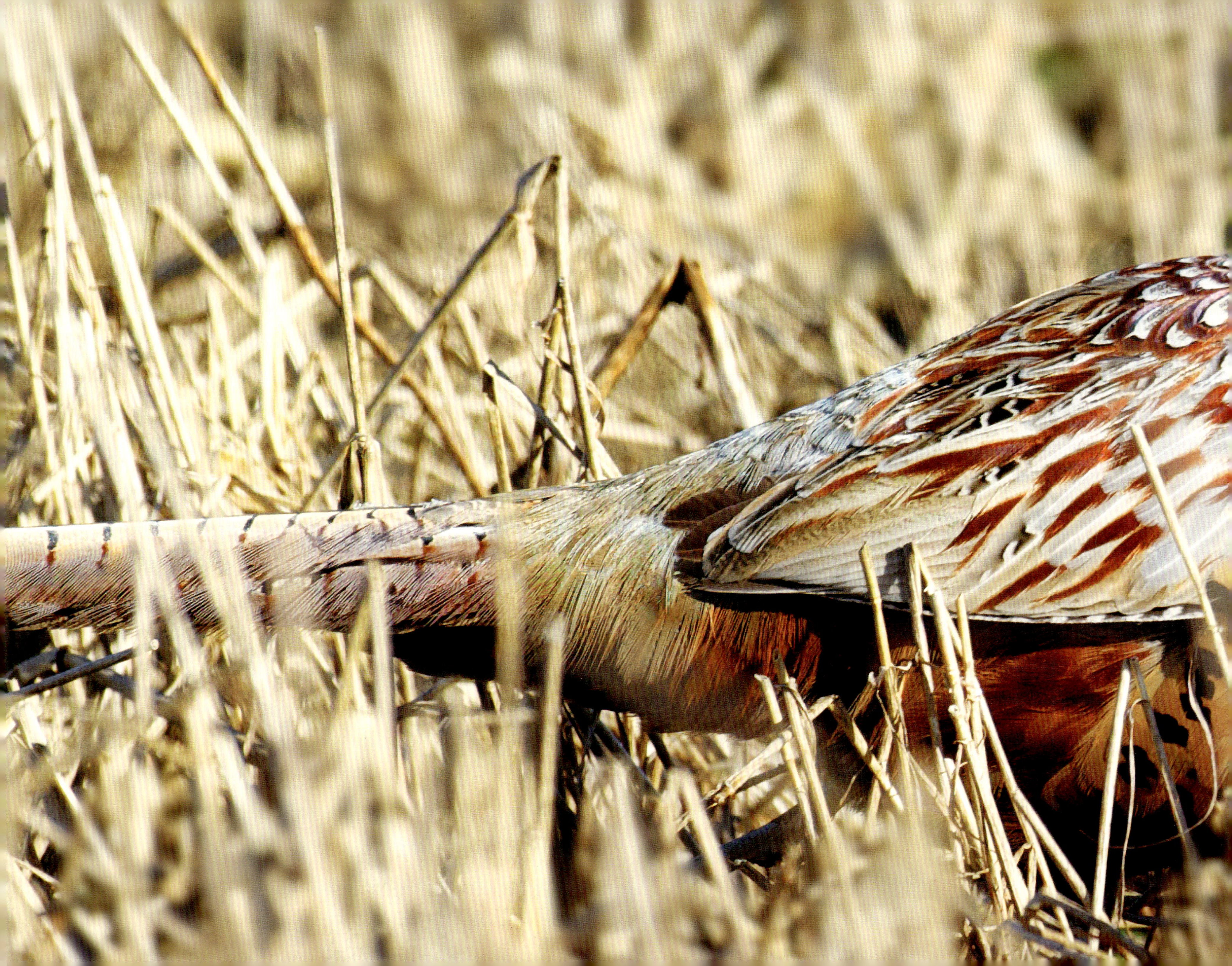

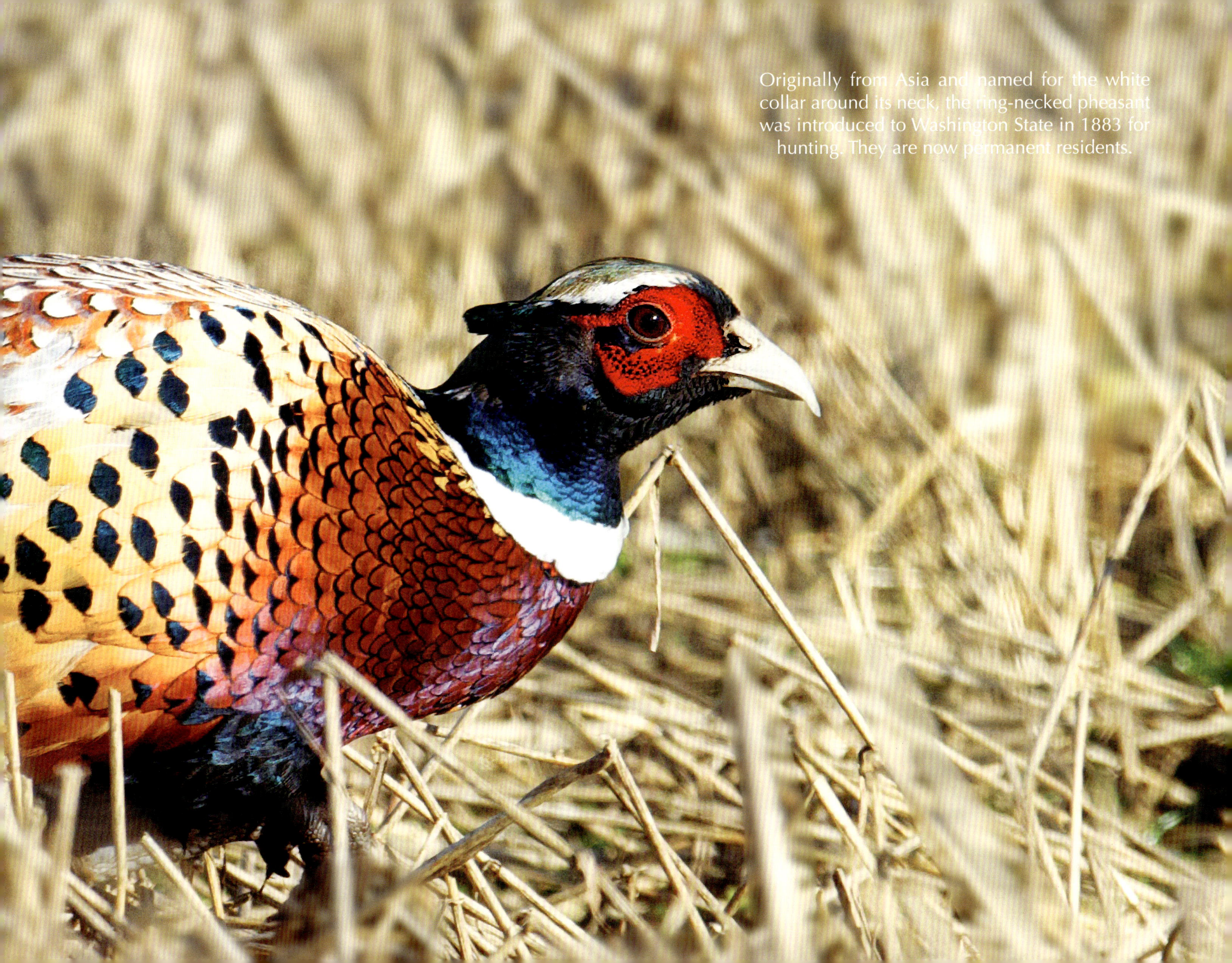

Originally from Asia and named for the white collar around its neck, the ring-necked pheasant was introduced to Washington State in 1883 for hunting. They are now permanent residents.

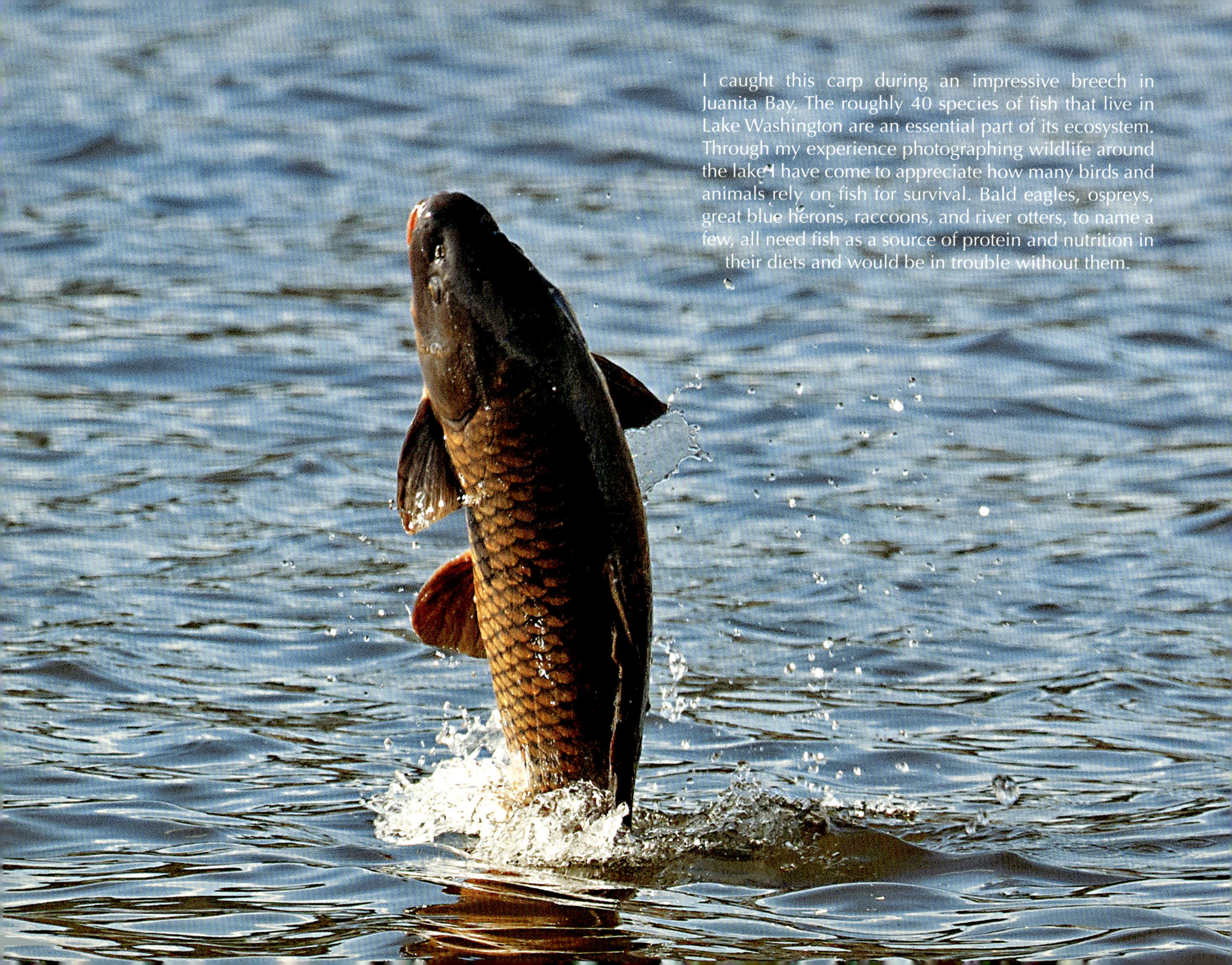

I caught this carp during an impressive breech in Juanita Bay. The roughly 40 species of fish that live in Lake Washington are an essential part of its ecosystem. Through my experience photographing wildlife around the lake I have come to appreciate how many birds and animals rely on fish for survival. Bald eagles, ospreys, great blue herons, raccoons, and river otters, to name a few, all need fish as a source of protein and nutrition in their diets and would be in trouble without them.

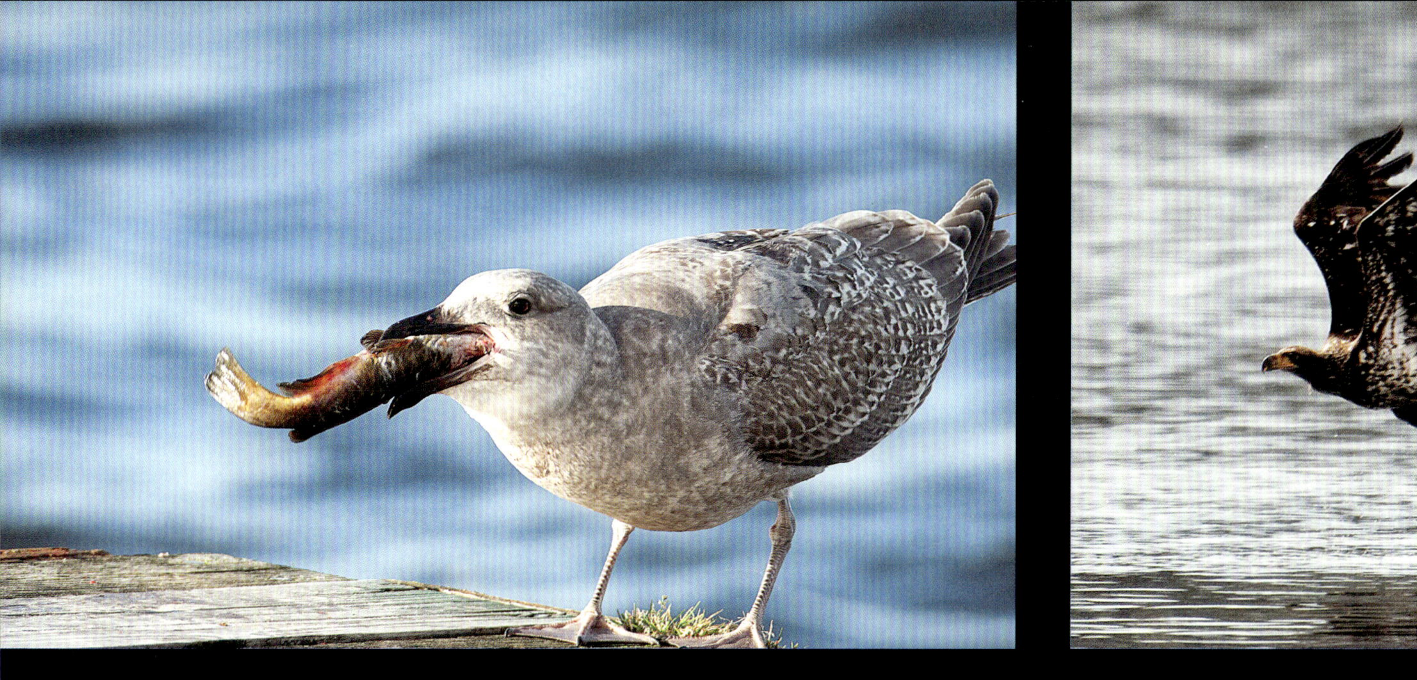

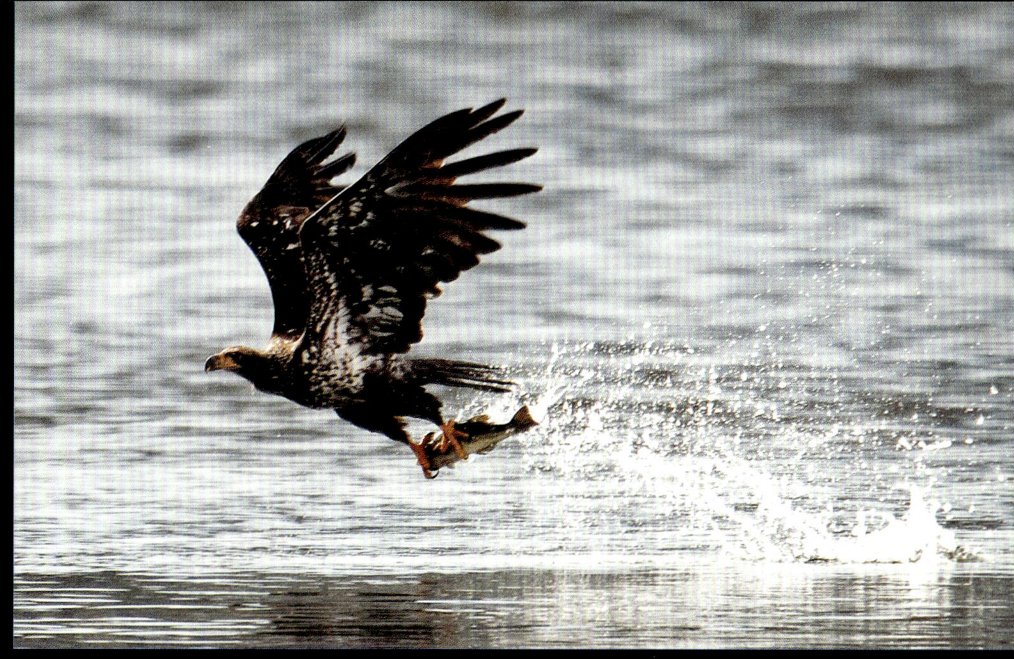

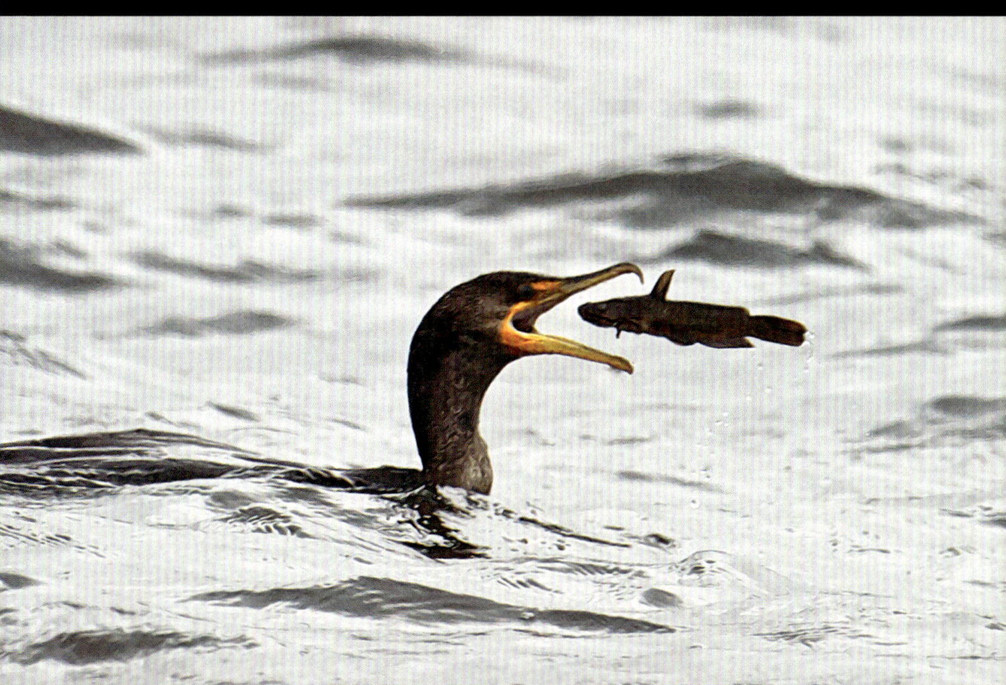

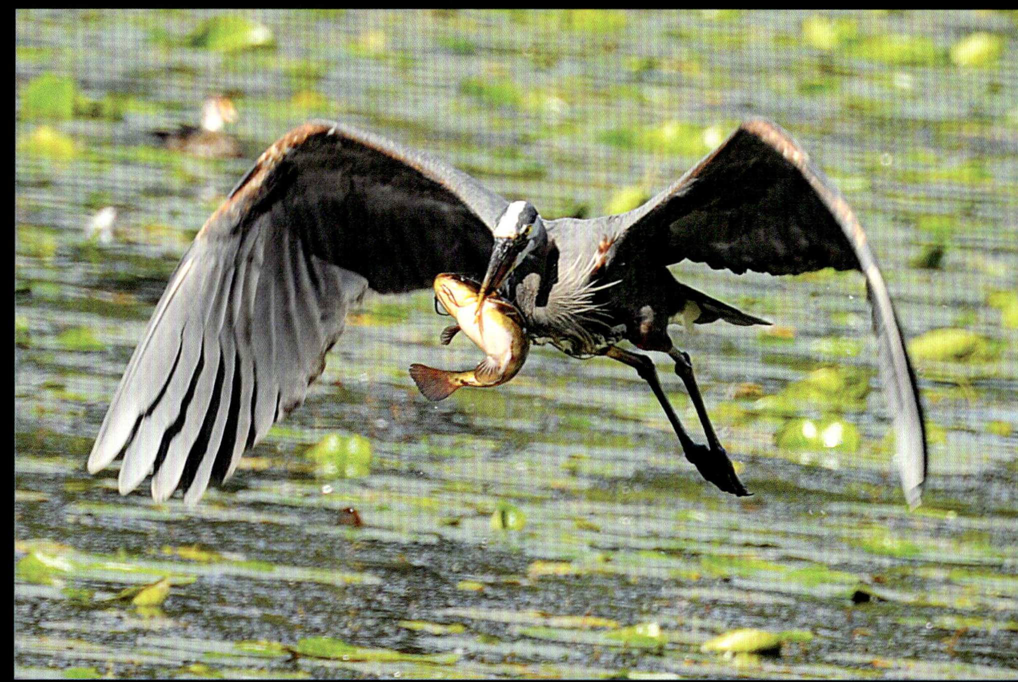

Top Left: A gull enjoys a fishy snack at Houghton Beach Park. *Top Right*: A juvenile bald eagle snatches a meal from the lake. *Bottom Left*: A double-crested cormorant flings its catch in the air at Union Bay. *Bottom Right*: A great blue heron takes flight after spearing a catfish.

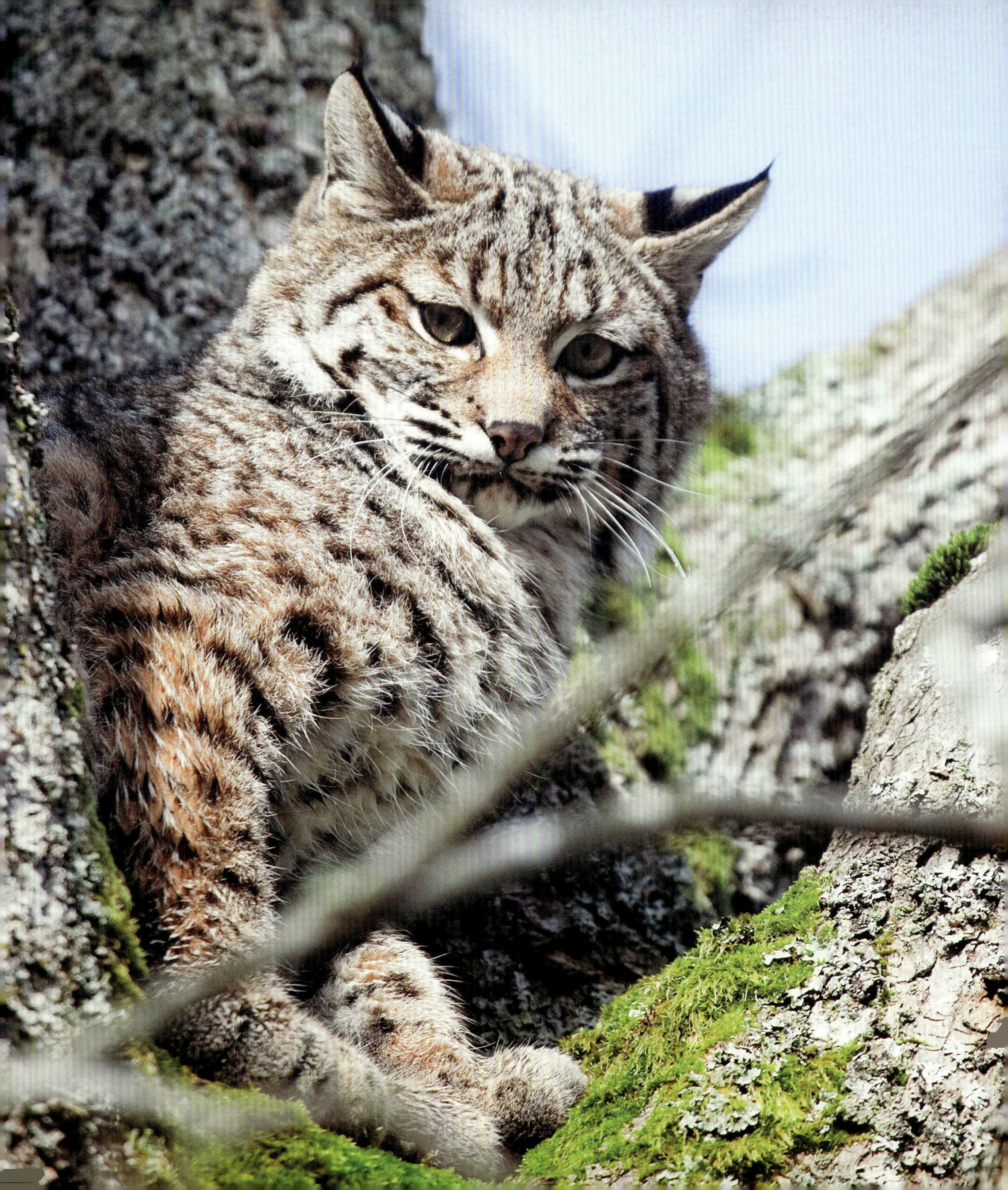

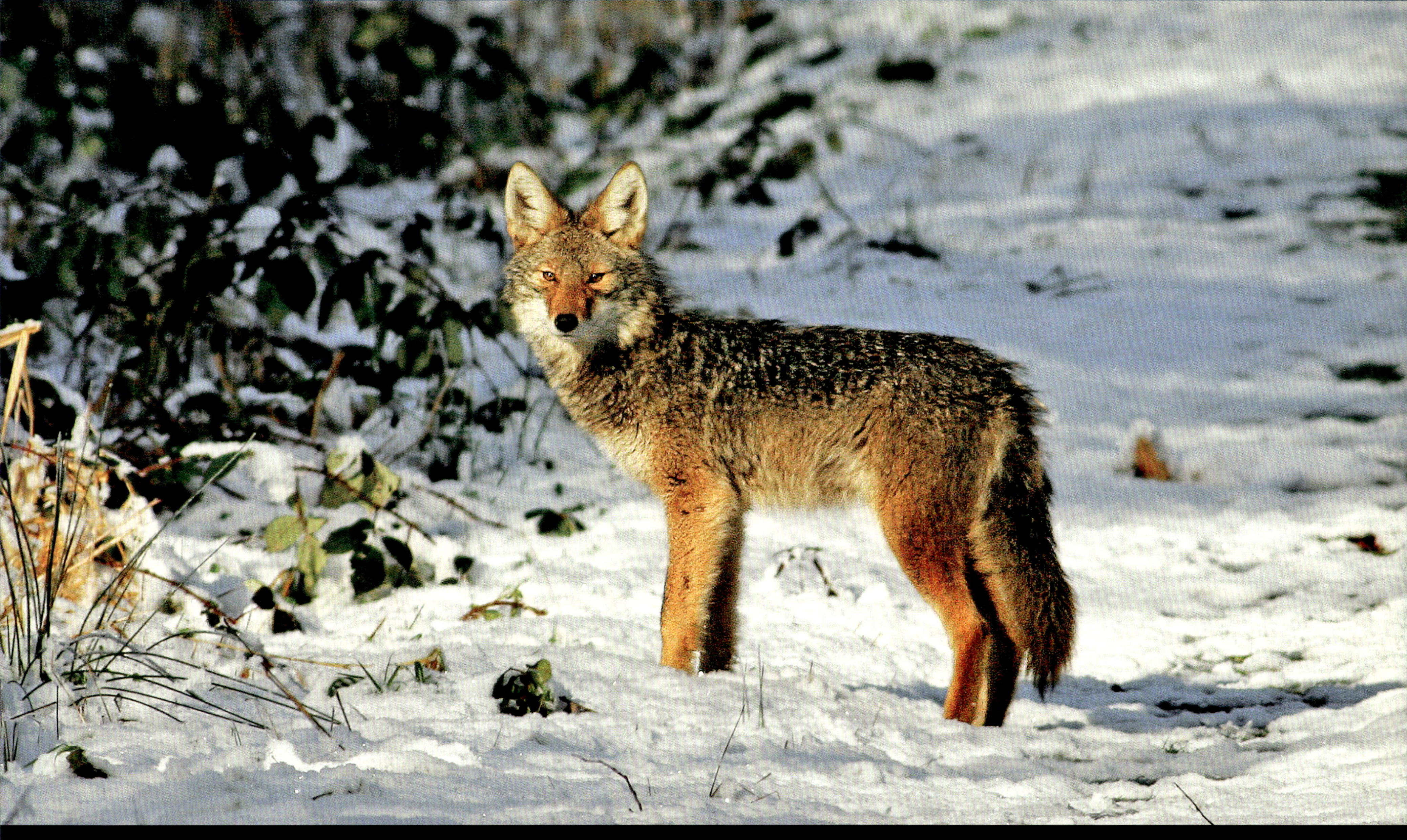

Facing Page: Bobcats are elusive and nocturnal, and therefore seldom seen by humans in the wild. Marc Hoffman took this photo during a rare encounter at Marymoor Park in December.

Above: Coyotes are clever animals that avoid human contact whenever possible. They are most active at night making them difficult to photograph. Larry Engles took this photograph behind Kirkland's Forbes Creek Fire Station.

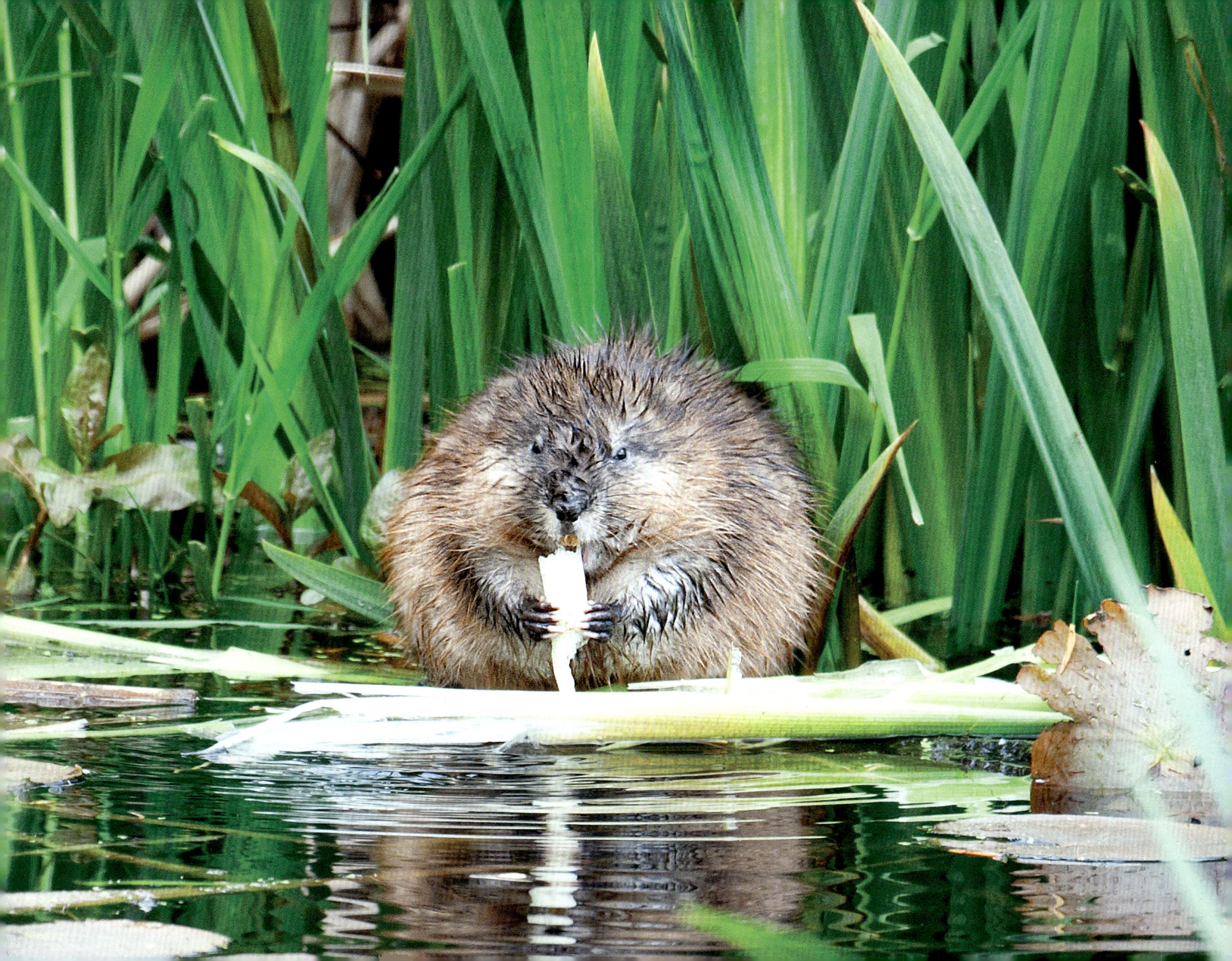

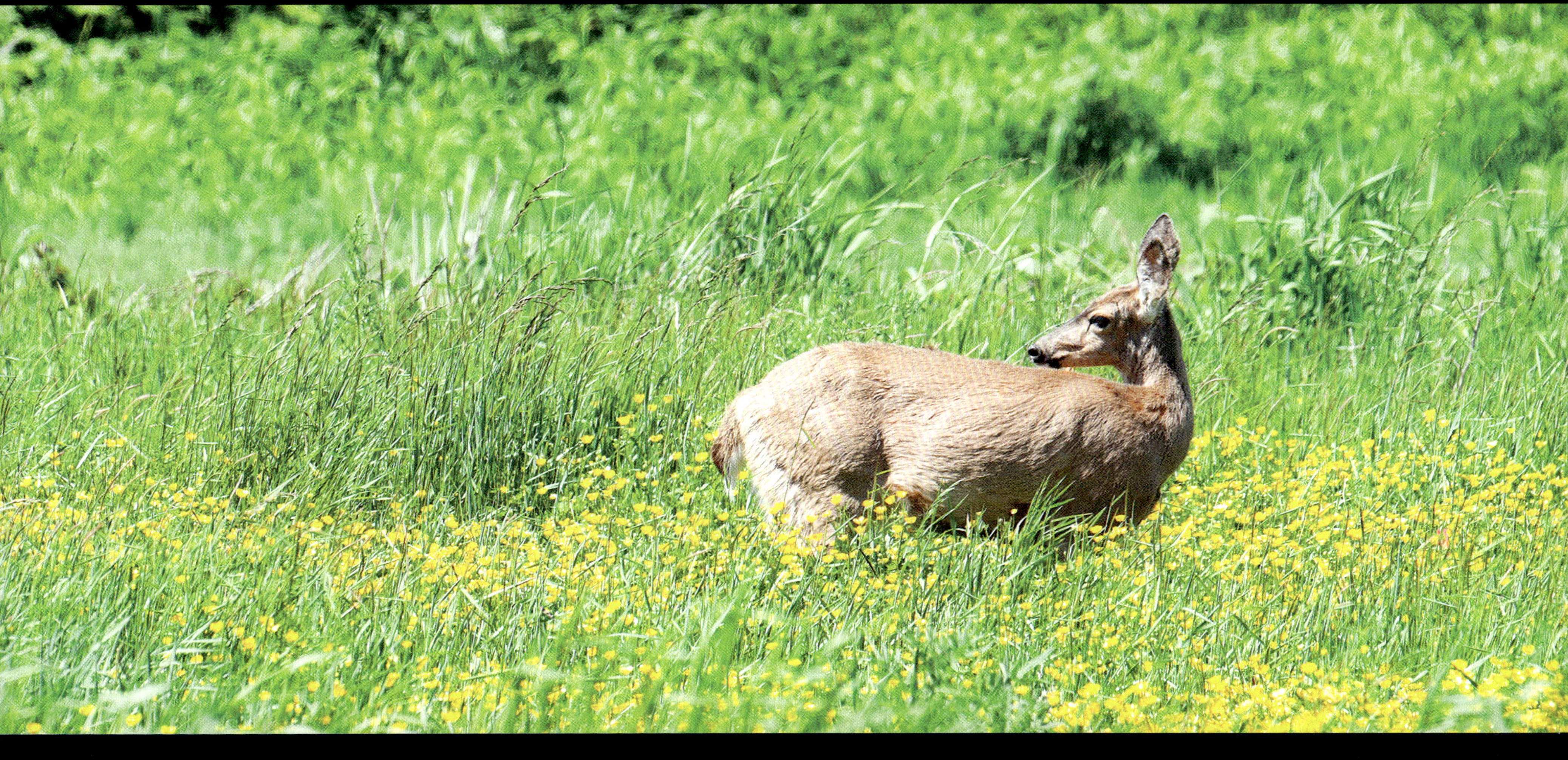

Facing Page: The muskrat is a semi-aquatic mammal that, like beavers, eats aquatic vegetation including cattails and water lilies. They can hold their breath an astonishing 15 minutes.

Above: This black-tailed deer on high alert scans a field of buttercup flowers in search of any sign of danger. Surprisingly, these deer can be found on Mercer Island.

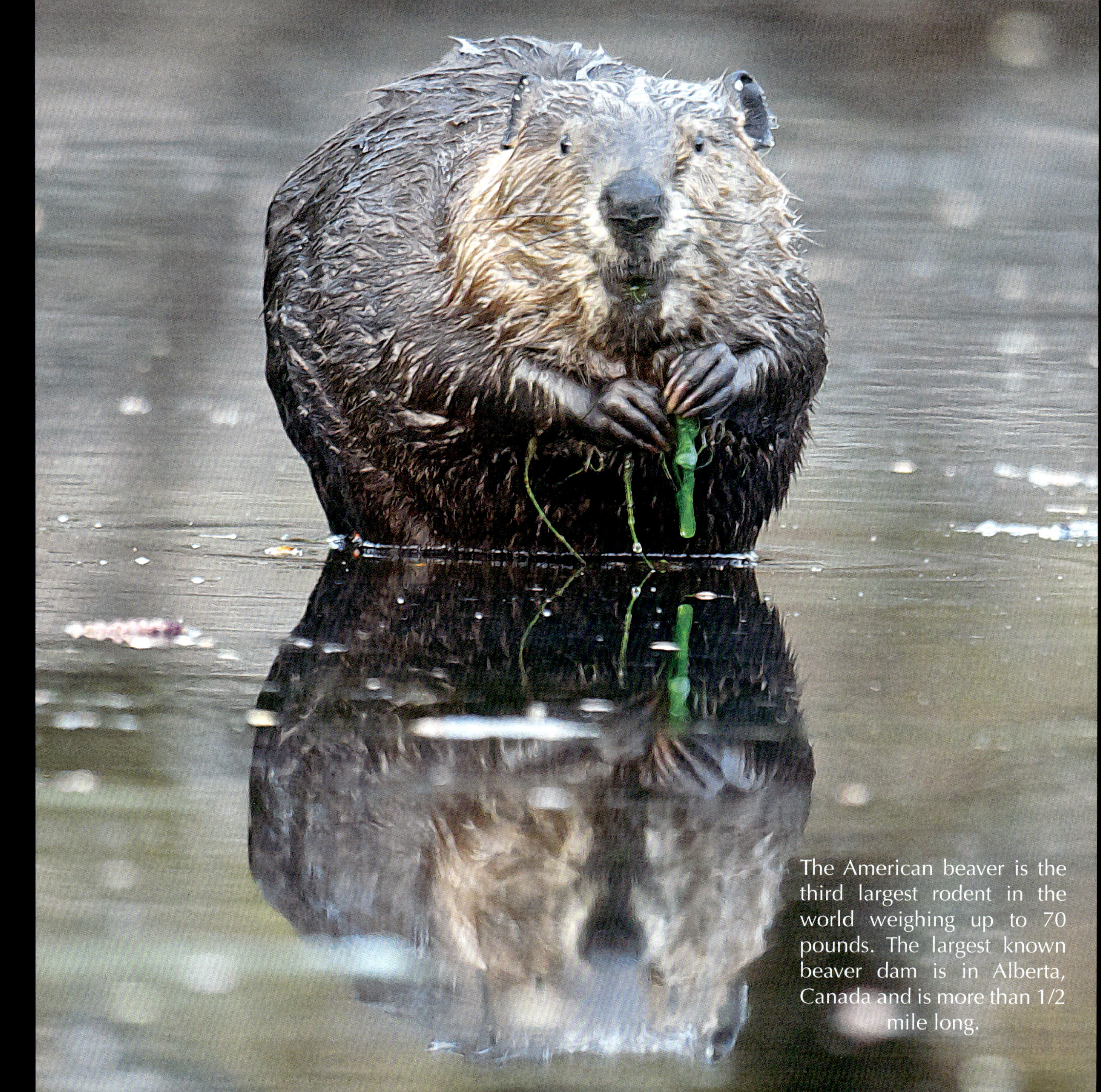

The American beaver is the third largest rodent in the world weighing up to 70 pounds. The largest known beaver dam is in Alberta, Canada and is more than 1/2 mile long.

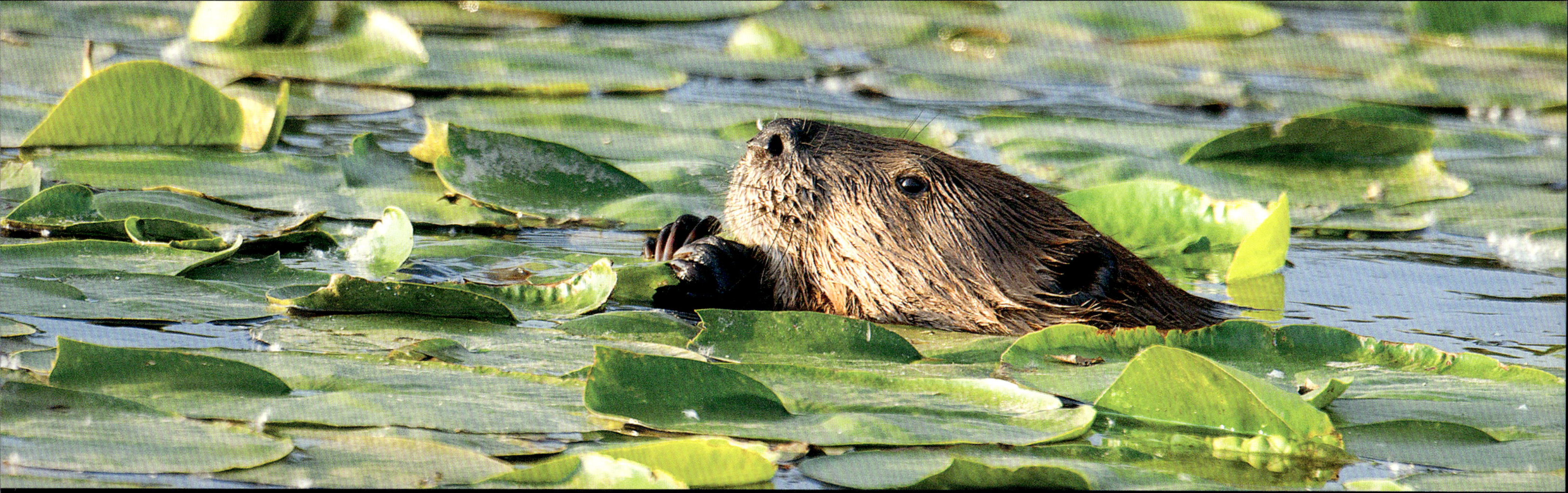

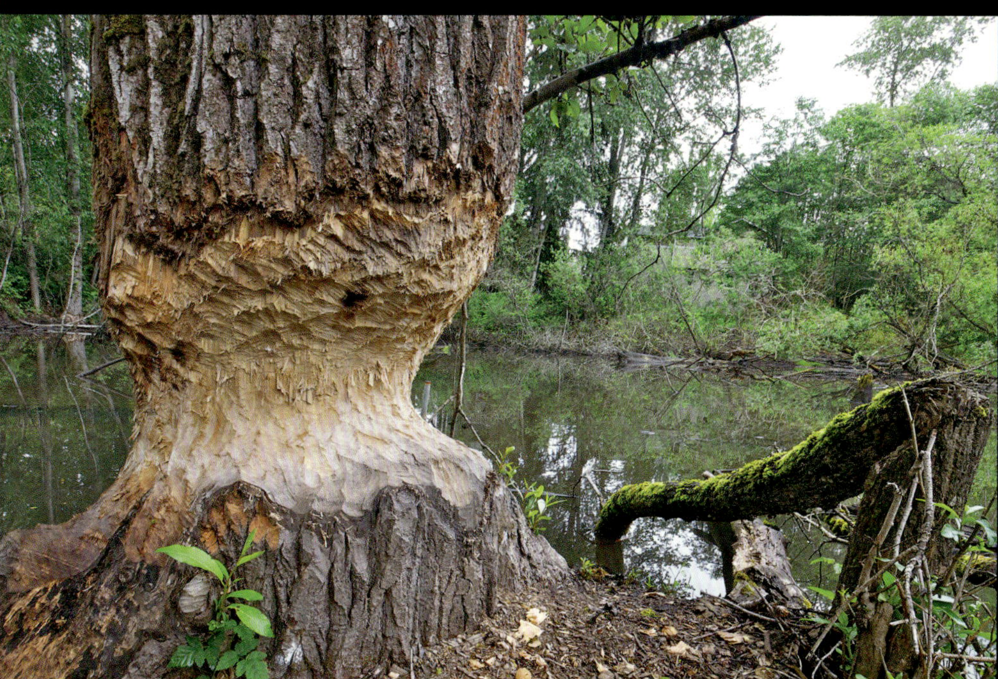

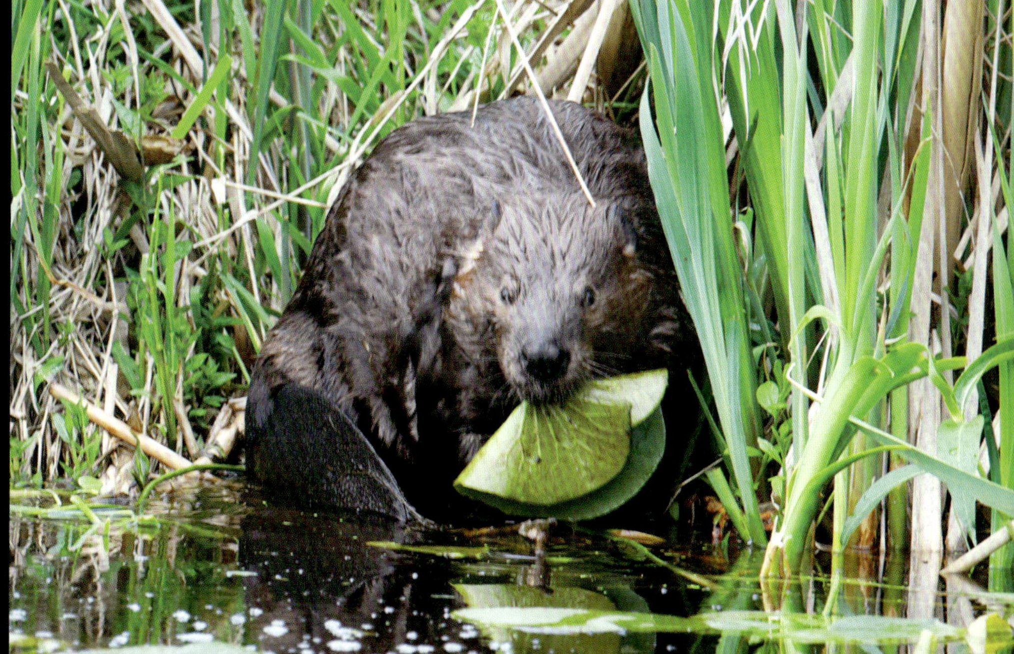

Top: Beaver make most of their diet from bark but also eat vegetation like roots, buds, and water lilies. Bottom Left: Less than a mile from the Costco in Kirkland a large tree shows obvious signs of beaver activity. Bottom Right: A beaver chews a recently collected water lily.

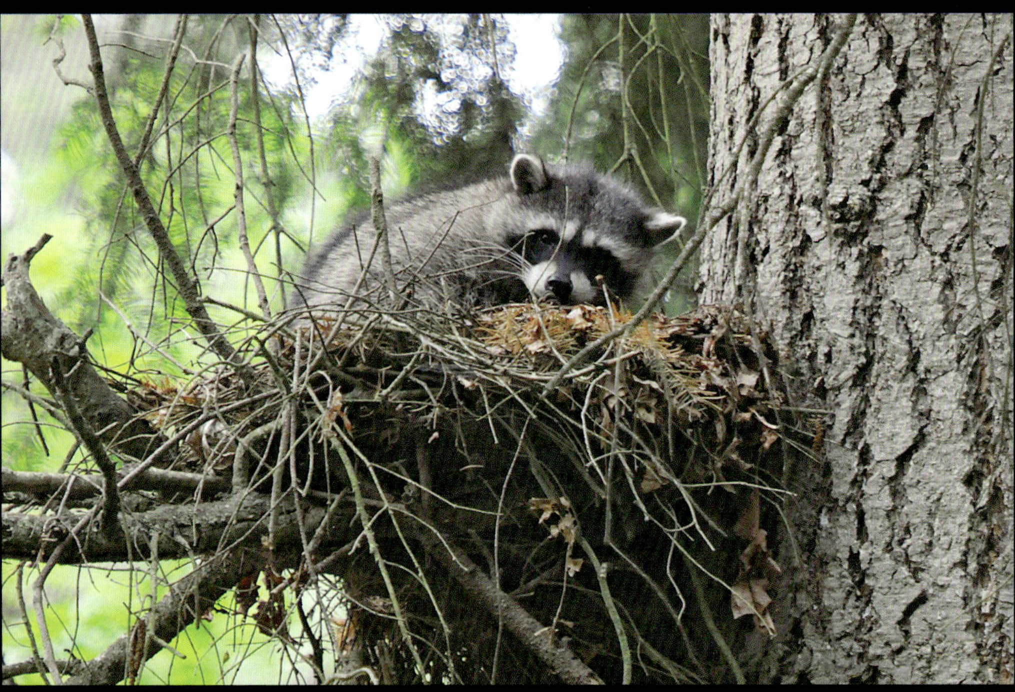

Raccoons, also known as "masked bandits" earn their name from mischief. They can surprisingly turn an unlocked doorknob without problem. They are very adaptable because they will eat almost anything, including human trash, which makes them very common in all types of environments including cities.

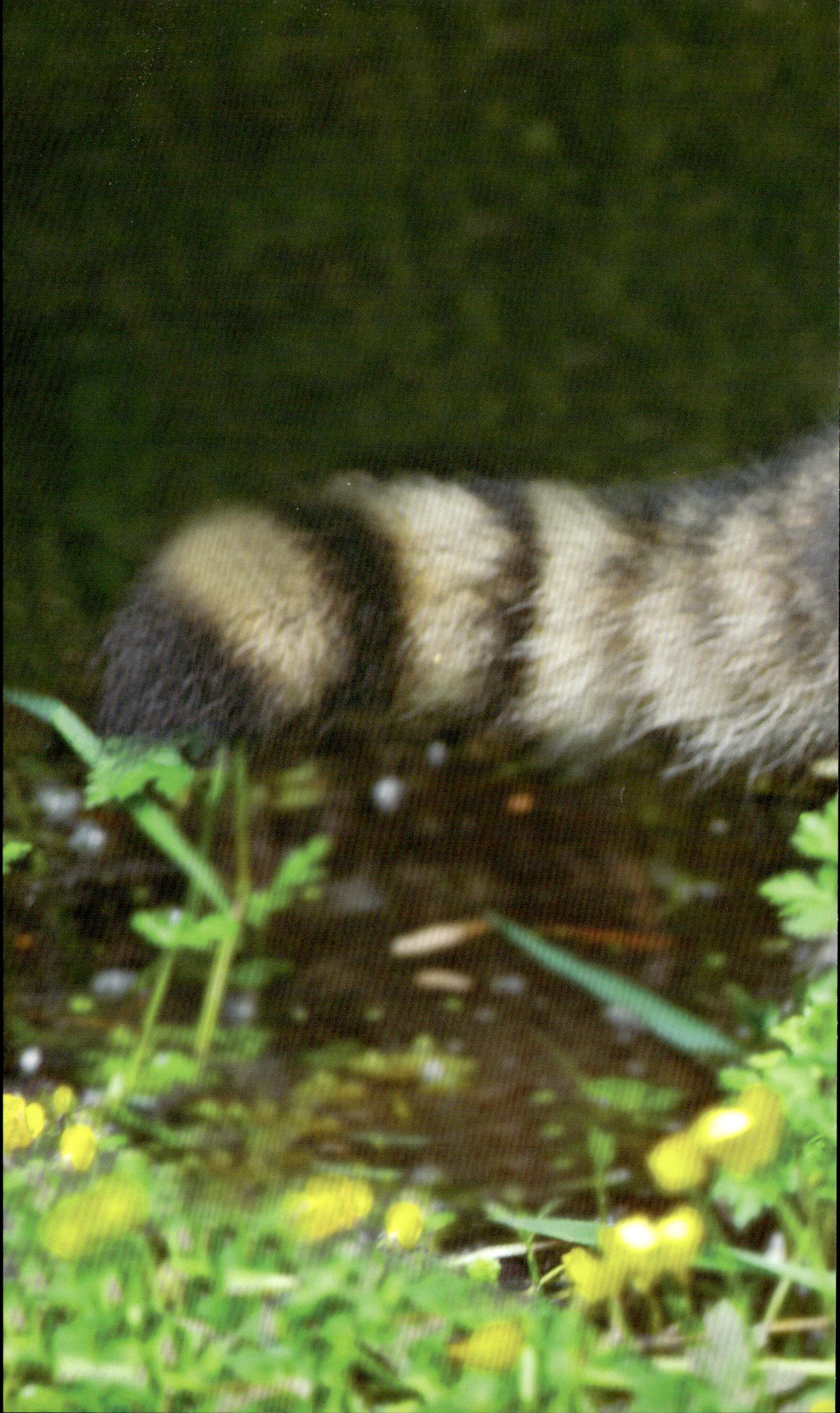

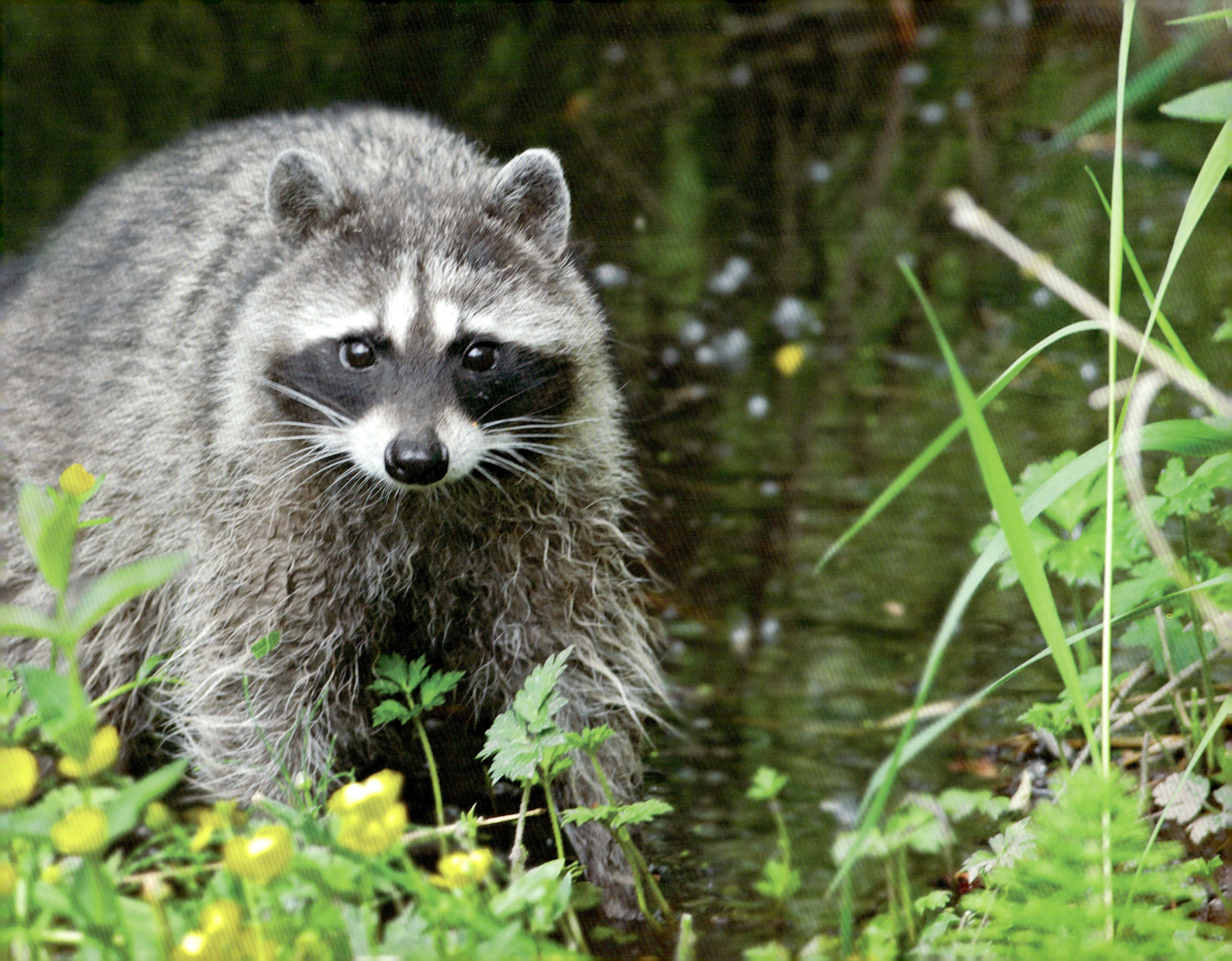

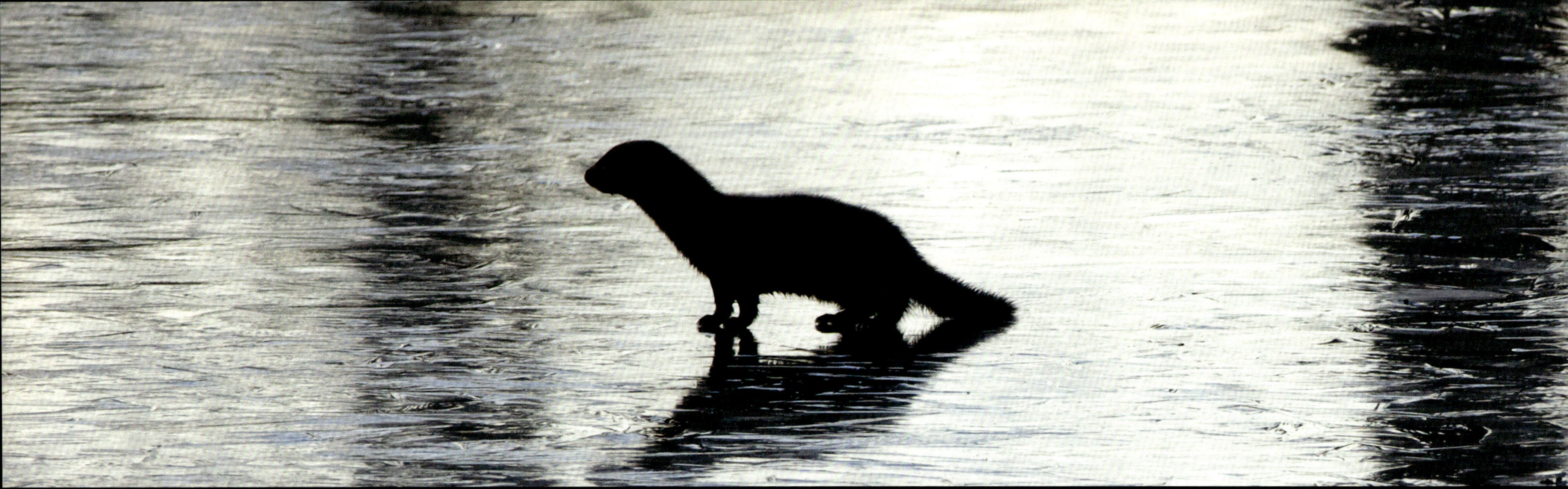

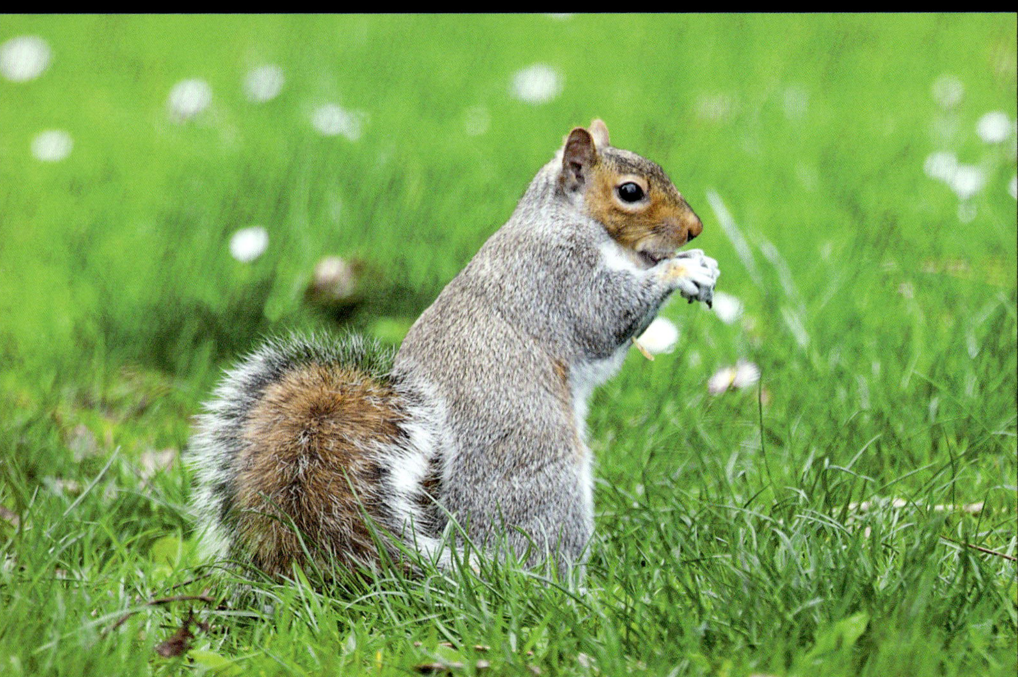

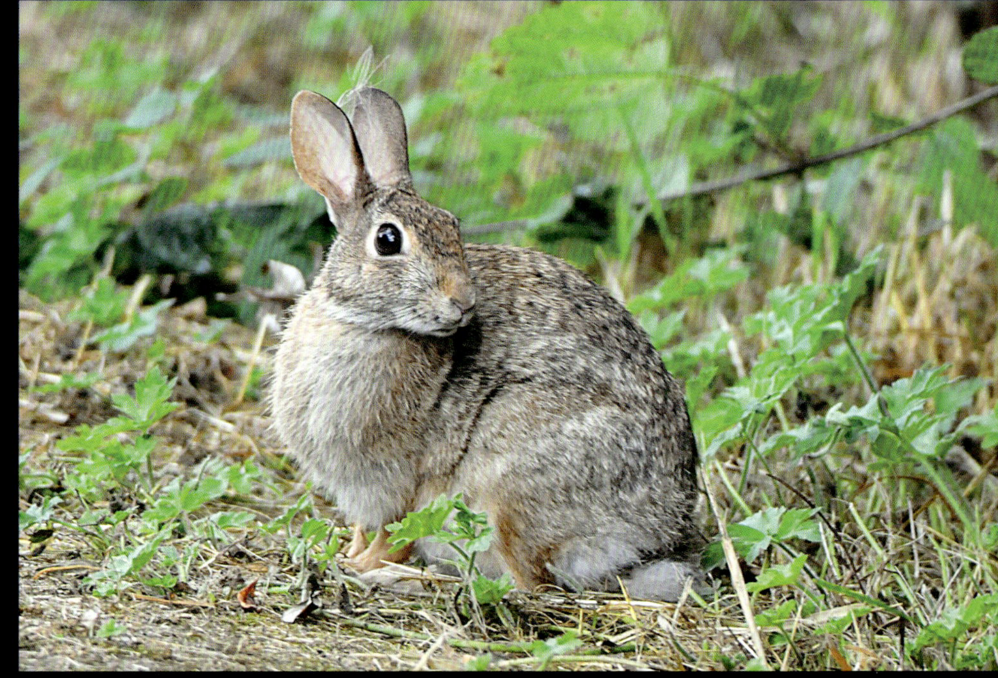

Top: An American mink pauses on the icy shores of Juanita Bay one frigid afternoon in December. Bottom Left: A western grey squirrel forages for seeds to deposit into multiple caches to dig up later when food is less abundant. Bottom Right: It is said that a single pair of cottontail rabbits could produce 350,000 rabbits in five years if no young were lost. However, few rabbits live more than one year.

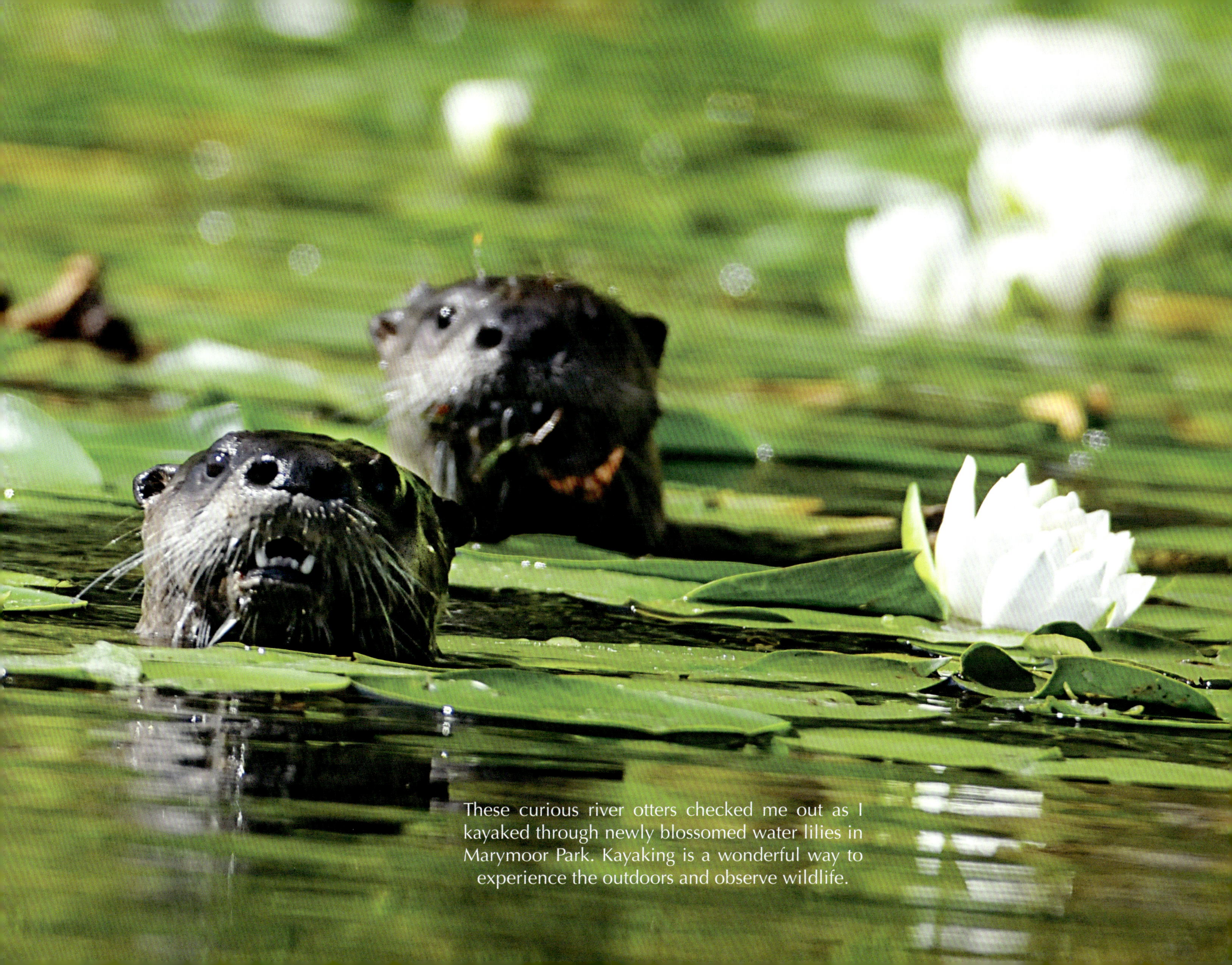

These curious river otters checked me out as I kayaked through newly blossomed water lilies in Marymoor Park. Kayaking is a wonderful way to experience the outdoors and observe wildlife.

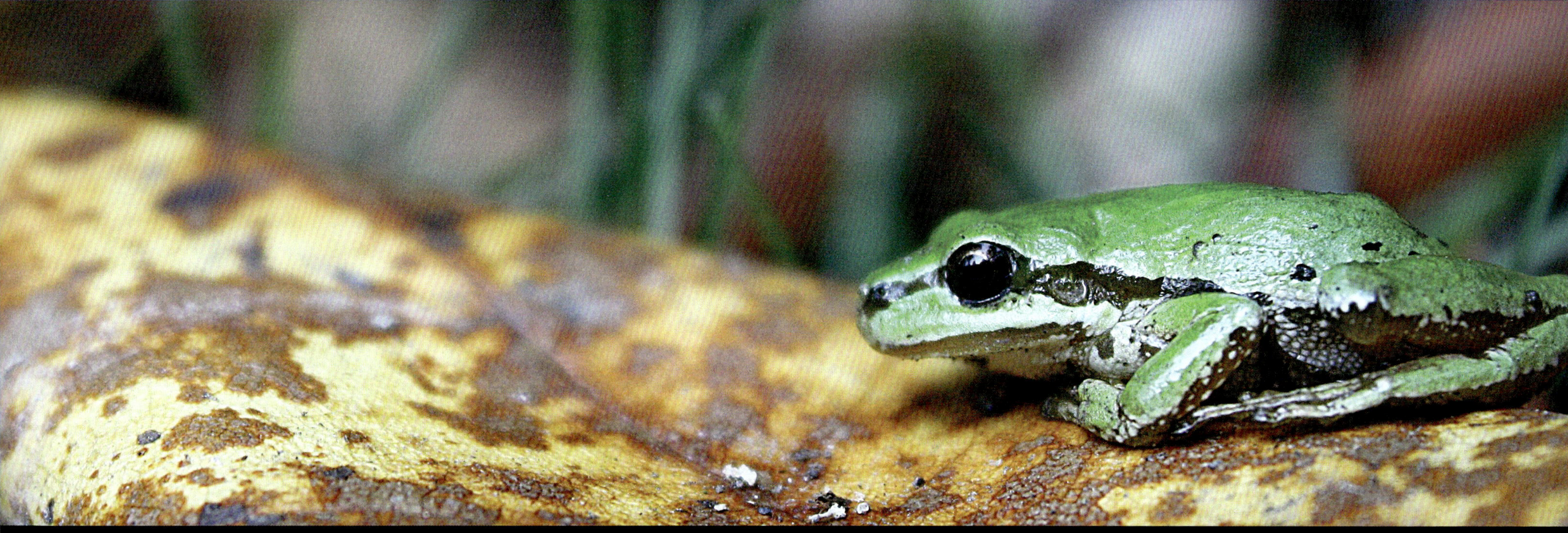

Above: The Pacific tree frog is the smallest but most commonly seen and heard frog in Washington. Individual tree frogs can change color between green and brown tones in a few minutes, depending on temperature and air moisture.

Facing Page: Bullfrogs are invasive and are believed to have contributed to the drastic decline of native frogs. For example, the northern leopard frog has been wiped out in much of the Pacific Northwest.

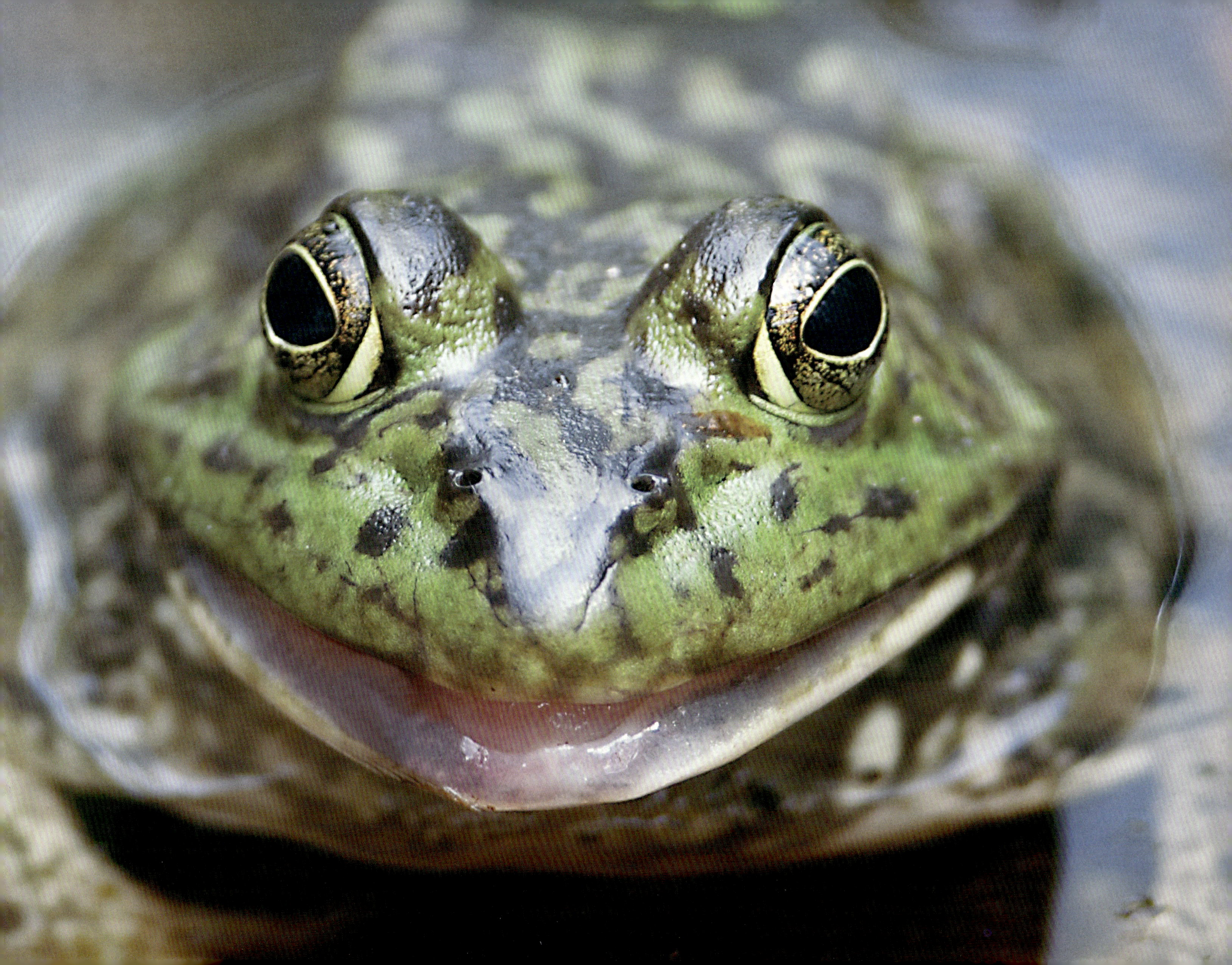

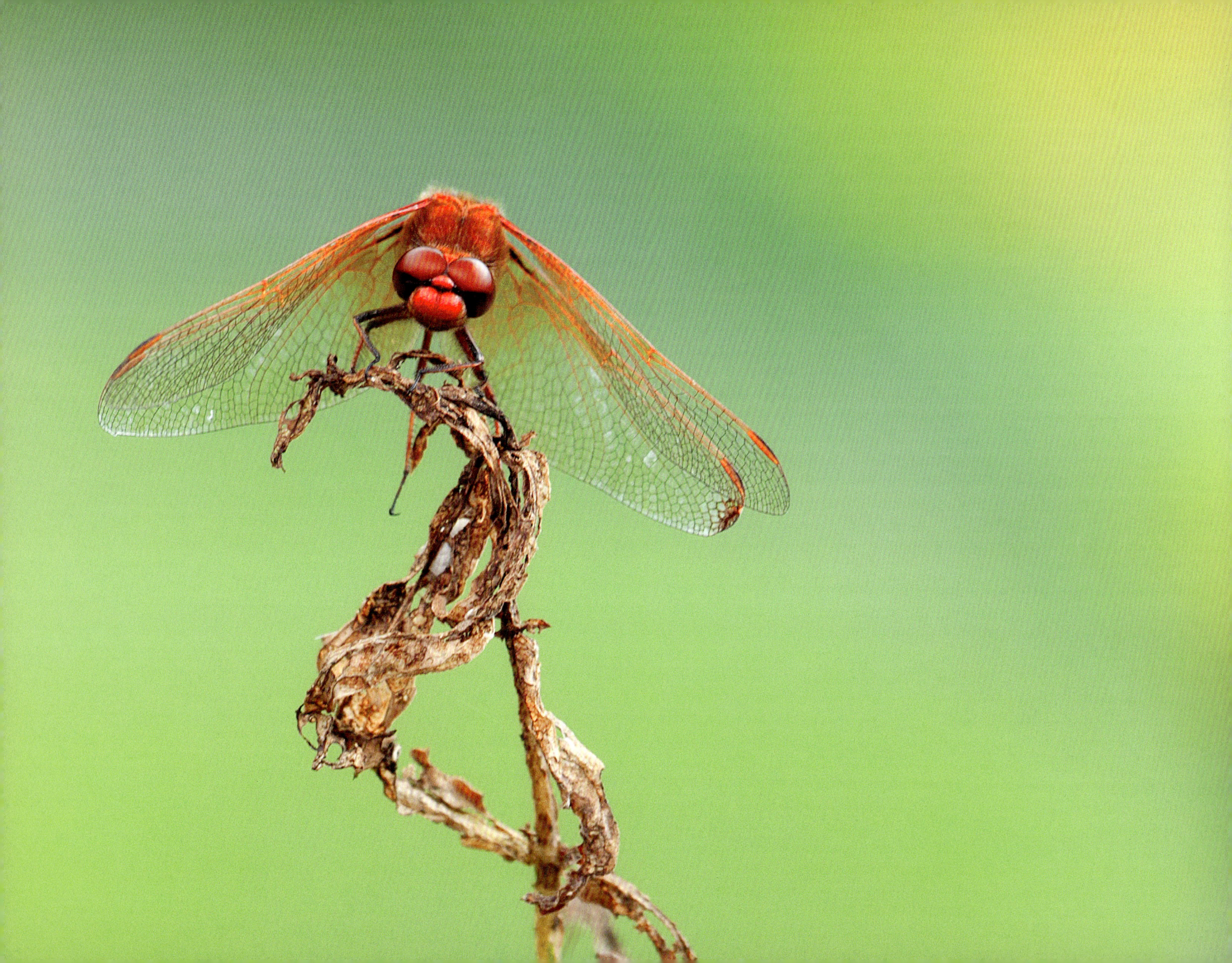

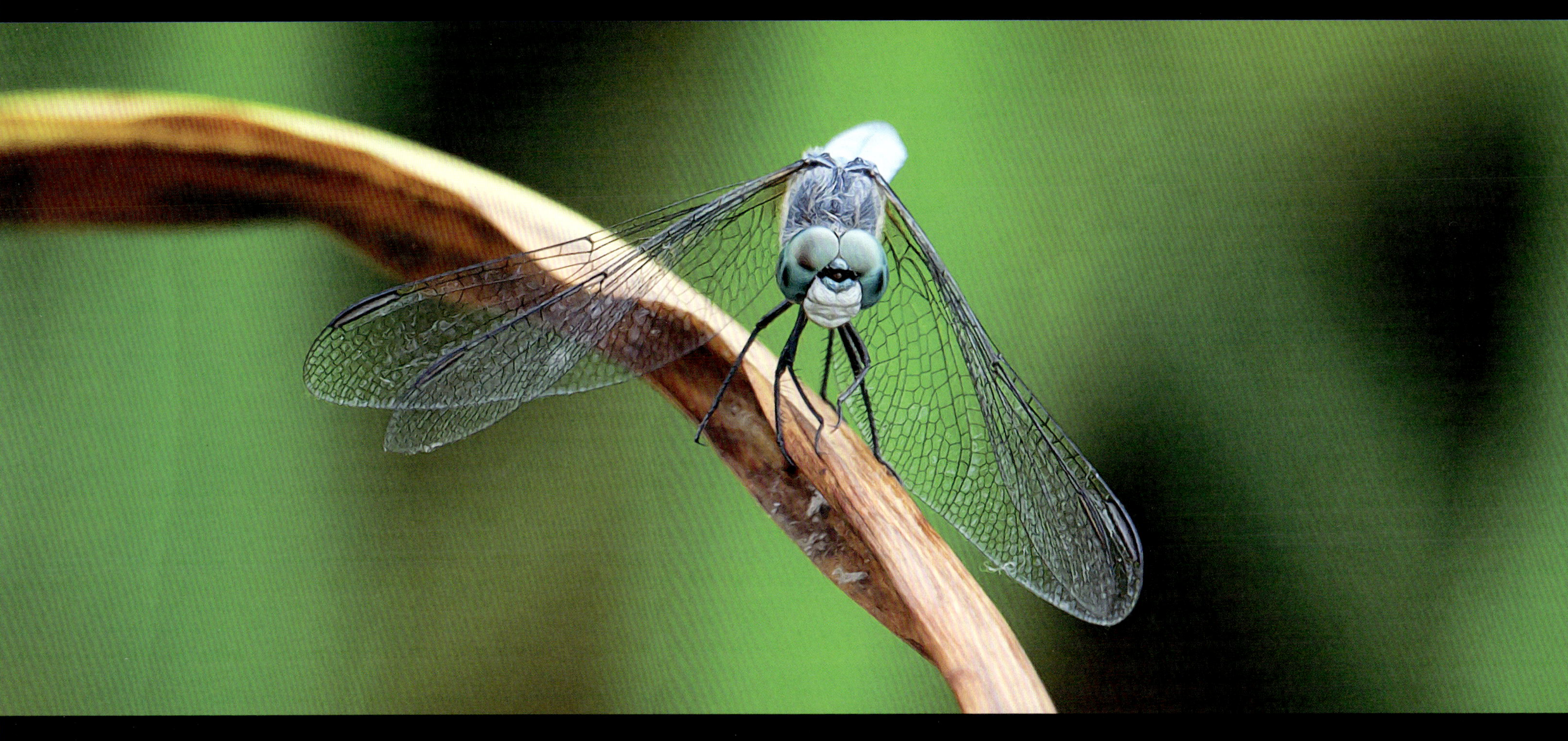

Facing Page: On a warm day sightings of at least 19 species of dragonflies, including this bright red cardinal meadowhawk, are possible at Magnuson Park.

Above: Dragonflies have been on earth for more than 250 million years, predating the dinosaurs. They have the finest vision and largest eye of any insect and can fly up to 30 miles an hour. This blue dasher dragonfly visits its favorite resting spot, a dying blade of grass along the shore of the lake.

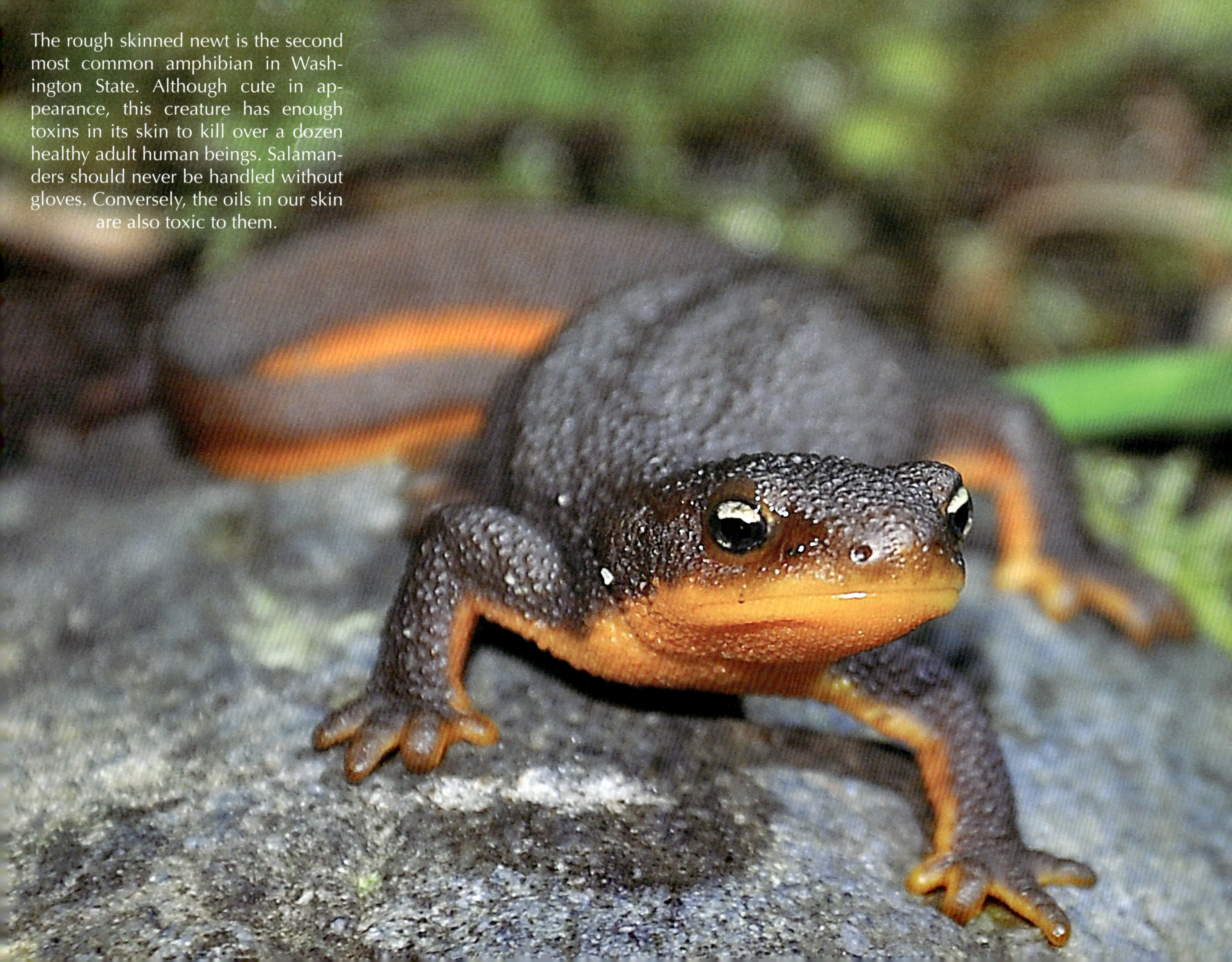

The rough skinned newt is the second most common amphibian in Washington State. Although cute in appearance, this creature has enough toxins in its skin to kill over a dozen healthy adult human beings. Salamanders should never be handled without gloves. Conversely, the oils in our skin are also toxic to them.

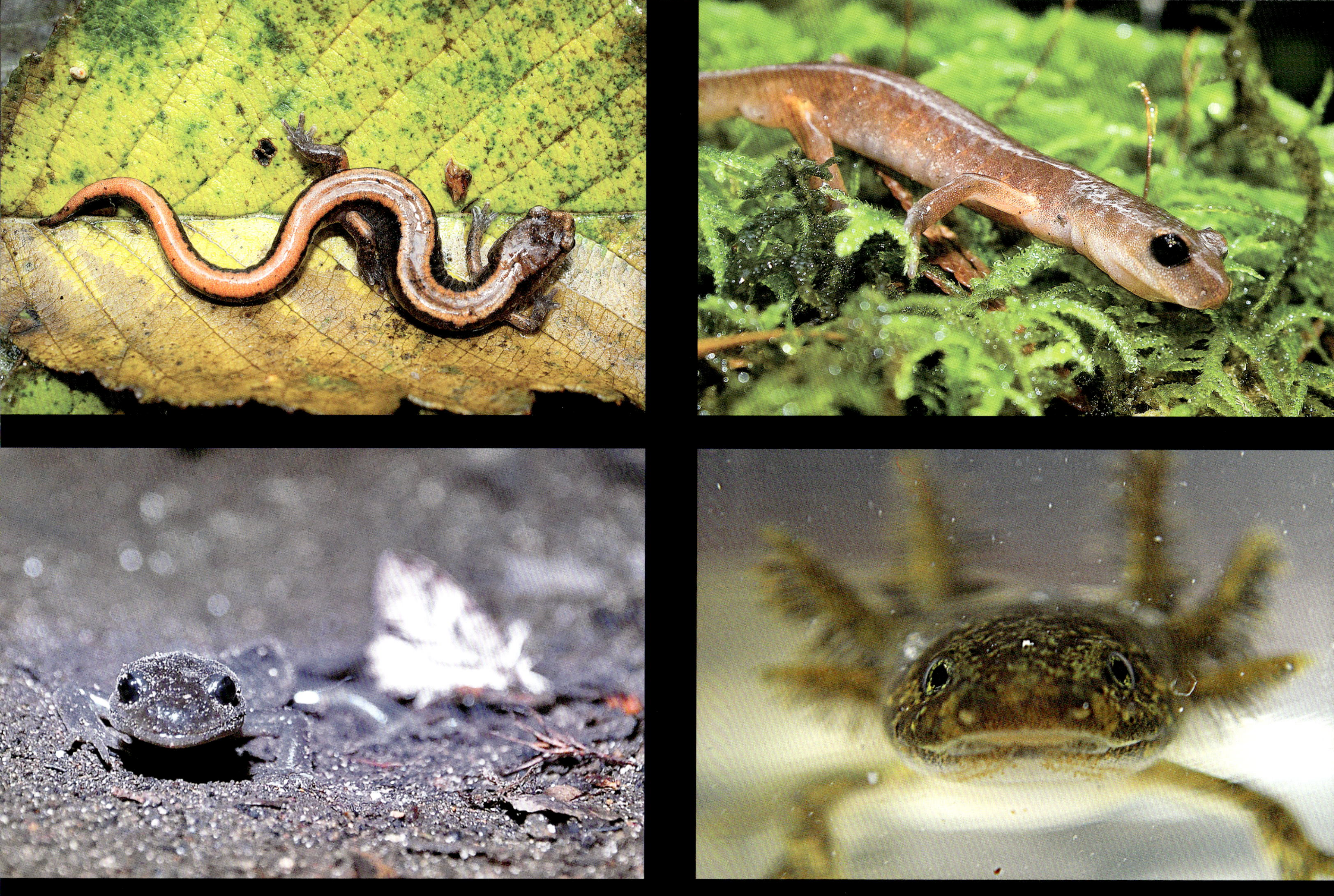

Top Left: Western Red-backed Salamander. *Top Right*: Ensatina Salamander.

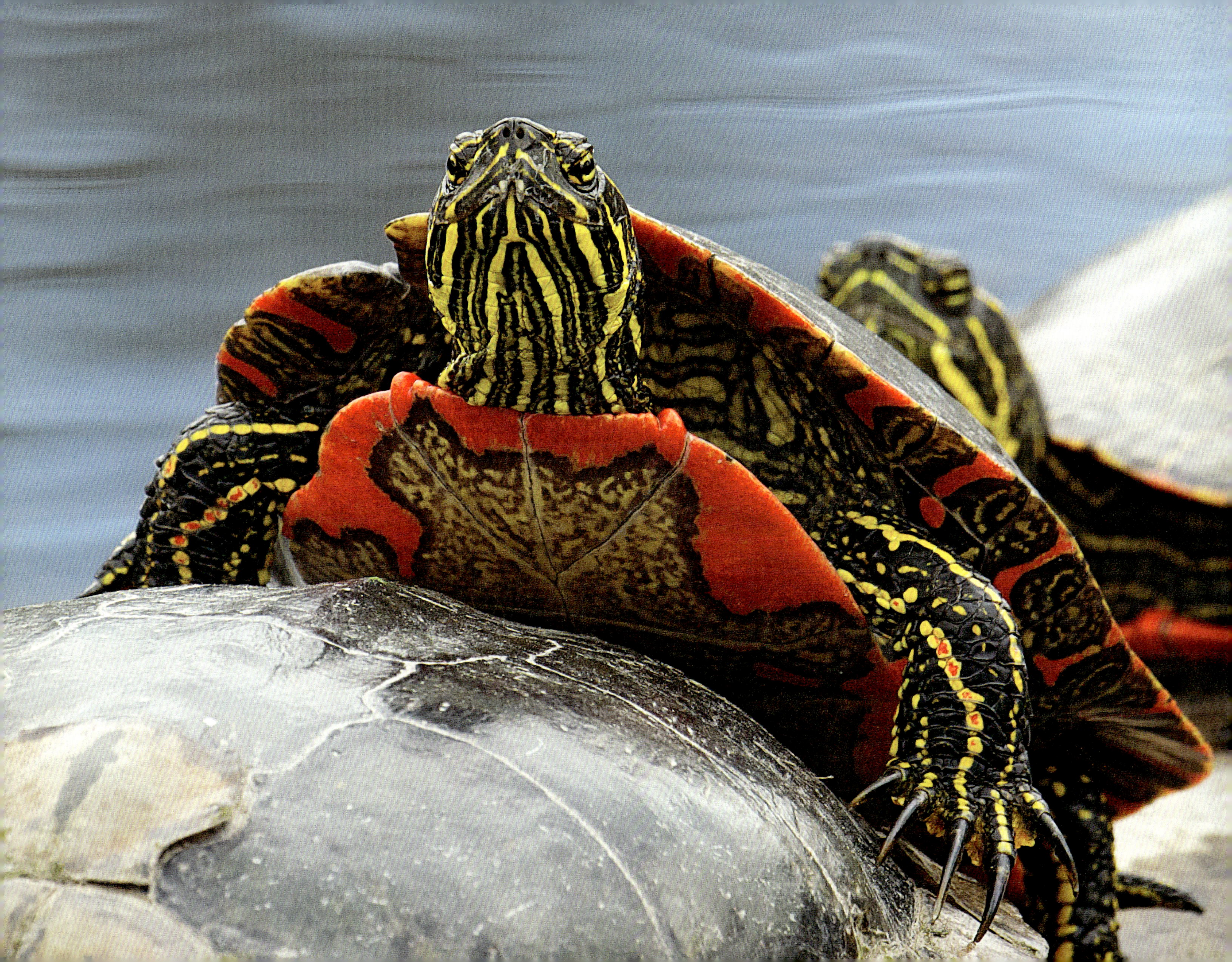

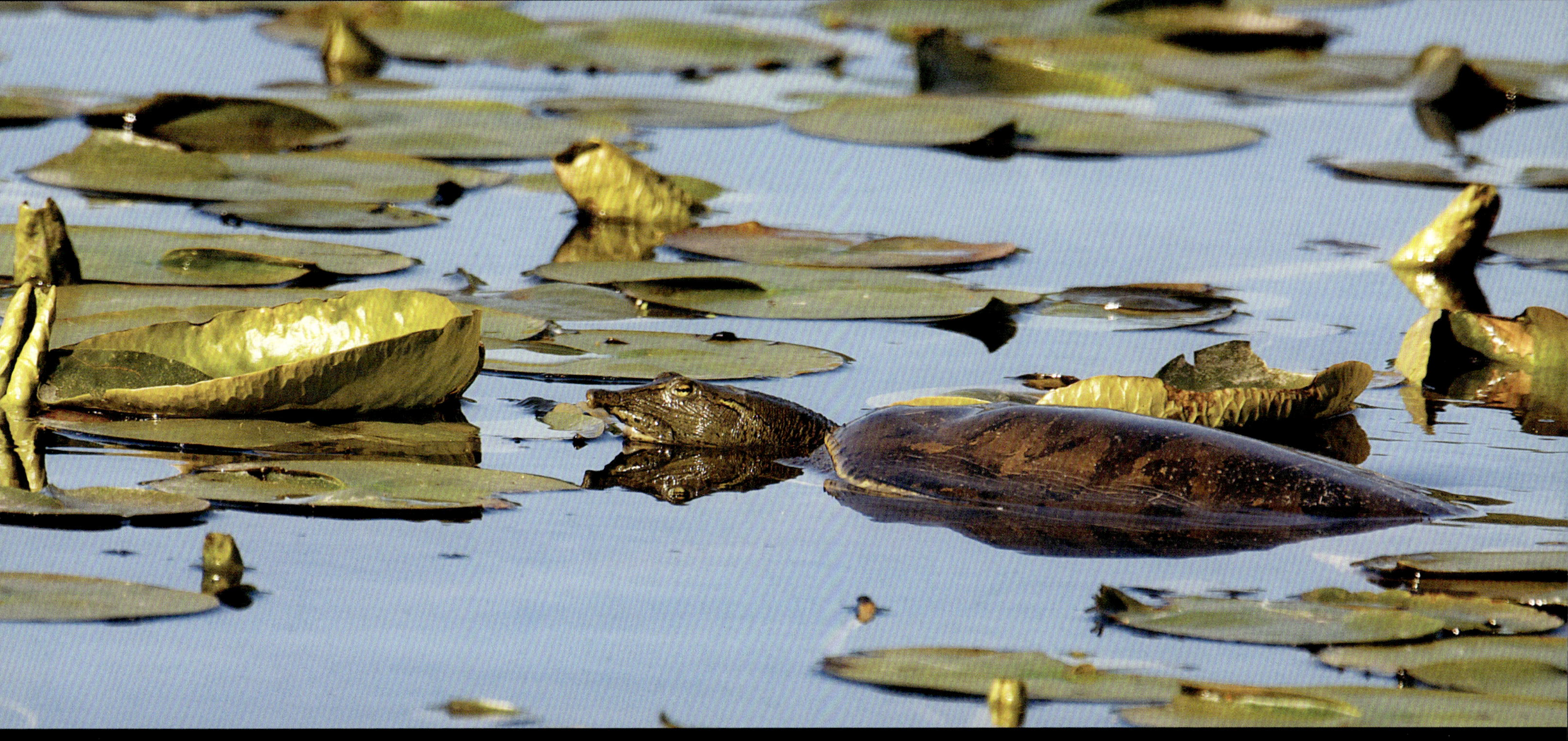

Facing Page: Western painted turtles earn their name from the bright orange and yellow markings that splash their undersides. My favorite place to photograph them is Juanita Bay Park, where they are abundant on sunny days. Look for them on logs near water or along the shoreline. It is easy to observe them from either of the park's boardwalks.

Above: Softshell turtles are not originally from Washington. They were probably released as pets and now inhabit the wild here.

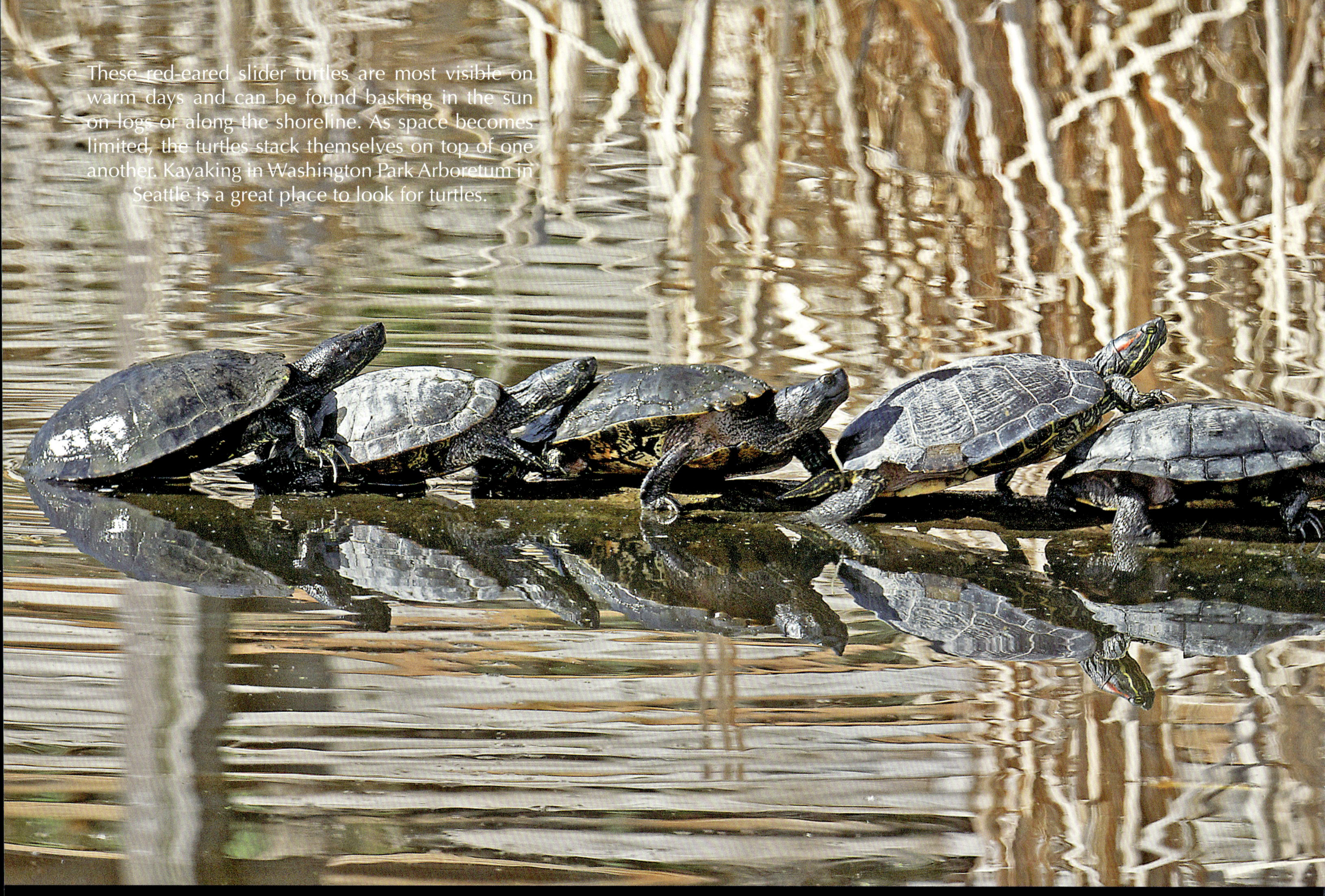

These red-eared slider turtles are most visible on warm days and can be found basking in the sun on logs or along the shoreline. As space becomes limited, the turtles stack themselves on top of one another. Kayaking in Washington Park Arboretum in Seattle is a great place to look for turtles.

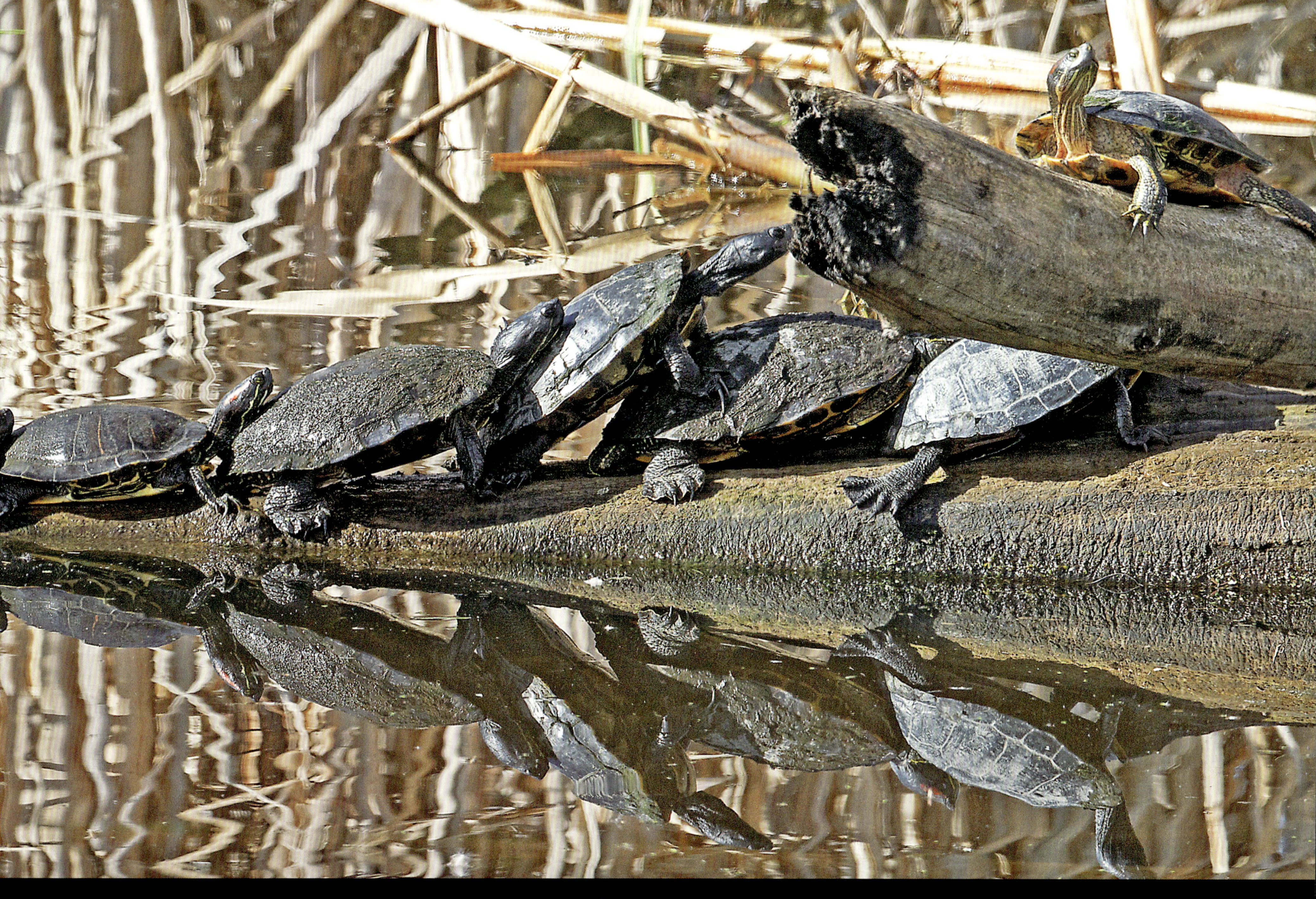

Test Your Knowledge

Challenge yourself to identify the six birds on the right.
For the solution go to:

aaronbaggenstos.com

Special thanks to:
Ed Doyne
Lorraine Weeks
Bryan Baggenstos
Melinda Baggenstos
Duke Coonrad
Marc Hoffman
Larry Engels
Michael Rohani
Jeff Hooper
Mike Young
Todd Humphrey
Deb Lyon
Mick Thompson
All of my friends at Juanita Bay
The Juanita Bay Park Rangers
All of the local park workers and volunteers

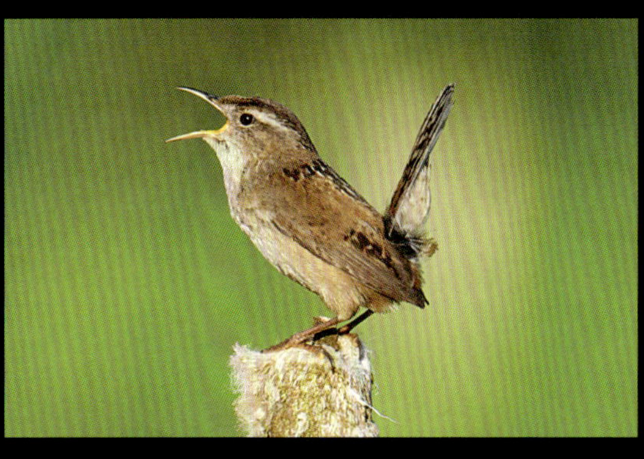

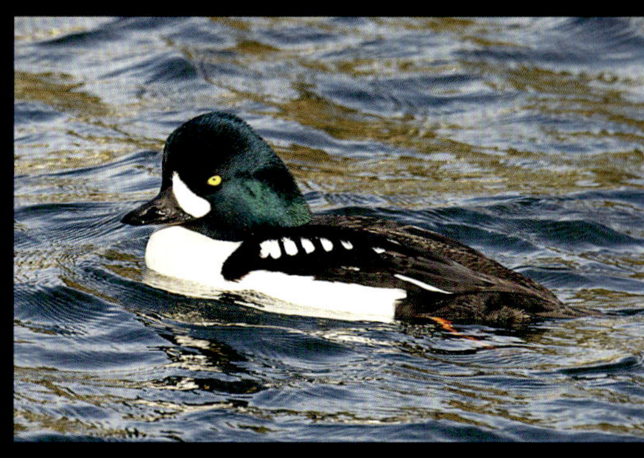

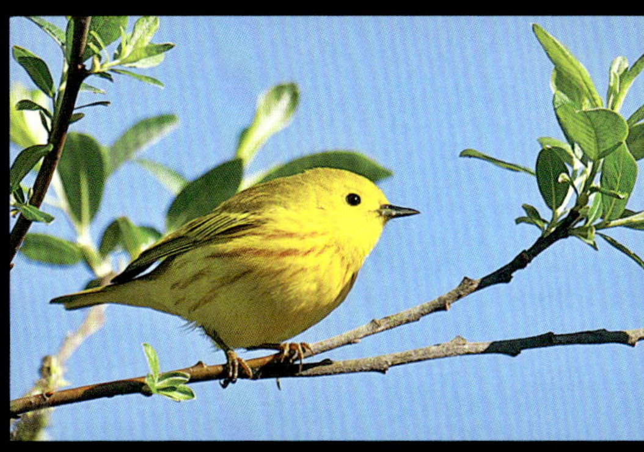

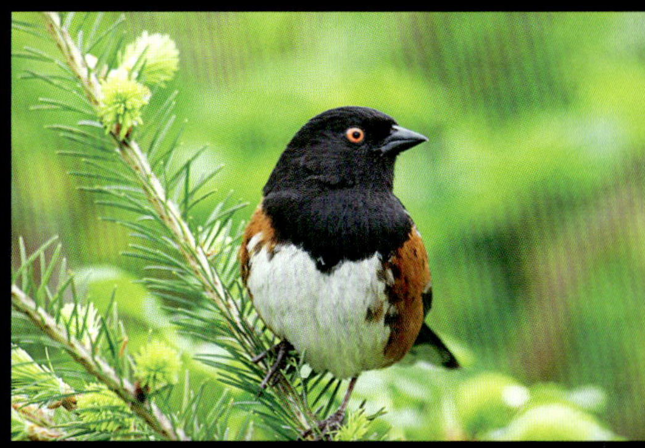

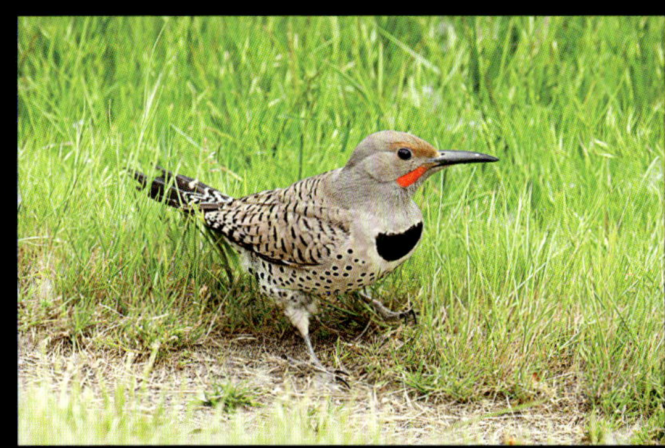

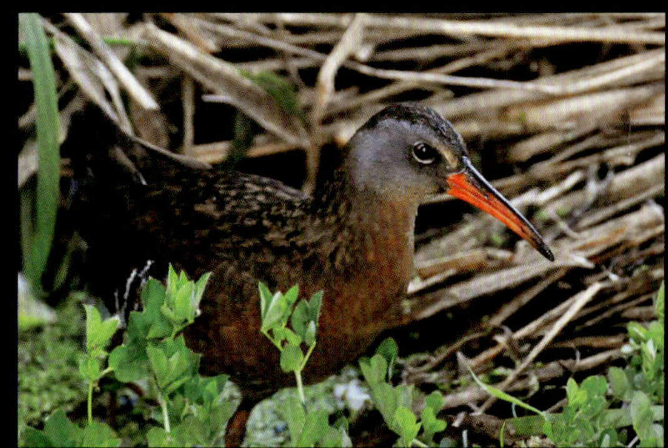